Morality Policies in Europe

The regulation of issues like abortion, euthanasia, gun control, same-sex unions, pornography, prostitution, drugs, or gambling is commonly referred to as a special class of so called morality policies. The distinctive feature of these policies is that politics are shaped by conflicts over first principle: When does life end? When does it begin? Is gambling, drug consumption or prostitution inherently malignant? The regulation of these value conflicts entails decisions about 'right' or 'wrong' and hence the 'validation of a particular set of basic values'. Yet there is still a remarkable lack of scholarly attention on morality policies, in particular with regard to general implications for the study of public policy.

To stimulate further research in this area, this book focuses on different concepts and theories of morality policy change in European countries. It is based on a broad and comparative empirical perspective on different morality issues, including, for instance, the regulation of prostitution, abortion, euthanasia, gambling, drugs, as well as gun control.

This book was previously published as a special issue of the *Journal of European Public Policy*.

Christoph Knill is Professor of Political Science and Public Administration at the University of Konstanz, Germany.

Journal of European Public Policy Series
Series Editor: Jeremy Richardson is a Professor at Nuffield College, Oxford University

This series seeks to bring together some of the finest edited works on European Public Policy. Reprinting from Special Issues of the *Journal of European Public Policy*, the focus is on using a wide range of social sciences approaches, both qualitative and quantitative, to gain a comprehensive and definitive understanding of Public Policy in Europe.

Towards a Federal Europe
Edited by Alexander H. Trechsel

The Disparity of European Integration
Edited by Tanja A. Börzel

Cross-National Policy Convergence:
Causes Concepts and Empirical Findings
Edited by Christoph Knill

Civilian or Military Power?
European Foreign Policy in Perspective
Edited by Helene Sjursen

The European Union and New Trade Politics
Edited by John Peterson and Alasdair R. Young

Comparative Studies of Policy Agendas
Edited by Frank R. Baumgartner, Christoffer Green-Pedersen and Bryan D. Jones

The Constitutionalization of the European Union
Edited by Berthold Rittberger and Frank Schimmelfenig

Empirical and Theoretical Studies in EU Lobbying
Edited by David Coen

Mutual Recognition as a New Mode of Governance
Edited by Susanne K. Schmidt

France and the European Union
Edited by Emiliano Grossman

Immigration and Integration Policy in Europe
Edited by Tim Bale

Reforming the European Commission
Edited by Michael W. Bauer

International Influence Beyond Conditionality
Postcommunist Europe after EU Enlargement
Edited by Rachel A. Epstein and Ulrich Sedelmeier

The Role of Political Parties in the European Union
Edited by Björn Lindberg, Anne Rasmussen and Andreas Warntjen

EU External Governance
Projecting EU Rules beyond Membership
Edited by Sandra Lavenex and Frank Schimmelfennig

EMU and Political Science
What Have We Learned?
Edited by Henrik Enderlein and Amy Verdun

Learning and Governance in the EU Policy Making Process
Edited by Anthony R. Zito

Political Representation and EU Governance
Edited by Peter Mair and Jacques Thomassen

Europe and the Management of Globalization
Edited by Wade Jacoby and Sophie Meunier

Negotiation Theory and the EU
The State of the Art
Edited by Andreas Dür, Gemma Mateo and Daniel C. Thomas

The Political Economy of Europe's Incomplete Single Market
Edited by David Howarth and Tal Sadeh

The European Union's Foreign Economic Policies
A Principal-Agent Perspective
Edited by Andreas Dür and Michael Elsig

The Politics of the Lisbon Agenda
Governance Architectures and Domestic Usages of Europe
Edited by Susana Borrás and Claudio M. Radaelli

Agency Governance in the European Union
Edited by Berthold Rittberger and Arndt Wonka

The EU Timescape
Edited by Klaus H. Goetz and Jan-Hinrik Meyer-Sahling

The EU's Common Foreign and Security Policy
Edited by Helene Sjursen

Economic Patriotism in Open Economies
Edited by Ben Clift and Cornelia Woll

The Power of the European Court of Justice
Edited by Susanne K. Schmidt and R. Daniel Kelemen

The Representative Turn in EU Studies
Edited by Sandra Kröger and Dawid Friedrich

Legislative Co-decision in the European Union
Edited by Anne Rasmussen, Charlotte Burns and Christine Reh

Frameworks of the European Union's Policy Process
Edited by Nikolaos Zahariadis

Morality Policies in Europe
Concepts, Theories and Empirical Evidence

Edited by
Christoph Knill

LONDON AND NEW YORK

First published 2014
by Routledge

Published 2014 by Routledge
2 Park Square, Milton Park, Abingdon, Oxfordshire OX14 4RN

and by Routledge
711 Third Avenue, New York, NY 10017

Routledge is an imprint of the Taylor and Francis Group, an informa business

First issued in paperback 2015

© 2014 Taylor & Francis

All rights reserved. No part of this book may be reprinted or reproduced or utilised in any form or by any electronic, mechanical, or other means, now known or hereafter invented, including photocopying and recording, or in any information storage or retrieval system, without permission in writing from the publishers.

Trademark notice: Product or corporate names may be trademarks or registered trademarks, and are used only for identification and explanation without intent to infringe.

British Library Cataloguing in Publication Data
A catalogue record for this book is available from the British Library

ISBN 978-0-415-71788-5 (hbk)
ISBN 978-1-138-95465-6 (pbk)

Typeset in Garamond
by Taylor & Francis Books

Publisher's Note
The publisher accepts responsibility for any inconsistencies that may have arisen during the conversion of this book from journal articles to book chapters, namely the possible inclusion of journal terminology.

Disclaimer
Every effort has been made to contact copyright holders for their permission to reprint material in this book. The publishers would be grateful to hear from any copyright holder who is not here acknowledged and will undertake to rectify any errors or omissions in future editions of this book.

Contents

Citation Information ix

1. The study of morality policy: analytical implications from a public policy perspective
   Christoph Knill 1

2. Public policy meets morality: conceptual and theoretical challenges in the analysis of morality policy change
   Stephan Heichel, Christoph Knill and Sophie Schmitt 10

3. The puzzle of permissiveness: understanding policy processes concerning morality issues
   Isabelle Engeli, Christoffer Green-Pedersen and Lars Thorup Larsen 27

4. Is morality policy different? Institutional explanations for post-war Western Europe
   Donley T. Studlar, Alessandro Cagossi and Robert D. Duval 45

5. From 'morality' policy to 'normal' policy: framing of drug consumption and gambling in Germany and the Netherlands and their regulatory consequences
   Eva-Maria Euchner, Stephan Heichel, Kerstin Nebel and Andreas Raschzok 64

6. Framing and policy change after shooting rampages: a comparative analysis of discourse networks
   Steffen Hurka and Kerstin Nebel 82

7. Diverging against all odds? Regulatory paths in embryonic stem cell research across Western Europe
   Isabelle Engeli and Christine Rothmayr Allison 99

8. Regulating prostitution and same-sex marriage in Italy and Spain: the interplay of political and societal veto players in two catholic societies
   Sophie Schmitt, Eva-Maria Euchner and Caroline Preidel 117

CONTENTS

9. Policy entrepreneurs and controversial science: governing human embryonic stem cell research
   Michael Mintrom   134

   Index   151

Citation Information

The chapters in this book were originally published in the *Journal of European Public Policy*, volume 20, issue 3 (2013). When citing this material, please use the original page numbering for each article, as follows:

Chapter 1
The study of morality policy: analytical implications from a public policy perspective
Christoph Knill
Journal of European Public Policy, volume 20, issue 3 (2013)
pp. 309–317

Chapter 2
Public policy meets morality: conceptual and theoretical challenges in the analysis of morality policy change
Stephan Heichel, Christoph Knill and Sophie Schmitt
Journal of European Public Policy, volume 20, issue 3 (2013)
pp. 318–334

Chapter 3
The puzzle of permissiveness: understanding policy processes concerning morality issues
Isabelle Engeli, Christoffer Green-Pedersen and Lars Thorup Larsen
Journal of European Public Policy, volume 20, issue 3 (2013)
pp. 335–352

Chapter 4
Is morality policy different? Institutional explanations for post-war Western Europe
Donley T. Studlar, Alessandro Cagossi and Robert D. Duval
Journal of European Public Policy, volume 20, issue 3 (2013)
pp. 353–371

Chapter 5
From 'morality' policy to 'normal' policy: framing of drug consumption and gambling in Germany and the Netherlands and their regulatory consequences
Eva-Maria Euchner, Stephan Heichel, Kerstin Nebel and Andreas Raschzok
Journal of European Public Policy, volume 20, issue 3 (2013)
pp. 372–389

CITATION INFORMATION

Chapter 6
Framing and policy change after shooting rampages: a comparative analysis of discourse networks
Steffen Hurka and Kerstin Nebel
Journal of European Public Policy, volume 20, issue 3 (2013)
pp. 390–406

Chapter 7
Diverging against all odds? Regulatory paths in embryonic stem cell research across Western Europe
Isabelle Engeli and Christine Rothmayr Allison
Journal of European Public Policy, volume 20, issue 3 (2013)
pp. 407–424

Chapter 8
Regulating prostitution and same-sex marriage in Italy and Spain: the interplay of political and societal veto players in two catholic societies
Sophie Schmitt, Eva-Maria Euchner and Caroline Preidel
Journal of European Public Policy, volume 20, issue 3 (2013)
pp. 425–441

Chapter 9
Policy entrepreneurs and controversial science: governing human embryonic stem cell research
Michael Mintrom
Journal of European Public Policy, volume 20, issue 3 (2013)
pp. 442–457

Please direct any queries you may have about the citations to
clsuk.permissions@cengage.com

The study of morality policy: analytical implications from a public policy perspective

Christoph Knill

ABSTRACT Morality policies generally refer to issues in which political conflicts are shaped by debates over first principle; i.e., value conflicts are more important than instrumental considerations of policy design. Yet there is still a remarkable lack of scholarly attention on morality policies, in particular with regard to general implications for the study of public policy. To stimulate further research in this area, the article discusses different concepts of morality policy and suggests a distinction between different morality policy types. Moreover, distinctive features of morality policy content and effects are discussed. The article concludes with sketching out promising areas of future research in this field of inquiry.

INTRODUCTION

The regulation of issues like abortion, euthanasia, gun control, same-sex unions, pornography, prostitution, drugs or gambling is commonly referred to as a special class of so-called morality policies. The distinctive feature of these policies is that politics are shaped by conflicts over first principle: when does life end? When does it begin? Is gambling, drug consumption or prostitution inherently malignant? The regulation of these value conflicts entails decisions about 'right' or 'wrong' and hence the 'validation of a particular set of basic values' (Mooney 1999: 675).

Yet there is still a remarkable lack of scholarly attention on morality policies. Comparative assessments of developments across countries or different morality policy subfields are rare. Research has been restricted to a small number of countries, with a strong geographical bias towards the United States of America (USA) (Meier 1994; Mooney 2001; Smith and Tatalovich 2003). It is only more recently that individual studies systematically have compared policy developments across a broader number of countries and over time, albeit often focusing on individual subfields (e.g., Banchoff 2011; Fink 2008; Schiffino *et al.* 2009).

Moreover, potential theoretical challenges emerging from the analysis of morality policies for the study of public policy in general have only been partially recognized and addressed. First, there is a still unsettled debate on the extent to which morality policy can be subsumed under existing policy typologies. Second, only a few attempts have been made to differentiate analytically between various types of morality policy. Third, distinctive features of morality policy contents and effects have not been investigated in a systematic way yet. In the following, each of these issues will be addressed in more detail, with the basic purpose of highlighting issues of particular theoretical interest and stimulating further research.

CONCEPTS OF MORALITY POLICY

When taking a closer look at the literature on morality policies, we can analytically distinguish between three different policy conceptions that either emphasize politics, framing or policy substance.

Policies determine politics: morality policy as policy type

With the emergence of morality policies on the research agenda, the central question was not so much on the explanation of policy variation and change, but on the politics of morality policy. Especially in the US context, research concentrated on the extent to which morality policies are characterized by typical process patterns and the question of whether morality policy constitutes a genuine policy type. More specifically, it was argued that morality policies share a number of process patterns that reach beyond existing policy typologies based on economic and class interests, like the distribution and redistribution of wealth or the regulation of economic activities.

The process patterns that have been identified to delineate morality from non-morality issues first of all relate to the presence of conflicts over first principle, typically entailing clashes of values that cannot be resolved by argument (Mooney 1999). Political conflicts centre on the question of which basic values a polity ought to acknowledge rather than questions of effective policy designs in order to achieve certain objectives. Second, given the dominance of principle rather than instrumental conflicts, morality policies are assumed to be technically less complex, hence favouring broader public participation in the policy process. Third, higher public participation and technical simplicity favour high political salience of morality policies (Mooney 2001). In view of these characteristics, Tatalovich and Daynes (2011) argued that morality policies constitute a new policy type of social regulatory policy that reflects highly conflictive and salient process patterns of redistributive policies, while defining regulatory rules governing social interaction and hence being regulatory in nature.

The use of this classification, however, can be questioned on several grounds. First, we can generally ask whether the distinction of policy types is actually the most promising way to improve our understanding of policy variation and policy change. To what extent do policy types explain differences and change of policy contents across countries and policy areas? Second, the perceived need to define a new policy type might simply emerge as a result of analytical inconsistencies in Lowi's (2011) typology. While his distinction between redistributive and distributive policies is based on different policy effects, i.e., the (re-)distribution of resources, Lowi emphasizes the regulation of human behaviour as the central criterion of the regulatory policy type. This creates the false impression that regulatory policies have no distributive or redistributive effects (Knill and Tosun 2012: 17).

Morality policy as frame

Departing from Lowi's (2011) suggestion of distinguishing between morality and instrumentally rational policies rather than trying to squeeze morality policy in his older categories, Mucciaroni (2011) argues that morality policies do not exist *per se*, but constitute a strategic approach to framing public policy issues. Rather than being inherently moral in substance, policies might be framed as moral issues. The basic feature of morality frames is that those who frame the issues place adherence to moral principles above instrumental considerations. Non-morality frames, by contrast, emphasize a rational instrumental view, in which policies are evaluated in light of their potential to achieve certain objectives.

Frames may vary in the extent to which competing advocacy coalitions define issues in moralistic or non-moralistic terms, with fully morality policies implying that all actors stick to morality frames and fully instrumental policies imply that all actors advocate non-morality frames. In hybrid constellations, by contrast, one side frames an issue using moral principles and the other uses instrumentally rational criteria. At the same time, morality frames might differ in the target of moral judgment; i.e., the extent to which they focus on the morality of private, social or governmental behaviour (Mucciaroni 2011: 193–4).

According to this conception, morality policies are not necessarily linked to specific policy fields. Rather their emergence, regardless of the policy area in question, depends on the extent to which advocates are willing and able to use moral principles to frame issues. This also implies that the prevalence of morality policies might vary over time, across countries and issues.

Policy content: fields of morality policy

Rather than conceiving of morality policy as a specific policy type or specific way of framing policy issues, the policy-based approach differentiates between morality and non-morality policies by focusing on policy contents (Heichel *et al.* 2013). Policies are considered as morality policies if their regulatory substance is closely related to public decisions over societal values, although the manifestation of this linkage might vary over time and across policies and countries. The policy-based approach avoids the problematic assumption inherent in the politics-based perspective that assumes distinctive process patterns, regardless of the political system in question (Engeli *et al.* 2013).

Which issues should then count as morality policies when taking this point of departure? In the literature we find long lists as well as various attempts of categorization (Mooney 2001). Basically, different morality subfields can be distinguished: (1) issues of 'life and death' (including abortion, euthanasia, artificial insemination, stem cell research and capital punishment); (2) issues of sexual behaviour (e.g., homosexuality, prostitution, pornography); (3) issues related to addictive behaviour (e.g., gambling, drug regulation); and (4) issues referring to basic decisions over the relationship between individual freedoms and collective values (e.g., religious education, gun control).

The existence of different lists, however, also indicates difficulties in clearly delineating morality and non-morality issues. While value conflicts reflect an obvious feature of the 'life and death category', their prevalence is less pronounced in the other subfields. The extent to which these differences can be taken into account by specifying different types of morality policies is addressed in the following section.

TYPES OF MORALITY POLICY

The above discussion indicates conceptual problems of defining morality policy in terms of a genuine policy type or distinctive policy fields. At the same time, the conception as policy frame remains indeterminate insofar as it hardly allows for *ex ante* identifying issues, countries or periods in which morality frames are particularly prevalent or not. To address these difficulties, the following distinction of types of morality policy takes an alternative point of departure. Based on the underlying interest constellations, a distinction is drawn between manifest and latent morality policies.

Manifest morality policies

Manifest morality policies refer to issues in which value conflicts constitute the standard mode of political decision-making. Economic costs and benefits are dispersed broadly across different societal groups; i.e., material gains and losses are of minor importance. Individual values and beliefs, by contrast, play a central role. On the one hand, they are inherently relevant, constituting the basic criterion that determines individual preferences. On the other hand, values are relevant as instrument of social and political power. Different actors and groups (e.g., liberals, conservatives or churches) may gain or lose power if certain values prevail or change.

As a result of this constellation, even minor issues referring to instrument choices or the calibration of instruments (e.g., shifts in the time frame after fertilization in which abortions are still considered legal) are very likely to trigger fundamental value conflicts. Typical cases are so-called 'life and death' issues, matters of family and sexuality or religious education. Often, these issues are closely related to religious orientations, also implying that conflicts refer to beliefs rather than scientific evidence.

Table 1 Types of morality policy

Policy feature	Manifest morality policy	Latent morality policy	Non-morality policy
Cultural opportunity structures	Favorable	Favorable	Restrictive
Relevance of economic costs/benefits	Low	High	High or low
Relevance of values	Inherent (as such); instrumental to political power	Instrumental to political power; instrumental to economic gains	No relevance

Latent morality policies

Latent morality policies, by contrast, refer to issues in which value conflicts are not the order of the day, but – under certain conditions – might break out. Similar to volcano eruptions, there is a potential that policy debates are framed as moral conflict. These issues are typically characterized by the combination of concentrated economic benefits and highly dispersed costs, hence implying an important economic dimension for certain groups. This constellation favours that political debates are framed as instrumental, focusing on the design of effective solutions to existing problems. At the same time, however, the regulatory matter contains elements that can easily be 'morally exploited'. Competing advocacy coalitions might try to shift the political debate from an instrumental one towards a value conflict in order to achieve their economic or political objectives. Actors opposing this strategy, by contrast, may seek to de-moralize political debates, e.g., by emphasizing health issues or economic matters.

Typical fields in which such constellations prevail refer to gambling, pornography, gun control or drug regulation. While values as such are of minor importance, they might be used instrumentally. As value conflicts are hardly accessible to compromise solutions, their activation might be an important strategy to block unpleasant reform initiatives. Gun producers, the tobacco industry or casinos, for instance, may resort to individual freedoms in order to fend off attempts of stricter regulation. At the same time, public interest groups might rely upon value frames as instruments of societal mobilization to get certain issues on the political agenda. Depending on actor preferences, policy moralization may either be used to increase the chances of decision gridlock for issues already on the agenda, or to get topics on the agenda in the first place.

Non-morality policies

Latent morality policies might either be framed as morality or non-morality issues, depending on the underlying constellation of interest. This does not mean, however, that each non-morality issue can easily become a morality policy. What distinguishes both manifest and latent morality policies from non-morality policies is their connectivity to value issues, or what I would refer to as *cultural opportunity structures*.

Cultural opportunity structures can be understood as specific configurations of cultural value dispositions and their institutional representation (via established interest groups, social movements, religious organizations, the institutional relationship between state and churches, the existence of confessional parties) that define issue- or country-specific resources for social mobilization. These resources can be considered high for both manifest and latent morality policies, but low for non-morality issues, like technical standardization or administrative reform policies. Hence, the existence of non-morality policies does not necessarily presuppose the prevalence of conflicts over tangible resources, but the presence of strong cultural constraints on value-based social mobilization.

Dynamics over time and space

Yet the characterization of a certain issue as a morality or non-morality policy is not set in stone. It is well conceivable that issues that started out as highly controversial value debates turn into latent morality policies in the course of time, when a basic political decision had been reached. In such cases, subsequent changes might follow a more instrumental process mode, albeit outbreaks of value conflicts are still very likely. Moreover, cultural opportunity structure might change over time, implying an increase or decrease in the extent to which issues might be successfully framed as morality policies. Secularization and associated cultural change, for instance, might reduce value conflicts on certain issues and hence change their 'morality charge'.

However, as cultural opportunity structures, like institutional opportunities and constraints, might differ across countries, it is possible that similar issues constitute different morality policy types in different countries. For instance, what is a manifest morality issue in country A, like abortion or euthanasia in countries belonging to the religious world as defined by Engeli *et al.* (2013), might constitute a latent type in country B that belongs to the secular world.

While non-morality policies and manifest morality policies reflect stable constellations, latent morality policies constitute a more volatile category, with a high potential for oscillation between instrumental and morality modes of policy-making. The extent to which such shifts may occur is affected by various factors. First, shifts in both directions can be triggered by new scientific evidence. On the one hand, new evidence (e.g., on the addiction potential of gambling) might favour an instrumental policy debate, emphasizing objective data rather than values and beliefs. On the other hand, new evidence might – somewhat paradoxically – trigger the relevance of morality frames. The more compelling the evidence, the more potential losers of evidence-based policy changes may resort to mobilizing societal resistance by reverting back to basic values. A case in point is Mayor Michael Bloomberg's recent move against obesity, proposing to ban oversized servings of sugary drinks in New York's food-service establishments. While scientific evidence underpins a causal link between can size and individual consumption, the food industry launched a broad campaign emphasizing intolerable liberty restrictions associated with Bloomberg's plans (Frum 2012). Second, shifts from instrumental to morality modes of policy-making can be triggered by moral panics (Cohen 2002), in which a certain event emerges to become defined as a threat to societal values. Moral panics hence mean an exaggerated reaction of the media, the government or the public to a type of behaviour that is seen as social problem. As shown by Hurka and Nebel (2013), public shootings can trigger such dynamics, which might lead to the tightening of gun control regulations.

GENERAL FEATURES OF MORALITY POLICY CONTENTS AND EFFECTS

Systematic differences between morality and non-morality policies can be observed not only for the politics dimension (Engeli *et al.* 2013; Studlar *et al.* 2013) or the causes of policy change and variation (Heichel *et al.* 2013; Schmitt *et al.* 2013), but also with regard to policy contents and policy effects. For policy contents, it is a distinctive feature of morality policies that in many instances regulation is not based on issue specific frameworks, but on general criminal law. Second, regardless of the existence of issue-specific regulations, sanctioning and criminal prosecution constitute crucial contents of morality policies. Policy change often takes the less visible route of changes in criminal law rather than the regulation of substance matters. A move towards permissive policies can be based on the decriminalization of conduct, implying that regulatory restrictions remain in place, but their disregard is no longer sanctioned. Third, value conflicts and inherent difficulties in compromising increase the probability of vague and open legal texture, offering regulatory authorities considerable discretion during the implementation stage. Although these patterns might also be observed for non-morality areas, they are particularly pronounced for morality policies.

These features also have consequences for the effects of morality policies; i.e., their implementation and evaluation. The relevance of criminal law and the limited development of issue-specific arrangements imply that implementation of morality policies is the task of general law enforcement authorities rather than specialized agencies. Given their broad spectrum of tasks, they enjoy considerable discretion in the allocation of resources for sanctioning and monitoring compliance in distinctive issue areas. This is reinforced by the tendency towards ambiguous legal rules on morality issues. In addition, compliance on the side of policy addresses is generally less certain than in non-morality areas, as individuals might be required to accept rules that are in conflict with their basic values and beliefs. This might favour different patterns of non-compliance, reaching from active or passive resistance to strategies of evasion by subterfuge or the exploitation of legal loopholes. Taken together, these aspects render it highly difficult to predict and measure effects of morality policy change. This refers not only to uncertainty in the extent to which public authorities actually sanction or tolerate non-compliant behaviour, but also to the assessment of behavioural changes in the first place, given high incentives and ample opportunities for circumventing legal rules.

AGENDA FOR FUTURE RESEARCH

Departing from the above discussion, several avenues for future research emerge that will be addressed in this collection. First, a crucial question refers to the extent to which classical explanations of policy change and variation still hold when it comes to morality policy (; Engeli *et al.* 2013; Engeli and Rothmayr Allison 2013: Heichel *et al.* 2013; Schmitt *et al.* 2013). Second, in addition to the analysis of differences in policy contents and effects, we still have no full understanding of the politics of morality and the extent to which they are distinct from non-morality issues. These questions are addressed by Studlar *et al.* (2013) and Engeli *et al.* (2013). Third, several papers place particular emphasis on the conditions of morality policy change. Starting from the argument that policy change in morality issues is highly difficult to achieve, Schmitt *et al.* (2013) and Mintrom (2013) focus on specific constellations and actors that might favour moral policy reforms. Fourth, several contributions place emphasis on the factors under which latent moral policies change their mode from instrumental to morality frames and *vice versa* (Engeli *et al.* 2013; Engeli and Rothmayr Allison 2013; Euchner *et al.* 2013; Hurka and Nebel 2013). In addressing these questions, the collection adopts a broad theoretical, methodological and empirical perspective.

Biographical note: Christoph Knill is Professor of Political Science and Public Administration at the University of Konstanz, Germany.

ACKNOWLEDGEMENTS

This research is based on generous funding of the European Research Council (ERC Advanced Grant). The project MORAPOL analyses patterns of morality policy for nine different policy subfields in 26 countries over a period of 50 years (1960–2010).

REFERENCES

Banchoff, T. (2011) *Embryo Politics. Ethics and Policy in Atlantic Democracies*, Ithaca, NY: Cornell University Press.
Cohen, S. (2002) *Folk Devils and Moral Panics*. 3rd ed. London: Routledge.

Engeli, I., Larsen, L. and Green-Pedersen, C. (2013) 'The puzzle of permissiveness: understanding policy processes concerning morality issues', *Journal of European Public Policy* 20(3), doi: 10.1080/13501763.2013.761500

Engeli, I. and Rothmayr Allison, C. (2013) 'Diverging against all odds? Regulatory paths in embryonic stem cell research across Western Europe', *Journal of European Public Policy* 20(3), doi: 10.1080/13501763.2013.761500

Euchner, E., Heichel, S., Nebel, K. and Raschzok, A. (2013) 'From "morality" policy to "normal" policy: framing of drug consumption and gambling in Germany and the Netherlands and their regulatory consequences', *Journal of European Public Policy* 20(3), doi: 10.1080/13501763.2013.761506

Fink, S. (2008) 'Politics as usual or bringing religion back in? The influence of parties, institutions, economic interests, and religion on embryo research laws', *Comparative Political Studies* 41(12): 1631–56.

Frum, D. (2012) 'Bloomberg's visionary move against obesity', CNN International, 4 June, available at http://edition.cnn.com/2012/06/04/opinion/frum-bloomberg-soda/index.html.

Heichel, S., Knill, C. and Schmitt, S. (2013) 'Public policy meets morality: conceptual and theoretical challenges in the analysis of morality policy change', *Journal of European Public Policy* 20(3), doi: 10.1080/13501763.2013.761497

Hurka, S. and Nebel, K. (2013) 'Framing and policy change after shooting rampages – a comparative analysis of discourse networks', *Journal of European Public Policy* 20(3), doi: 10.1080/13501763.2013.761508

Knill, C. and Tosun, J. (2012) *Studying Public Policy: A New Introduction*, London: Palgrave Macmillan.

Lowi, T.J. (2011) 'Foreword: new dimensions in policy and politics', in R. Tatalovich and B.W. Daynes (eds), *Moral Controversies in American Politics*. Armonk, NY: M.E. Sharpe.

Meier, K. (1994) *The Politics of Sin*. Armonk, NY: M.E. Sharpe.

Mintrom, M. (2013) 'Policy entrepreneurs and controversial science: governing human embryonic stem cell research', *Journal of European Public Policy* 20(3), doi: 10.1080/13501763.2012.761514

Mooney, C.Z. (1999) 'The politics of morality policy: symposium editor's introduction', *policy studies journal* 27: 675–80.

Mooney, C.Z. (ed.) (2001) *The Public Clash of Private Values*. New York: Chatham House.

Mucciaroni, G. (2011) 'Are debates about "morality policy" really about morality? Framing opposition to gay and lesbian rights', *Policy Studies Journal* 39(2): 187–216.

Schiffino, N., Ramjoué, C. and Varone, F. (2009) 'Biomedical policies in Belgium and Italy', *West Euopean Politics* 32(3): 559–85.

Schmitt, S., Euchner, E. and Preidel, C. (2013) 'Regulating prostitution and same-sex marriage in Italy and Spain: the interplay of political and societal veto players in two Catholic societies', *Journal of European Public Policy* 20(3), doi: 10.1080/13501763.2013.761512

Smith, T.A. and Tatalovich, R. (2003) *Cultures at War. Moral Conflict in Western Democracies*. Peterborough, ON: Broadview Press.

Studlar, D.T., Cagossi, A. and Duval, R.D. (2013), 'Is morality policy different? Institutional explanations for postwar Western Europe', *Journal of European Public Policy* 20(3), doi: 10.1080/13501763.2013.761503

Tatalovich, R. and Daynes, B. (eds) (2011) *Moral Controversies in American Politics*. 4th ed. Armonk, NY: M.E. Sharpe.

Public policy meets morality: conceptual and theoretical challenges in the analysis of morality policy change

Stephan Heichel, Christoph Knill and Sophie Schmitt

ABSTRACT This contribution examines morality policies from the perspective of the comparative public policy literature. We analyse which concepts, theories and explanatory factors are useful given the peculiarities of this policy field. We answer the question to what extent morality policies are different by analysing these central aspects from a policy *change* perspective. In view of the identified problems in morality policy research, we suggest an alternative concept of measurement. It is based on the assumption that the constitutive cleavage underlying morality policies refers to a single dimension on which changes occur, namely, the degree of restrictiveness of a given regulatory provision. As such, this paper contributes to the emerging field of morality policy research by outlining future venues of research along with an overview of the different existing approaches.

INTRODUCTION

The study of policy change can be considered a core area of public policy (Howlett and Cashore 2009) which focuses on the description and explanation of changes in dominant regulatory patterns in different policy fields. Scientific discussion on policy change is not only centred on conceptual core issues such as the definition and operationalization of 'policy change' but also focuses on its theoretical explanation including the timing of change. We find a variety of suggestions to address these conceptual and theoretical issues in the literature.

It is the objective of this paper to contribute to this discussion by focusing on policy change in morality policy – an area that is generally ascribed specific analytical features that distinguish it from classical fields of regulation. The latter refers in particular to the fact that societal value conflicts shape political processes rather than diverging material interests. Starting with morality policy change as the central analytical focus, we address the three research issues mentioned above.

In so doing, we review the existing policy change literature. We analyse which concepts, theories and types of explanatory factors seem particularly appropriate for the study of morality policies, as well as which peculiarities have to be taken into account. This way, we will also answer the question of whether and to what extent morality policies really differ analytically from other policy areas.

The contribution proceeds as follows. The subsequent sections deal with the field of morality policy at large by focusing on what constitutes change in this area, including how morality policies change can be measured. Next we discuss the explanatory factors we consider crucial to explaining morality policy change.

ASSESSING MORALITY POLICY CHANGE: CONCEPTS AND MEASUREMENT

In order to address questions of how to conceptualize morality policy change, we first need to define morality policy. Second, we address particular problems associated with measuring morality policy change. To pinpoint these issues, we finally suggest an alternative measurement approach.

Morality policy: definitions and subfields

In the literature, we find two different approaches to defining morality policies (e.g., Engeli *et al.* 2012; Knill 2013). The first approach focuses on the regulatory matter as such (i.e., the policy dimension) as the decisive criterion. Here, policies are considered morality policies if they address topics that are generally assumed to refer to decisions and conflicts about societal values. The analytical starting point is the matter of regulations, which might be dominated by value concerns to different degrees. As such, this approach adopts a nominal perspective, classifying policies *a priori* as morality or non-morality issues.

This policy-based definition has to be distinguished from the politics-oriented approach prevalent in United States (US)–American research on morality issues. Here, the analytical point of departure is that morality policies are made and result from the policy-making process. A first group of authors focuses on the framing of policies as morality or non-morality issues (cf., Mucciaroni 2011; Euchner *et al.* 2013). Policies are considered morality issues if they are framed as such by at least one (important) advocacy group. Scholars, however, disagree on what degree of morality framing (e.g., when, by whom and with what terminology) is required to qualify a policy as a morality policy. A second perspective stresses that the decision of whether to treat an issue as a matter of conscience in the political debate depends on the conflict lines that divide political actors within political parties. In the absence of any clear-cut party position on a policy issue, Members of Parliament are asked to trust their own conscience when voting on morality law proposals (Cowley 1998). This situational definition of 'issues of conscience' precludes any *ex ante* specification of morality policy that is applicable over time and space.

Instead, situational cleavages between political actors determine policy-making dynamics and, hence, policy decisions.

In many cases, both conceptual approaches might yield similar classifications because the nature of the policy favours specific process patterns. Notwithstanding the potential linkages between both approaches, we base our following discussion on the policy-based definition. Accordingly, we speak of morality policies whenever the regulation of value conflicts rather than conflicts over tangible resources constitutes the core feature of a policy (Knill 2013).

In addition, we distinguish between four major subfields of morality policy. The first subfield refers to issues of 'life and death' and includes policies on abortion, assisted suicide and all aspects of stem cell treatment. The second subfield covers issues of sexual behaviour (including homosexuality, same-sex recognition, prostitution and pornography). The third subfield encompasses addictive behaviour or substances, including gambling and drug consumption. A fourth subfield encloses all policies defining public limitations on individual self-determination; i.e., where the major tension arises from the clash between conflicting goals, like personal liberties and other persons' basic rights. A typical policy example of the fourth type is the regulation of firearm possession.

Issues of conceptualization and measurement

In the literature, we find various approaches to measure policy change. As a consequence, the theoretical and empirical findings are hardly comparable, as the dependent variable is conceptualized and measured very differently. In this context, a first basic decision refers to the question for which stages in the policy cycle change should be measured. A basic distinction can be drawn between policy outputs and policy effects (Knill and Tosun 2012).

Policy outputs are the direct result of the decision-making process, which usually involves the adoption of a certain programme, law or regulation. They are hence defined by the content of a policy, as it is fixed in legal or administrative documents. Policy effects, by contrast, are closely related to the stages of policy implementation and evaluation. Here, the focus is on the way policies induce behavioural change with the targeted actors. Do policy addressees alter their previous behaviour in concert with the objectives of a public policy? For example, do increased charges on slot machine establishments lower their usage in pubs and consequently reduce the number of gambling addicts? In general, there are many factors that affect how a certain policy output actually yields the expected effects. In addition to potential intervening variables that may play a role in this regard, particular emphasis has to be placed on the soundness of underlying causal assumptions regarding the policy design. To what extent does the policy actually tackle the real causes of a problem and to what extent does it rely on effective steering instruments?

While the assessment of such questions can be considered as difficult in general, it is particularly challenging when it comes to morality issues. Triggering behavioural change might be particularly difficult if behavioural patterns are deeply rooted in the moral values and convictions of the targeted individuals. Individuals, for instance, who strongly advocate abortion as a result of personal values or beliefs are unlikely to change their behaviour in light of stricter regulations. This holds in particular, as in morality policy-making, bargaining for compromise is only rarely a feasible strategy in view of the fundamental value conflicts involved (Mooney 2001; Patton 2007). At the same time, drug or gambling addicts will stick to their behaviour independent of regulatory changes and knowingly accept the penalties. Individuals who consider the supply and demand of commercial sex as an ordinary business might hardly be deterred from their behaviour by tighter laws, but may instead look for regulatory loopholes or continue their activities illegally. In short, both the potential interference with individual core values and the high challenges of monitoring and sanctioning compliance for a broad range of individual actors pose considerable problems for effectively designing morality policies in such a way that policy outputs actually result in expected policy effects. Although compliance and monitoring deficits characterize processes of policy implementation in many sectors, the link between policy outputs and policy effects can hence be considered as particularly precarious in the case of morality policies. This is why morality policies are associated with the presence of systematic implementation deficits (Meier 1994). This pattern is reinforced by the fact that, in light of fundamental conflicts between opposing advocacy coalitions, compromise solutions, if possible at all, typically involve the reliance on rather vague and open legal formula and broad legal terms. Ambiguous policy outputs, however, favour deviations from initial policy objectives during the implementation stage.

Hence, while in other policy studies (e.g., on environmental policy change) policy effects are often used as proxies for changes in policy outputs, such measurement approaches seem hardly feasible for morality policies. However, even if we concentrate on policy outputs as basic indicator of policy change, morality policies pose particular challenges.

A focus on policy outputs as a measure of policy change generally assumes that policy outputs reflect the preferences and intentions of the government. Changes can hence be interpreted as an indication of political willingness to change morality policies in a certain direction, regardless of the effectiveness of these attempts. In this context, a widely accepted typology has been suggested by Hall (1993), who distinguishes between three components of policy outputs: (1) policy paradigms; (2) policy instruments; and (3) the precise setting or calibration of those instruments.

This distinction is a useful starting point for measuring change in morality policy outputs across policy subfields and countries. Paradigm changes would refer to fundamental changes in the regulatory regime, i.e., a transition in legal status from, for instance, the total prohibition to the partial legalization of certain activities (e.g., 'big changes' in abortion or prostitution decriminalization). These kinds of paradigm shifts in morality policy have found considerable scholarly attention so far (see Green-Pedersen 2007; Haider-Markel 2001).

Instrument changes, by contrast, refer to changes in the means undertaken to achieve existing morality policy objectives (e.g., new elements for 'harm reduction' within drug policy), while setting adjustments as the slightest form of change refers to issues like, for instance, the number of gestation weeks during which legal termination of pregnancy is possible or the amount of cannabis tolerated for personal consumption.

However, although the distinction between different orders of change should, in principle, also work for morality policy outputs, certain limitations to its general applicability may emerge from the distinctive nature of the policy field. Morality policies – by definition – entail decisions on the regulation of societal value conflicts. This implies that minor adjustments in instrument settings might be discussed in a paradigmatic manner as they affect the involved actors' deeply rooted core beliefs. In other words, the strong dominance of value conflicts may imply that any morality policy change is *per se* paradigmatic. As long as decisions over societal values are at stake, policy change is always about paradigmatic core issues rather than instrumental aspects. For instance, minor adjustments of the time limits for legal abortion might be considered a paradigmatic change by the involved actors, although this would only touch the calibration of a given policy in Hall's terms. Similar debates can be observed in many countries when it comes to the decisions about the amount of drugs that can be legally purchased or owned by individual actors. Another example is the current debate in Germany with regard to the legal status of same-sex unions. Although the question of whether same-sex unions should have equal inheritance and tax entitlements as heterosexual couples merely refers to instrumental aspects of the underlying policy, these issues are debated in a paradigmatic way (Debus *et al.* 2012).

Compared to other policy areas, the link between different forms of morality policy change (paradigms, instruments, settings) and the degree of change is generally more complex. The extent to which even minor changes might be associated with fundamental paradigmatic value decisions, however, should of course vary across morality policy subfields, depending on the dominance of value conflicts.

An alternative measurement approach

In view of these problems, we suggest an alternative concept for measuring morality policy change. Rather than assessing policy change in terms of distinct dimensions that reflect different degrees of change, like the distinction between paradigms, instruments and setting suggested by Hall (1993) and its further development by Howlett and Cashore (2009), we argue that in the case of morality policy such classifications are to a lesser extent feasible. Therefore, we focus on the degree of change of a certain direction rather than the underlying policy dimensions. Our concept is based on the assumption that the constitutive cleavage underlying morality policies refers to a single dimension on which changes occur and are observable, namely, the degree of restrictiveness or liberality of a given regulatory or penal provision. Such a focus implies that both the degree and direction of change needs to be assessed from the perspective of an individual and the extent to which her behaviour is legally tolerated. On this basis, we propose a differentiated concept and measurement of morality policy change, which has not yet been systematically implemented in the morality policy literature, though it is sometimes addressed implicitly (see Flowe [2010] for an example in prostitution regulation).

First, changes in the restrictiveness of morality policies may affect both the demand and the supply of certain activities. This enables a distinction, for instance, between women seeking an abortion and the physicians providing the service, or between a drug consumer and a drug dealer. Such an approach reduces the risk of overlooking important changes (consider, for instance, the case of Sweden, where prostitution was re-criminalized for men buying sex but not women offering it [Gould 2001]).

Second, for a systematic assessment of morality policy change, we need to distinguish between the regulation and criminalization of certain behaviour. For example, many jurisdictions have abolished the criminality of abortion for the pregnant women, while abortion as such remained illegal. In short, morality policy change often occurs on the sanctioning dimension (i.e., the extent to which illegal behaviour is actually enforced), rather than the regulatory dimension.

A third consideration refers to the fact that – compared to other policy fields – change in morality policies is more often triggered by various forms of judicial intervention, such as judicial review, case law or court interpretations of statutes in civil law system. This is not only relevant for the general explanation of morality policy change (see below) but also has conceptual implications. A particular challenge in this regard is that judicial choices can be made in isolation from politics and the policy process. For example, court rulings have been responsible for the decriminalization of abortion in many states (Gindulis 2003), paved the way for the legalization of physician assisted suicide (Smith 2002) and ended gambling prohibitions in Europe (Littler 2007). The country- and field-specific impact of courts on morality policy change implies that the dependent variable is often heavily 'contaminated' by a factor that is actually outside of the realm of democratic politics. This is particularly salient in common-law systems. Given this particularity of morality politics, a perspective is needed that looks at policy change from different angles covering both legislative/executive activity and judicial policy change.

EXPLAINING MORALITY POLICY CHANGE: ANALYTICAL PECULIARITIES

Next, we concentrate on select explanatory peculiarities that potentially distinguish accounts of morality policy change from that of other areas. These peculiarities emerge from the distinctive nature of morality policies; i.e., the reference to values rather than material issues. Adopting this perspective, analytical attention is paid to the role of problem pressure, religion, societal values and public option, party positions and cleavages, institutional peculiarities emerging from the influence of the judiciary, and international influences.

Problem pressure: 'fundamental problems', 'threshold problems' and 'moral shocks'

Generally, studies mostly adopt an accumulative logic with regard to the role of problem pressure as a trigger of policy change, hence assuming a linear relationship between changes in problem indicators (like, for instance, unemployment rates or public debt levels) and the level of problem pressure. It is, however, questionable whether this logic also holds for morality issues.

First, morality policies – as a matter of fact – might address fundamental problems; i.e., decisions about principal aspects that are societally acceptable or not. This kind of 'fundamental policy' is especially relevant in the subfield of 'life and death'. Here, even one single case, like a court ruling on euthanasia or on abortion, might be sufficient to trigger broad societal mobilization and political debate. With 'fundamental policies', the application of quantifiable indicators for problem pressure, such as the total number of late abortions or the total number of people who die because of gunshots per year, is therefore of limited use. A societal phenomenon might trigger far-reaching policy change, even though it is exceptional or irregular.

A second type of morality policies, that can be distinguished in terms of its problem pressure implications, are so-called 'threshold policies'. Such policies concern the regulation of (the amount of) morally deviant behaviour that is still socially acceptable, e.g., the degree of prostitution presence or gambling. Rather than the acceptability of certain activities *per se*, the underlying problem here is one of 'critical mass'. Thus, for this second type of morality policies, objective problem indicators become more relevant. However, while the problem accumulation might occur in a linear manner, we assume that problem pressure needs to surpass a certain threshold before policy change occurs. As long as the problem remains rather hidden, in the sense that the moral mobilization potential is low, a policy response is rather unlikely.

Third, compared to other policy areas, both 'fundamental' and 'threshold' types of morality policy are especially prone to external shocks (Birkland 1997) in the form of moral shocks or public scandals that help induce policy change. While external shocks, like massive policy failures, often provide a window of opportunity to trigger policy change, morally shocking events that arouse public attention could be considered even more extreme in that regard. Examples include the recent tightening of pornography regulations in the UK owing to a single incidence of necrophilia pictures (Johnson 2010) or the attempt to legalize physician-assisted suicide following two prominent court cases involving terminally ill women in the UK (Greasley 2010). One of the most illustrative examples is (legal) gun possession: dramatic policy change has only followed rampages (Hurka and Nebel 2013).

The complex relevance of religion

The influence of religion on morality policies is one of the most extensively studied factors. There are several access points that allow this broad factor to take effect. First, religious affiliations or societal structures might indirectly affect governmental or legislative policy choices. At a remote level, this factor affects politicians' cost–benefit considerations for different morality policy options in terms of their expected (re-)election effects.

Morality policies are particularly sensitive to a society's religious stratification. Contrary to other policy fields, morality policies often touch upon issues that are central elements of various religious doctrines: e.g., the regulation of sexuality (e.g., sexual orientation, sexual conduct, prostitution and pornography); issues of life and death (e.g., abortion, euthanasia, stem cell research and assisted reproduction techniques); or activities with high addictiveness (e.g., the Islamic position on gambling or alcohol). Through their very content, morality policies can reinforce religious doctrine, express certain indifference on specific issues (consider for instance the liberalization of sexual orientation of most Western societies) or stand in contrast with religious dogmas (e.g., the liberalization of abortion regulation). We assume that the electorate rewards certain morality policies depending on the prevailing religious doctrines. The more an issue is of religious importance, the more influential this factor will be in the decision-makers' cost–benefit considerations.

Religious denomination and degree of religiosity of society are factors that have been studied as relatively remote sources of influence. While Castles (1994) finds a positive relationship between Catholicism and, among other things, liberal divorce laws, Minkenberg (2003) provides in-depth analyses of different configurations of Church–State relations and their impact on the restrictiveness of abortion policies. The author finds that religion matters in both respects: the degree of institutionalization of Protestantism or Catholicism and the level of religiosity in society. These results are also corroborated by in-depth qualitative research.

Other scholars have elaborated on this notion of 'religion' by trying to tease out the precise mechanisms of influence (on the meso level). Warner (2000) emphasizes the structural advantages of organized religion that enables, for instance, the Catholic Church to have a say in the debates on morality issues in most European countries. Thus, she conceives of the Church as a powerful *interest group* that acts rationally given the institutional context of the respective nation-states. In this context, Minkenberg (2003) emphasizes the impact of Church–State patterns on policy-making and outputs in morality politics. He argues that high public esteem for the values articulated by the Church and their independence from economic interests give organized religion a structural advantage compared to other lobbying organizations (cf., Schwartz and Tatalovich 2009).

Fink (2008) takes a slightly modified perspective on the nexus between religion and policy-making. Historical analyses of the regulation of assisted reproduction techniques and stem cell research provide evidence for the impact of religious institutions such as the Catholic Church as an *institutional actor* in morality politics. In this context, the author emphasizes the role of religious parties that enable the more direct articulation of religious interests in all stages of the policy cycle.

This reasoning is also characteristic of the work of Green-Pedersen (2007) and Engeli *et al.* (2012). These scholars provide a theoretical framework for comparing morality policy-making across secular party systems and those characterized by the existence of a religious cleavage (hence the presence of at least one strong religious party). They focus on the decisive stage of agenda-setting by arguing that in order for a morality issue to appear on the policy agenda, the nation-state's party system needs to be characterized by a conflict between religious parties and secular parties (see below).

While most research on the impact of religion on morality policy change takes a macro or meso perspective, few attempts have been made to focus on the decision-making behaviour of political actors according to their personal denomination. Most empirical studies of this category compare the voting behaviour of individual Members of Parliament in American states. Yamane and Oldmixon (2006), for instance, model the result of roll-call voting in the Wisconsin legislature on the issue of abortion by examining, among other things, the religious affiliation and religious group advocacy. They find evidence for Protestant religious denomination as being a strong determinant for individual voting behaviour (see also Calfano 2010).

As the examples illustrate, students of morality policy rely on a number of different approaches to assess the influence of religion on change and decision-making processes. First, from the macro perspective, religiosity and religious denomination of the electorate or population are regularly considered as proxies for values prevailing in society and, hence, decisive for understanding political actors' choices on moral issues. Second, meso approaches take into account the organizational structures of religion by either focusing on interest group activities or institutional foundations of influence (through, for example, Church–State relations). Finally, micro-level studies focus on the impact of religious affiliation on the individual decision-making by analysing voting behaviour on morality policies in legislatures.

Societal values and public opinion

The discussion above illustrates that the influence of religion on policy-making roots in a society and the policy-makers' degree of religious affiliation or openness towards religious concerns. With respect to the relationship between social values and (morality) policies, however, the mechanisms or direction of causality are arguably more hazy (see Wetstein and Albritton 1995). There is broad consensus that, by definition, morality policies respond to clashes of incompatible 'core values' between subgroups of society. As a consequence of this assumption, the impact of social values on morality policies has been left under-explored.

Research on the nexus between social values and morality politics is largely limited to comparisons of policy-making patterns in American states. Based on existing research, we argue that morality politics are more sensitive to social and personal values than other – regulatory or (re)distributive – policies.

In this context, it is interesting to note that early research on morality politics did not measure the actual impact of social or personal values on the content or direction of policy-making (see Mooney and Lee 1995). Later studies, however, explored this relationship by correlating public opinion on moral issues with actual policy outputs in American states. These include, for instance, Mooney and Lee (2000) on death penalty policies and Norrander and Wilcox's (1999) analyses of abortion policies. Further, Haider-Markel and Kaufman (2006) find a positive impact of public opinion and the protection of sexual orientation rights.

Recent research lends evidence to the expectation that personal values and personal opinions on different issues are related concepts (Kilburn 2009). Notwithstanding this finding, we still lack studies that systematically link analyses of public opinion or values (Inglehart and Welzel 2010) with those of morality policy-making. Based on the discussion on the influence of religion, we expect social values and public opinion to have a direct effect on the content of the policy and hence to be relevant during policy formulation and decision-making.

Do parties matter?

Party positions and cleavages are classical, explanatory factors in public policy. Yet it is questionable whether they are of equal relevance when it comes to morality issues. Regarding the left–right alignment of parties, we expect more left-leaning parties to take a more liberal stance on core morality issues and values and right-wing parties to advocate conservative positions (cf., Lindaman and Haider-Markel 2002) on questions related to sexual orientation, identity and conduct, abortion, stem cell research or ART. In contrast, we expect the left–right cleavage to be rather irrelevant for policies such as gun control, drug regulation or gambling. Still, there is disagreement within the research community on the impact of political parties on morality policies. Highton (2004), for instance, finds that parties have an indirect effect by shaping the voters' behaviour in Senate elections in American states when it comes to the highly politicized issue of abortion politics. On the same issue and with similar conclusions, Jaenicke (2002) studies the effect of partisanship on Congress decision results. Overby *et al.* (1998) corroborate these results when concluding that political partisanship is the best predictor for votes cast on abortion regulation in Canadian Parliament. Thus, on the micro level, partisan influence is generally found to matter with regard to abortion. From a macro perspective, however, the aggregate effect of (predominantly left-leaning) political parties on morality politics cannot be confirmed by existing studies (Blofield 2006).

One possible reason for this might be the fact that decisions on morality issues cut across party political orientations, implying that members of the legislature vote according to their personal convictions rather than party political positions (see Cowley [1998] for an empirical illustration of morality policy-making in the British case). This argument is supported by the fact that informal rules of party-disciplinary voting behaviour (that are applied especially in countries with proportional voting systems) are abandoned when it comes to decisions on morality issues.

On the other hand, political parties might matter for morality policies in a distinctive way that goes beyond the classical left–right dimension, namely in their degree of religious affiliation or secularization. In this context, it is interesting to note that only limited attention has been paid to analysing the role of, for instance, Christian Democratic parties in morality policy-making so far. While research is devoted to studying the impact religious actors have on morality policies (i.e., as interest groups, lobbying organization or opinion leader on different issues, see above), we still lack systematic research on the impact of religious parties on morality policies.

A first step towards filling this research gap has been made by Green-Pedersen (2007) and Engeli *et al.* (2012), who, however, deliberately shift attention from the explanation of morality policy choices towards the processes of agenda-setting and policy formulation. The authors argue that morality policy-making is contingent upon the existence of a political conflict between two political parties. They expect this morality conflict to be institutionalized if the party system includes a strong religious political party that takes restrictive positions on morality issues by default. As Green-Pedersen (2007) empirically demonstrated, secular parties take advantage of this institutionalized opinion of religious parties by putting morality issues on the agenda. While Engeli *et al.* (2012) do not seek to explain single morality policy choices, the authors convincingly analyse the dynamics of agenda-setting and conflict emergence. In addition to what has been demonstrated by the latter authors, we argue that the structure of the party system and the relative strength of liberal, conservative and religious parties matter in order to understand both political attention for morality issues and subsequent policy-making (Schmitt *et al.* 2013).

Institutional peculiarities: the role of the judicial branch and the special function of courts

A central feature of morality politics is the role of policy changes that have been brought about by judicial intervention. It is an inherent characteristic of morality policies that they often concern human rights and individual freedoms, as well as equal treatment and (anti-)discrimination. These fundamental principles are codified in constitutional and other civil rights, while courts are assigned the responsibility to define, interpret and delineate in litigations the concrete substance of these rights. These circumstances provide a fruitful ground for judicial activism (e.g., Epp 1998). A large body of research has found a profound impact of courts on morality policies. This refers first to the subfield 'life and death', including abortion (e.g., Gindulis 2003) and assisted suicide. For the latter, several contributions showed how early and progressive court decisions in the Netherlands (Van Hees and Steunenberg 2000) eventually paved the way for its legalization in 2002. In particular, Steunenberg (1997) provides an ambitious model of how the courts interacted with the Dutch legislature and were able to exploit their room to manoeuvre.

The regulation of sexuality is a further field that is affected by court rulings to a large degree, owing to the fact that most subfields therein are strongly intertwined with concerns of human rights, equal treatment and anti-discrimination. This was already observed for the decriminalization of consensual sex among adult men (e.g., Dunphy 1997). In recent years, the legal recognition of same-sex-partnerships became a central field of judicial activism worldwide (Keck 2009; Smith 2005). However, Pierceson et al. (2010) recently showed that the judicial push for the legal recognition of gay and lesbian marriage in Latin America is far from being uniform. Constitutional courts, despite being confronted with similar cases, differ with respect to their activism to further the recognition of same-sex partnerships.

In general, courts can trigger morality policy change in four distinctive ways. First, they may act as agenda-setters by creating a situation where the legislature is either forced to react (judicial review which declares an act unconstitutional) and challenged (e.g., case law or statutory interpretation that breaks with the *status quo*). Second, courts might also be central to initial problem definition. Third, courts are decisive actors when it comes to policy implementation, hence strongly affecting policy change in terms of effects. Finally, there is an enormous relevance for strategic interaction between the judicial and the legislative or executive branch. While courts, on the one hand, might sometimes be willing to step in where legislatures are unwilling or unable to act (perhaps to follow an own policy agenda), they might, on the other hand, on other occasions be very reluctant to do so. In contrast, governments and legislatures might intentionally refrain from intervening in a certain field because of high polarization and the resultant high political costs and hence deliberately leave the issue 'to the judges'.

International and transnational influences

The influence of international or transnational mechanisms on domestic morality policies has barely been systematically analysed so far. While a number of scholars give descriptive accounts of the content, bindingness, potential and limitations of different institutional norms, mainly with regard to the international drug regime (e.g., Elvins 2003) or European gambling regulation (Littler 2007), we still lack approaches to link these findings with morality policy choices on a national level (but see, for example, Sanders [2002]).

The policy consequences of international norms and transnational communication are only being addressed in recent studies. Kollman (2009), for instance, illustrates how European Union institutions and the European Court of Human Rights, together with strong transnational homosexual lobbying organizations, have shaped policy-making on the issue in a number of European countries. Frank *et al.* (2010) try to reconstruct international dynamics in morality politics by analysing the diffusion and change of sex-laws based on a global sample and a time frame of 60 years. Applying an event-history design, they identify broad patterns of change – that is, increasing criminalization of child-related and violent practices accompanied by more leniency towards adults' consensual sexual behaviour.

The findings of these studies suggest that different channels of international influence are of importance, including first, international law and norms (hard and soft law); second, international court rulings (e.g., through the European Court of Justice or the European Court of Human Rights (see above); and third, transnational communication and the globalization of ideas and social movements that lead to emulation and diffusion dynamics in morality policy-making.

Despite a shortage of systematic research, this brief account illustrates that morality policies are likely to differ in their exposure to international and transnational sources of influence. While a large body of international laws and treaties already shapes national regulation of addictive behaviour and substances (drugs or gambling), social ideas and norms on, for example, sexual freedom are likely to spread through transnational networks and relevant court rulings. In this context, we expect diffusion and international courts to be relevant in national agenda-setting processes as they increase public awareness of certain morality issues. International soft or hard law, in turn, has the potential to reach farther, also shaping policy formulation and decision-making processes. As this brief presentation suggests, international factors of influence should not be neglected in future attempts to analyse and explain morality politics and policy choices.

CONCLUSION

This contribution offered a conceptual and empirical discussion of morality politics and policy-making. We provided a structured account in order to ease future research in the field of morality politics in general and morality policy change in particular. By summarizing the state of the art and outlining possible research gaps, we provided a starting point and guidance for future theoretical and empirical analyses of this field. Given the extensiveness of morality politics as such, and in order to reduce complexity, we mainly focused on the actual decision-making of political actors. We are aware that other processes precede this stage of the policy cycle, such as agenda-setting or policy formulation (see Engeli *et al.* 2012). While different explanatory factors might be important at different stages of the policy-making process, we put analytical emphasis on explaining the way in which morality policy choices are made. In this regard, we placed particular emphasis on the peculiar role of problem pressure, religion, societal values and public opinion, party cleavages, the role of the judiciary, and international influences. Our results are only a first step for exploring the fascinating and neglected field of morality policy-making.

Biographical notes: Stephan Heichel is Assistant Professor at the Chair of Comparative Public Policy and Administration, University of Konstanz, Germany. Christoph Knill is Professor of Political Science and Public Administration at the University of Konstanz, Germany. Sophie Schmitt is Postdoctoral Research Fellow at the Institute for Research Information and Quality Assurance in Berlin, Germany.

ACKNOWLEDGMENTS

This article is based on the project MORAPOL (ERC Advanced Grant). Generous funding by the European Research Council is gratefully acknowledged.

REFERENCES

Birkland, T.A. (1997) *After Disaster: Agenda Setting, Public Policy, and Focusing Events*, Washington, DC: Georgetown University Press.
Blofield, M. (2006) *The Politics of Moral Sin: Abortion and Divorce in Spain, Chile and Argentina*, New York/London: Routledge.
Calfano, B.R. (2010) 'The power of brand: beyond interest group influence in U.S. state abortion politics', *State Politics and Policy Quarterly* 10(3): 227–47.
Castles, F.G. (1994) 'On religion and public policy: does Catholicism make a difference?', *European Journal of Political Research* 25(1): 19–40.
Cowley, P. (ed.) (1998) *Conscience and Parliament: Moral Issues in British Politics*, London: Frank Cass.
Debus, M., Knill, C. and Tosun, J. (2012) 'Drum zahle, wer sich ewig bindet: Eine Analyse der Gebührenhöhe für eingetragene Lebenspartnerschaften in Baden-Württemberg', *Politische Vierteljahresschrift* 53(1): 1–28.
Dunphy, R. (1997) 'Sexual identities, national identities: the politics of gay law reform in the republic of Ireland', *Contemporary Politics* 3(3): 247–65.
Elvins, M. (2003) *Anti-Drugs Policies of the European Union: Transnational Decision-Making and the Politics of Expertise*, Basingstoke: Palgrave Macmillan.
Engeli, I., Green-Pedersen, C. and Larsen, L.T. (eds) (2012) *Morality Politics in Western Europe: Parties, Agendas and Policy Choices*, Basingstoke: Palgrave Macmillan.

Epp, C.R. (1998) *The Rights Revolution: Lawyers, Activists, and Supreme Courts in Comparative Perspective*, Chicago, IL: University of Chicago Press.

Euchner, E.-M., Heichel, S., Nebel, K. and Raschzok, A. (2013) 'From "moral" policy to "normal" policy: framing of drug consumption and gambling in Germany and the Netherlands and their regulatory consequences', *Journal of European Public Policy* 20(3), doi: 10.1080/13501763.2013.761506

Fink, S. (2008) 'Politics as usual or bringing religion back in? The influence of research laws parties, institutions, economic interests, and religion on embryo', *Comparative Political Studies* 41(12): 1631–56.

Flowe, M. (2010) 'The international market for trafficking in persons for the purpose of sexual exploitation: analyzing current treatment of supply and demand', *North Carolina Journal of International Law and Commercial Regulation* 35(3): 669–722.

Frank, D.J., Camp, B.J. and Boutcher, S.A. (2010) 'Worldwide trends in the criminal regulation of sex, 1945 to 2005', *American Sociological Review* 75(6): 867–93.

Gindulis, E. (2003) *Der Konflikt um die Abtreibung: Die Bestimmungsfaktoren der Gesetzgebung zum Schwangerschaftsabbruch im OECD-Ländervergleich*, Wiesbaden: Westdeutscher Verlag.

Gould, A. (2001) 'The criminalisation of buying sex: the politics of prostitution in Sweden', *Journal of Social Policy* 30(3): 437–56.

Greasley, K. (2010) 'R(Purdy) v DPP and the case for wilful blindness', *Oxford Journal of Legal Studies* 30(2): 301–26.

Green-Pedersen, C. (2007) 'The conflict of conflicts in comparative perspective: euthanasia as a political issue in Denmark, Belgium, and the Netherlands', *Comparative Politics* 39(3): 273–91.

Haider-Markel, D.P. (2001) 'Policy diffusion as a geographical expansion of the scope of political conflict: same-sex marriage bans in the 1990s', *State Politics and Policy Quarterly* 1(1): 5–26.

Haider-Markel, D.P. and Kaufman, M.S. (2006) 'Public opinion and policy making in the culture wars: is there a connection between opinion and state policy on gay and lesbian issues?', in J.E. Cohen (ed.), *Public Opinion in State Politics*, Standford, CA: Stanford University Press, pp. 163–82.

Hall, P.A. (1993) 'Policy paradigms, social learning, and the state: the case of economic policymaking in Britain', *Comparative Politics* 25(3): 275–96.

Highton, B. (2004) 'Policy voting in Senate elections: the case of abortion', *Political Behavior* 26(2): 181–200.

Howlett, M. and Cashore, B. (2009) 'The dependent variable problem in the study of policy change: understanding policy change as a methodological problem', *Journal of Comparative Policy Analysis: Research and Practice* 11(1): 33–46.

Hurka, S. and Nebel, K. (2013) 'Framing and policy change after shooting rampages: a comparative analysis of discourse networks', *Journal of European Public Policy* 20(3), doi: 10.1080/13501763.2013.761508

Inglehart, R. and Welzel, C. (2010) 'Changing mass priorities: the link between modernization and democracy', *Perspectives on Politics* 8(2): 551–67.

Jaenicke, D.W. (2002) 'Abortion and partisanship in the US Congress, 1976–2000: increasing partisan cohesion and differentiation', *Journal of American Studies* 36(1): 1–22.

Johnson, P. (2010) 'Law, morality and disgust: the regulation of "extreme pornography" in England and Wales', *Social & Legal Studies* 19(2): 147–63.

Keck, T.M. (2009) 'Beyond backlash: assessing the impact of judicial decisions on LGBT rights', *Law and Society Review* 43(1): 151–85.

Kilburn, H.W. (2009) 'Personal values and public opinion', *Social Science Quarterly* 90(4): 868–85.

Knill, C. (2013) ' The study of morality policy: analytical implications from a public policy perspective', *Journal of European Public Policy* 20(3), doi: 10.1080/13501763.2013.761494

Knill, C. and Tosun, J. (2012) *Public Policy: A New Introduction*, Basingstoke: Palgrave Macmillan.

Kollman, K. (2009) 'European institutions, transnational networks and national same-sex unions policy: when soft law hits harder', *Contemporary Politics* 15(1): 37–53.

Lindaman, K. and Haider-Markel, D.P. (2002) 'Issue evolution, political parties, and the culture wars', *Political Research Quarterly* 55(1): 91–110.

Littler, A. (2007) 'The regulation of gambling at European level: the balance to be found', *ERA Forum* 8(3): 357–71.

Meier, K.J. (1994) *The Politics of Sin: Drugs, Alcohol, and Public Policy*, Armonk, NY: ME Sharpe.

Minkenberg, M. (2003) 'The policy impact of Church–State relations: family policy and abortion in Britain, France, and Germany', *West European Politics* 26(1): 195–217.

Mooney, C.Z. (ed.) (2001) *The Public Clash of Private Values: The Politics of Morality Policy*, Chatham, NJ: Chatham House.

Mooney, C.Z. and Lee, M.-H. (1995) 'Legislating morality in the American states: the case of pre-Roe abortion regulation reform', *American Journal of Political Science* 39(3): 599–627.

Mooney, C.Z. and Lee, M.-H. (2000) 'The influence of values on consensus and contenious morality policy: U.S. death penalty reform, 1956–82', *Journal of Politics* 62(1): 223–39.

Mucciaroni, G. (2011) 'Are debates about "morality policy" really about morality? Framing opposition to gay and lesbian rights', *Policy Studies Journal* 39(2): 187–216.

Norrander, B. and Wilcox, C. (1999) 'Public opinion and policymaking in the States: the case of post-Roe abortion policy', *Policy Studies Journal* 27(4): 707–22.

Overby, L.M., Tatalovich, R. and Studlar, D.T. (1998) 'Party and free votes in Canada: abortion in the House of Commons', *Party Politics* 4(3): 381–92.

Patton, D. (2007) 'The Supreme Court and morality policy adoption in the American states', *Political Research Quarterly* 60(3): 468–88.

Pierceson, J., Piatti-Crocker, A. and Schulenberg, S. (eds) (2010) *Same-sex Marriage in the Americas: Policy Innovation for Same-sex Relationships*, Lanham, MD: Lexington Books.

Sanders, D. (2002) 'Human rights and sexual orientation in international law', *International Journal of Public Administration* 25(1): 13–44.

Schmitt, S., Euchner, E.-M. and Preidel, C. (2013) 'Regulating prostitution and same-sex marriage in Italy and Spain: the interplay of political and societal veto players in two Catholic societies', *Journal of European Public Policy* 20(3), doi: 10.1080/13501763.2013.761512

Schwartz, M.A. and Tatalovich, R. (2009) 'Cultural and institutional factors affecting political contention over moral issues', *Comparative Sociology* 8(1): 76–104.

Smith, J.D. (2002) *Right-to-Die Policies in the American States: Judicial and Legislative Innovation*, New York: LFB Scholarly Publishing.

Smith, M. (2005) 'Social movements and judicial empowerment: courts, public policy, and lesbian and gay organizing in Canada', *Politics and Society* 33(2): 327–53.

Steunenberg, B. (1997) 'Courts, cabinet and coalition parties: the politics of euthanasia in a parliamentary setting', *British Journal of Political Science* 27(4): 551–71.

Van Hees, M. and Steunenberg, B. (2000) 'The choices judges make: court rulings, personal values, and legal constraints', *Journal of Theoretical Politics* 12(3): 305–23.

Warner, C.M. (2000) *Confessions of an Interest Group: The Catholic Church and Political Parties in Europe*, Princeton, NJ: Princeton University Press.

Wetstein, M.E. and Albritton, R.B. (1995) 'Effects of public opinion on abortion policies and use in the American states', *Publius* 25(4): 91–105.

Yamane, D. and Oldmixon, E.A. (2006) 'Religion in the legislative arena: affiliation, salience, advocacy, and public policymaking', *Legislative Studies Quarterly* 31(3): 433–60.

The puzzle of permissiveness: understanding policy processes concerning morality issues

Isabelle Engeli, Christoffer Green-Pedersen and Lars Thorup Larsen

ABSTRACT The growing interest in morality politics has spurred a large number of studies on individual morality issues and the gradual shift from restrictive to permissive regulation across Western Europe. Several studies have further pointed to the changing role of religion as the main cause of permissive policy shifts. However, seen in a comparative perspective across four countries and five morality issues, the move towards permissiveness poses more of a puzzle than a simple shift. Religion and secularization do not impact on regulation directly, but are filtered through a policy dynamic in which the essential factor is whether or not the party system contains a conflict line between secular and confessional parties. Countries without confessional parties, here the United Kingdom and Denmark, surprisingly end up less permissive than countries with strong confessional parties, here the Netherlands and Spain, because the former group lacks the conflict line necessary to politicize morality issues

INTRODUCTION

Long kept off the agenda, morality issues now gain increasing importance across most Western countries. Abortion was the first morality issue to attract broad political attention in the 1960s, but since then a growing number of issues have raised public attention to morality conflicts, including same-sex marriage, euthanasia, embryo research and assisted reproductive technology (ART).

While most Western European countries have addressed these morality issues in the last decades, the permissiveness of regulation varies substantially. A growing literature has emerged on what can explain such cross-national differences in policy, but most studies so far focus on a single issue, like abortion (Minkenberg 2002; Stetson 2001), stem cell research (Banchoff 2011; Fink 2008), euthanasia (Green-Pedersen 2007), same-sex marriages (Kollmann 2007) and ART (Bleiklie *et al.* 2004; Monpetit *et al.* 2007). The focus on single issues leaves open the question of whether there is a consistent policy pattern across the different morality issues, and as a result these studies may leave an unclear and contradictory picture of what causes cross-national variation in permissiveness.

To improve our understanding of what causes variation in the permissiveness of morality issues, there is a need to clarify the nature of the policy processes concerning morality issues. We therefore present a model with two ideal types of the policy process in what we term 'the two worlds of morality politics'. One is called the religious world and applies to countries where the party system embodies a significant conflict between secular and confessional parties – either Christian Democratic or Conservative parties with a confessional orientation. Morality issues often play a significant role in party competition in the religious world and consequently receive a great deal of political attention, sometimes because they evoke deep historical conflicts about the role of religion in society. In the religious world, politics thus matters for morality issues in the sense that permissive regulation may be passed when confessional parties are not in government, whereas this is unlikely to happen when they are in government. Furthermore, the varying degrees of secularization can explain cross-national differences in permissiveness here, since it provides secular parties with electoral support for increasingly permissive regulation.

Conversely, in what we label the secular world, policy processes on morality issues are distinctively different. There is no significant conflict between secular and confessional parties that can generate political attention to morality issues, which are often seen as being essentially non-political, ethical questions falling outside the realm of normal politics. As a result, the composition of parties in government is not central to understanding policy decisions on morality issues, which depend on issue-specific coalitions with no unifying tendency towards permissive regulation across all issues.

Empirically, the contribution compares policies and policy processes across four countries (the Netherlands, Spain, the United Kingdom and Denmark) and five morality issues (abortion, same-sex marriage, euthanasia, stem cells and ART). First, we present a detailed analysis of how permissive policies are on each of the five policy issues and in each of the four countries. Among our cases, the Netherlands and Spain exemplify the religious world owing to the significant conflict between secular and confessional parties in their respective party systems. We then show how party conflict and party competition have driven the policy processes in these countries, where permissive legislation has generally been implemented when confessional parties were out of government. The Netherlands has seen a much earlier secularization than Spain and is therefore more permissive in general, while Spain is clearly catching up. Denmark and the United Kingdom (UK) both exemplify the secular world because there is no religious base underneath party conflict and morality issues have never played an important role in party competition. These countries passed some fragments of permissive regulation very early on, especially on abortion, but were much later in making permissive regulation on same-sex marriages and remain very restrictive on euthanasia. On ART and stem cell research, they vary even more. In other words, there is no macro-party conflict structuring morality policy processes in these countries, but rather specific dynamics on each issue.

EXISTING EXPLANATIONS OF CROSS-NATIONAL DIFFERENCES IN MORALITY POLICIES

Previous literature on morality policies in Western Europe and the United States (e.g., Mooney 2001; Smith and Tatalovich 2003; Tatalovich and Daynes 2011) has increased our detailed knowledge of each individual issue, but the predominance of single-issue studies tends to leave a diverging or even contradictory picture of morality policy in general. These studies may overestimate issue-specific characteristics, such as the impact of medical communities on ART and stem cell regulation or the mobilization of LGBT groups on same-sex marriage. As a result, while explanations of morality policies point to a complex interaction of multiple factors, the underlying causal mechanism is not always clearly identified. One is easily left with a somewhat fuzzy picture of how morality issues are currently governed in Western Europe. This is particularly the case with the two most 'usual suspects' in comparative policy studies, i.e., party politics or institutions as general explanations.

A number of single-case studies portray leftist parties as being more liberal on morality issues than right-wing parties. However, comparative research on abortion, reproductive technologies and stem cell research does not identify such a systematic pattern (Banchoff 2011; Blofield 2006; Mazur 2002; Rothmayr et al. 2004; Stetson 2001). The picture is somewhat similar with institutions, since previous studies seem to agree that institutional configurations alone do not exert direct impact on policy content (Engeli, Green-Pedersen and Larsen 2012; Fink 2008; Montpetit et al. 2007; Rothmayr et al. 2004; Stetson 2001; Varone et al. 2006). Rothmayr et al. (2004), Stetson (2001) and Fink (2009) systematically review the impact of institutional settings and veto points according to the classic typologies of political systems (consensus versus majoritarian democracies, federalist versus unitary systems, parliamentary versus presidential systems), but fail to identify a clear and consistent explanatory pattern.

Comparative research on morality politics has increasingly turned to the role of religious actors such as Christian Democrats and the Roman Catholic Church. Again, however, findings are mixed. While comparative research on ART contests that the field is governed by Christian Democracy (Rothmayr et al. 2004), studies on stem cell research emphasize how the Catholic Church has been able to establish a 'societal veto' of permissive policies and with strong partisan backup (Fink 2009). The impact of religion on abortion regulation is equally fuzzy, because whereas Minkenberg (2002, 2003) pays great attention to the relationship between state and church, Stetson (2001) argues that religious culture exerts no direct and systematic impact on abortion liberalization.

In sum, the comparative literature has opened our eyes to the role of religious actors, but still with no clear theoretical idea about how religion impacts on both policy choices and the underlying political conflicts. Religion seems to be important to the politics of morality issues, but we need a clear and comparatively consistent picture of how it exerts this influence.

THE POLICY PROCESS OF MORALITY ISSUES

A key requisite for making better explanations of morality policy is to be able to theorize the underlying policy dynamic rather than merely relating cross-national differences to static factors like institutional structures or the existence of Christian Democratic parties. While still important, such factors may not necessarily impact directly upon policy, but instead structure the policy process in a way that makes a politicization of morality issues much more likely. In the following, we present a model of the policy process structured around the 'two worlds of morality politics' (cf., Engeli, Green-Pedersen and Larsen 2012). The model draws on and combines insights from both policy agenda setting theory (Baumgartner and Jones 1993) and recent literature on religion and party conflict in Western Europe (van Kersbergen and Manow 2009).

A key tenet in policy agenda-setting theory is the distinction between subsystem and macro politics (Baumgartner and Jones 1993). Policy-making at the subsystem level is characterized by a limited number of actors with little outside interest, whereas macro politics designates situations where issues attract attention from the wider public and macro-political actors like presidents, party leaders, etc. Attention is thus the key variable, which differentiates subsystem from macro politics. A crucial dynamic in agenda-setting according to Baumgartner and Jones (1993) is a so-called 'Schattschneider mobilization' where an issue expands from the quiet life of sub-system politics to the macro-political agenda, in which case it is also likely to become relevant for party competition and electoral concerns. A weakness of the agenda-setting approach, however, has been the inability to explain why the same issue is delegated to subsystem politics in one country but is macro political in another country. We therefore also need to look beyond this approach to develop a dynamic model of the policy process for morality issues.

The literature on religion and party politics is an obvious place to start, given the increasing knowledge on the importance of religion. This literature takes its key point of departure in the cleavage tradition, especially the State–Church cleavage, which in some countries led to the formation of strong Christian Democratic parties (Ertman 2009), whereas in other countries religion disappeared completely from the party system. Thus, the presence or absence of strong Christian Democratic parties is the key to understanding religious influence on contemporary party politics, because they establish an essential conflict line between secular and confessional parties.

In the post-war period, many Christian Democratic parties successfully transformed from a largely confessional voter base to broad catch-all parties (van Kersbergen 1999). Put under pressure by increased secularization, several Christian Democratic parties have developed what Kalyvas and van Kersbergen (2010: 204) call 'unsecular' strategies focused on family values and the welfare state and without mentioning religion. Although it may sound counter-intuitive, Christian Democratic parties may therefore often try to avoid rather than appreciate morality issues, because morality debates can easily mobilize the confessional voters and grass-root activists and thereby threaten the broad appeal of the party. A similar dynamic is likely to take place in party systems without formally Christian Democratic parties, but where Conservative parties have confessional associations and are thus functional equivalents of Christian Democratic parties. What matters here is not the name of the party but whether a confessional profile or legacy is part of the common perception of the party, in which case it is also likely to pursue an 'unsecular' strategy and view morality issues as a liability in light of increased secularization.

The existence of a conflict line in the party system between secular and confessional parties is the key determinant of whether morality issues are likely to become part of 'macro politics' or whether they only exist in policy subsystems with limited macro-political attention. In what we label the 'religious world', the conflict line between confessional and secular parties generates macro-political attention to morality issues, because they are seen as new battlegrounds for the role of religion in an increasingly secularized society, which again attracts the secular side to challenge their opponents on morality issues. In sum, our expectations for the policy process around morality issues in the religious world are:

- First, politics is likely to matter for policy. When in government, confessional parties will seek to avoid more permissive legislation on morality issues. On the other hand, secular parties in opposition are likely to challenge a confessional government by demanding, for instance, free abortion or same-sex marriage. In turn, secular parties in government have strong incentives to govern morality issues permissively and distance themselves from previous governments.[1]
- Second, secularization is an important variable for explaining cross-national variation in permissiveness across the religious world. Secularization accentuates the problems of the 'unsecular' strategy of confessional parties while attracting secular challenges to the strategy. The more the median voter supports permissive polices, which is likely to increase with secularization, the stronger the pressure on confessional parties and the more likelihood of permissive policies.
- Third, the different morality issues are likely to experience a similar policy process, despite differences in the nature of the issues, a process shaped by the conflict between secular and confessional positions. Abortion has typically

been the first subject of this conflict and once settled with some form of permissive policy, the struggle will move on to other morality issues.

In what we label the secular world, the policy process is distinctively different. There is no conflict between secular and confessional parties that can draw morality issues onto the macro-political agenda. Instead, each issue will likely experience its own and more issue-specific dynamic at the subsystem level. Parties in the secular world generally pay very little attention to morality issues, and the colour of government is usually not important for policy decisions. The different morality issues are also much less connected in the sense that the end of the abortion struggle creates no pattern for other issues to follow. Policy decisions will be affected by the dynamics of subsystem politics. With the absence of religious actors in the political system, proposals for permissive policy changes will not necessarily be met with strong resistance, but the absence of strong resistance is not enough to generate a push for permissive regulation. This depends on interest groups to push for permissive regulation and their ability to form alliances with individual Members of Parliament (MPs) who can raise the issue in parliament. The likelihood that such interest groups will form depends upon the characteristics of the particular morality issue. Women's groups are likely to push for free abortion as gay and lesbian groups are likely to push for same sex marriage. However, a strong interest group pushing for euthanasia is less likely. Finally, secularization is unlikely to explain cross-national differences in permissiveness in the secular world, because, while it does make the median voter more supportive of permissive regulation, this has little or no impact on the policy process owing to the lack of electoral competition on morality issues.

CASE SELECTION AND MORALITY ISSUES

To test our expectations about policy processes and permissiveness, we have selected four cases: two countries with a conflict between secular and confessional parties and two countries without. In our first case, the Netherlands, the conflict in the party system between Christian Democratic parties, primarily the CDA (Christen-Democratisch Appèl), and secular parties (PvdA [Partij van de Arbeid – Social Democrats]), VVD (Volkspartij voor Vrijheid en Democratie – Liberals) and D66 (Politieke Partij Democraten 66 – Social Liberals) is well established (Andeweg and Irwin 2009). The second case is Spain, where the Conservative Party has a strong historical association with the Catholic Church and where party competition between the socialist party (PSOE, Partido Socialista Obrero Español) and the Conservative Party (PP, Partido Popular) represents the conflict between secular and confessional (Chaques and Roqué 2012). Our two cases of the secular world are the UK and Denmark, where there is no conflict between confessional and secular parties and where politics is strongly dominated by a traditional competition between left and right.

As argued, we expect to find a variation in policy processes that will in turn affect policy decisions. To evaluate this claim, we need a fine-grained measure of permissiveness that will work across all the issues, countries and in different periods. We have analysed the policy content of each authoritative decision taken at the national level from the end of the 1960s to 2010 and identified quantitative indicators on a number of dimensions of the issue at stake.[2] These indicators were first coded quantitatively on a scale from 0 to 3 for each dimension and then aggregated into a single composite index for each policy issue. For the sake of simplicity, we present here only the qualitative regulatory continuum from a very permissive ideal-type of regulation to a very restrictive ideal-type of regulation.[3] Figures 1 and 2 present the policy patterns in morality regulation across the religious world (Spain and the Netherlands) and the secular world (Denmark and the United Kingdom).

In the literature, abortion is often considered the 'mother' issue of morality politics that addresses women's reproductive freedom and the right to choose to terminate pregnancy. Permissive policies make abortion available upon women's request and provide financial coverage for the medical procedure. In contrast, restrictive policies limit access to abortion to medical and/or social grounds and restrict public funding. As Figures 1 and 2 reveal, the abortion issue was resolved much earlier in the secular than in the religious world. The UK was the first Western European country to liberalize abortion in 1967 by largely extending the medical grounds, and was followed by Denmark in 1973. In comparison, countries in the religious world took much longer to settle the abortion issue. The Netherlands opted for a permissive regulation in 1981, while Spain did not liberalize abortion fully until 2010, after a very moderate 1985 reform.

ART emerged with the invention of in vitro fertilization (IVF) in 1978, which allows for the creation of embryos outside a woman's body. The development of ART provided treatment to infertile couples, but has also created new forms of parenthood, such as same-sex parenthood where only one parent is also the biological parent, or single-woman parenthood with no father registered.[4] Governing ART thus involves decisions about access for different groups of patients and the degree of medical autonomy regarding technical procedures. Policies are qualified as permissive if there is large medical autonomy to practice and full financial coverage. A restrictive policy bans several ART techniques or puts

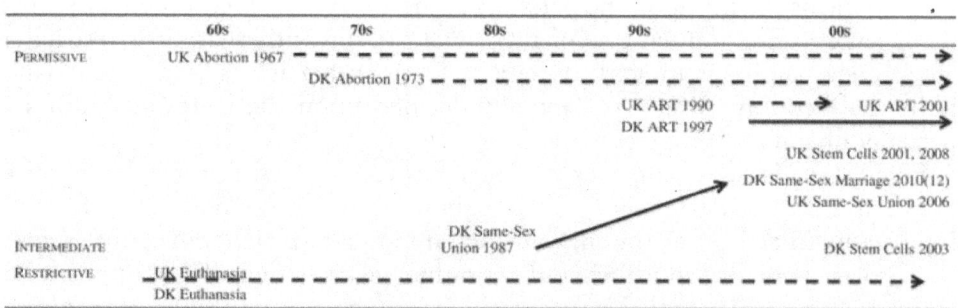

Figure 1 Policy pattern in the secular world: the United Kingdom and Denmark

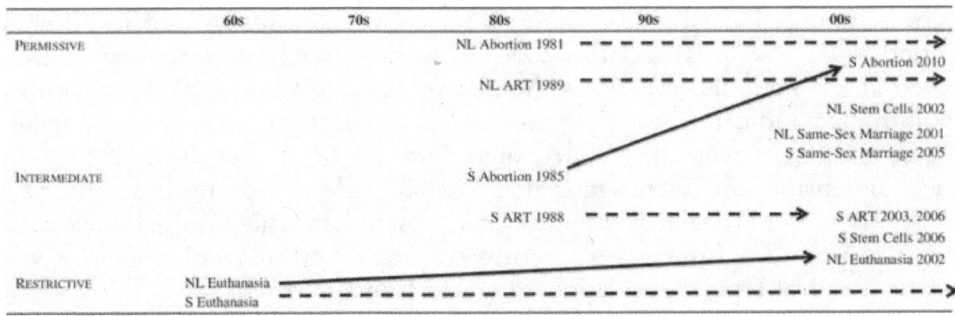

Figure 2 Policy pattern in the religious world: the Netherlands and Spain

conditions on their use and provides limited financial coverage. The United Kingdom opted for a comparatively permissive regulation on ART as early as in 1990, and Denmark followed in 1997 with a permissive regulation. The Netherlands first left ART in the hands of the medical community, which adopted very permissive self-regulatory guidelines that were later directly integrated into the 1989 policy decision. The Spanish regulatory approach has remained less permissive over time. While a large number of techniques are allowed, the financial coverage has remained very limited.

More recently, new technological development has raised a new set of regulations covering embryonic stem cell research. A permissive policy grants the medical and scientific communities broad autonomy to conduct stem cell research and therapeutic cloning, while a restrictive policy bans some or all forms of research on human embryos. Stem cell regulation presents a contrasting pattern to ART in that the UK is the only country to actively promote stem cell research through very permissive legislation, even allowing for therapeutic cloning. The other three are relatively restrictive: stem cell research is allowed under strict conditions, while therapeutic cloning is banned.

In our analysis, we focus solely on the two most serious forms of euthanasia: assisted suicide and active euthanasia. Assisted suicide provides assistance to patients to end their life through voluntary self-administration of lethal medication. Active euthanasia implies the direct involvement of the physician, who performs the act upon the patient's request. A policy is considered permissive if patients are granted one of these two options, otherwise it is restrictive. The policy pattern is in stark difference to the other issues. The Netherlands is the only country which has actually decided upon the issue (in 2002) and partially liberalized active euthanasia.

Finally, the issue of same-sex marriage has recently led to a vivid conflict in Western Europe. Permissive policies grant same-sex couples some form of legal status (marriage or union) and the same range of rights in terms of taxation, social benefits, adoption and reproductive rights (ART) as opposite-sex couples. Restrictive policies constrain the legal recognition of same-sex couples to a limited number of rights only. Our four countries have all entitled same-sex couples to very similar rights as opposite-sex couples. Spain and the Netherlands opened up for actual marriage and provided similar rights to homosexual couples in the early/mid-2000s. Denmark was the first country to establish legal status in 1989, but did not provide equal reproductive rights until 2010, and has just recently (2012) introduced same-sex marriage in the Danish national church. The UK introduced same-sex unions in 2006 and has also granted equal rights, but it does not have the same marriage ceremony for hetero- and homosexual couples.

EXPLAINING POLICY PATTERNS IN THE RELIGIOUS AND SECULAR WORLDS

The pattern of permissiveness across the four countries and five issues presented in Figures 1 and 2 does not distinguish clearly between the religious and secular worlds. The most permissive country exemplifying the religious world is the Netherlands. Today, Dutch regulation is permissive on all morality issues except euthanasia, where it is intermediate. The other country belonging to the religious world, Spain, was the least permissive overall. Regulation is permissive in terms of abortion and same-sex marriage, but intermediate with regard to ART and stem cells, and restrictive on euthanasia. Denmark and the UK fall somewhere in between. The UK is similar to the Netherlands except that regulation of euthanasia is restrictive. Denmark differs from the UK by having only an intermediate regulation of stem cells.

The greatest difference between the religious and secular worlds lies in the temporal dynamic, where the UK and Denmark were the first to move in a permissive direction with abortion laws introduced around 1970. This did not, however, start a clear permissive trend, since nothing happened until the 1989 introduction of same-sex legal rights in Denmark and permissive British policy on ART in 1990, and euthanasia remains restrictive. The Netherlands did not move in a more permissive direction until the 1981 abortion law, but has since then become the most permissive country. Spain liberalized abortion much later, in 2010, but had already 'caught up' with the other countries on same-sex marriage in 2005. This temporal variation points to the importance of the underlying policy dynamic, even if the two worlds of morality politics do not directly translate into policy differences. Rather, the policy dynamic determines which variables will be able to explain cross-national differences in policy choices. This can be shown by looking in more detail at the policy processes in connection with morality issues.

THE NETHERLANDS AND SPAIN – POLICY DYNAMICS IN THE RELIGIOUS WORLD

Since both the Dutch and the Spanish party systems have a conflict between confessional and secular parties, we would expect morality issues to be subject to party competition, which is indeed the case. In the Netherlands, morality issues have attracted substantial party attention in party manifestoes and in parliamentary activities. Furthermore, both abortion and euthanasia have been central issues in negotiations over Dutch government coalitions (Timmermans and Breeman 2012). In Spain, abortion has been a central political issue since the 1980s, and after 2000 other issues like same-sex marriage, ART and to a lesser extent euthanasia have attracted attention in party competition (Chaques and Roqué 2012). Our expectation about policy processes in the religious world should thus apply here, i.e., periods without confessional parties in government should matter for the policy decisions, while cross-national patterns of secularization could be significant explanatory factors.

Table 1 shows cross-national measures of church attendance from the World Values Surveys (WVS), a standard measure of secularization (cf., Norris and Inglehart 2004: 33–52). The two countries in the religious world experienced a later shift towards secularization in the 1980s, but Spain later than the Netherlands. In the 2000s, both the Netherlands and Spain have caught up with the UK and Spain with the Netherlands. The secularization of the two countries in the religious world should generate strong pressure towards more permissive polices, though much earlier in the Netherlands than in Spain. Although missing from the latest WVS data, Denmark still appears as the most secularized country, a picture also supported by the European Social Survey (see Engeli, Green-Pedersen and Larsen 2012: 33–4).

In the Netherlands, the pressure for more permissive regulation of abortion had started already in the late 1960s with pressure from the women's movement and secular political parties, especially PvdA (Outshoorn 2001). However, the Christian Democrats participated in all Dutch coalition governments through the 1970s, most often in coalition with VVD, and systematically tried to avoid a government decision on the issue, for example by setting up a commission to investigate the issue. In the end, the CDA and VVD compromised on a permissive abortion law in 1981 (Timmermans and Breeman 2012).

After the abortion conflict settled, the religious–secular conflict on morality issues did not end; it simply shifted to euthanasia. The issue had gained public attention through court cases in the 1970s, but was now taken into party politics. A bill to allow euthanasia was tabled by D66 in 1984. For the CDA and its secular coalition partners, the VVD until 1989 and then PvdA until 1994, euthanasia became a precarious issue. However, the CDA managed to avoid a decision on the issue while in government until 1994 (Green-Pedersen 2007). Same-sex marriage resembles euthanasia, with growing pressure from the secular parties, including PvdA in government after 1989, for permissive legislation. The CDA did accept the introduction of a same-sex union in 1994, but not same-sex marriage. Nineteen ninety-four saw the first government coalition without the CDA, more or less since 1918, which consisted of PvdA, VVD and D66. It seized on morality issues and implemented permissive legislation on euthanasia in 2000, same-sex marriage in 1997 and a relatively permissive embryo act in 2002. The regulation of ART was left with the quite permissive regulation of 1991 (Timmermans and Breeman 2012).

Table 1 Percentage of people reporting that they attend religious services at least once a month

	1981	1989/1990	1995/1996	1999	2006/2007
Denmark	12.7 (1182)	10.8 (1028)	–	11.9 (1017)	–
UK	22.3 (1167)	23.4 (1483)	–	18.9 (989)	23.5 (1034)
Netherlands	39.9 (1221)	30.4 (1012)	–	25.2 (1002)	19.1 (989)
Spain	53.6 (2303)	41.0 (4134)	37.4 (1183)	35.9 (1190)	22.5 (1179)

Source: World Values Survey/Values Surveys Databank.
Note: Total number of cases (N) in parentheses.

In sum, politics clearly mattered for permissive morality policies in the Netherlands, especially on the question of government participation. Conflicts over morality issues have been split between secular and confessional parties and with CDA using its government power to avoid decisions on issues where its coalition partners would support permissive legislation. On abortion, the CDA gave in while in government, but other permissive policies, like allowing euthanasia and same-sex marriage, had to await a government without Christian Democratic participation.

In addition to late democratization, Spain differs from the Netherlands regarding the secularization process. The political debate on morality issues only started in the 1980s and the Social Democratic government that took office in 1982 only introduced minor permissive changes on abortion owing to a sceptical public opinion (Chaques and Roqué 2012). This had all changed radically when the Social Democrats regained office in 2004 led by Zapatero, who dedicated a great deal of attention to morality issues during the campaign in order to profile the PSOE as the 'modern' party in Spanish politics. Once in power, the government first introduced same-sex marriage in 2005 (Platero 2007) and then a permissive abortion law in 2010. These laws met fierce resistance from the Conservative party and the Roman Catholic Church, but had the support of the majority of the Spanish population (Chaques and Roqué 2012). Policies on ART and stem cells have been subject to much of the same party political battles, although the issues were first seen as strictly medical. The first policies introduced in the 1980s and 1990s were thus relatively permissive, but were later restricted by the Conservative government in 2003. The PSOE government from 2004 turned these policies back in a permissive direction, although the end result today is intermediate (see Figure 1). Finally, euthanasia remains restrictive, although it is slowly emerging as a political issue (Chaques and Roqué 2012).

As we expected for the religious world, who governs has great impact on permissiveness in Spain. This is quite similar to the Netherlands, even if the two countries vary on the timing of individual issues. Spain is much later than the Netherlands in terms of secularization, and where the latter settled the abortion question in 1981, it took another 30 years for the same to happen in Spain owing to hesitance in public opinion. Differences in secularization can thus explain the variation in permissiveness today, even if Spain is now clearly catching up.

ISSUE VARIATION IN THE SECULAR WORLD

Denmark and the UK have no conflict between confessional parties in their party systems and our expectation of limited political attention dedicated to morality issues is confirmed in both countries. Morality issues are most often seen as non-partisan issues outside of normal party competition and they rarely find their way into party manifestoes or parliamentary activities like interpellations in Denmark or Prime Minister's Questions in the UK. Instead, decisions on these issues typically depend on the activities of interest groups and individual MPs and the colour of government has little impact on the success of these activities (Albæk *et al.* 2012; Cowley 2000; Larsen *et al.* 2012).

In Denmark, abortion reached the political decision-making process in the late 1960s and early 1970s owing to pressure from women's organizations and individual left-wing MPs. The proposal was met with some hesitation, but no strong resistance from any political parties. First, a broad majority of the parties agreed on having a commission investigate the issue, which led to a more permissive regulation in 1971 under a right-wing government and then the very permissive law in 1973 under a left-wing government. When this law was passed, the parties allowed their MPs to vote freely on the issue, with strong internal divisions within the major right-wing parties and to some extent the Social Democrats (Albæk *et al.* 2012).

The early settlement of the abortion issue did not have much impact on other morality issues in Denmark. In fact, they did not receive any political attention until the mid-1980s, when a debate about same-sex marriage emerged owing to pressure from gay rights interest groups and individual MPs from the Social Liberals, who seized on the issue to appear more progressive than the right-wing government (which included the very small Christian Democratic Party). Finally, in 1989, Denmark, as the first country, introduced same-sex unions with several legal rights for homosexuals (Albæk 2003). ART started to emerge as a political issue from the mid-1980s, mainly pushed by left-wing politicians who called for very restrictive legislation in opposition to medical and economic interests. Parliament passed a very restrictive moratorium on embryo research in 1987, with partial liberalizations in 1992 and 1997 (Albæk *et al.* 2012). The policy processes were often quite chaotic because parties allowed free votes and thereby cancelled the normal partisan structure of decision-making. Although relatively permissive, the 1997 law excluded lesbians and singles from ART, based on an amendment proposal from three Social Democratic MPs (Albæk 2003). On stem cell research, a partial liberalization was passed in 2003 with broad support, although the far left retained some of its scepticism towards new technologies.

The major gay rights organization pressured for lifting the exclusion of homosexuals from ART and adoption rights, which reached the decision agenda in the late 2000s by way of a new small libertarian party that managed to get MPs from the right-wing government parties to break rank and support the bills. The government tolerated this because of the non-political understanding of the question. Finally, there has been no political debate in Denmark about allowing euthanasia, which remains restively regulated (Green-Pedersen 2007).

The policy process concerning morality issues in the UK resembles that of Denmark in many respects. The UK was an early mover in terms of abortion when a permissive law was passed in 1967. Like in Denmark, this law was not the result of party politics but of pressure from interest groups that had support from individual MPs, like the Liberals' MP David Steel, who introduced the private member bill that ultimately passed. The Labour government allowed the bill to come to a vote, but the Labour party never moved the issue into party competition (Larsen *et al.* 2012; Lovenduski 1986; Millns and Sheldon 1998).

Like in Denmark, the early passing of an abortion law did not lead to pressure for more permissive regulation of morality issues. The next issue to gain political attention was ART in the late 1980s. The Conservative government was reluctant to introduce regulation, partly because of internal conflict, but in 1990 it finally introduced a quite permissive regulation. Since then, Labour governments have introduced several further steps in a more permissive direction, and the UK is the most permissive of all countries on ART and stem cell regulation. Behind this is a lack of party conflict and a focus on the economic growth potential of these new technologies. Further, the British medical community has played an important role in pressing for permissive regulation (Larsen *et al.* 2012).

The issue of same-sex marriages and further rights of homosexual couples was not raised until under the Labour government in the 2000s, which introduced same-sex unions, adoption rights and ART for homosexuals. These questions were more actively promoted as partisan questions by Labour, although a real partisan conflict failed to emerge as the Conservatives had no clear party position on the question and allowed free votes (Larsen *et al.* 2012). Like in Denmark, a debate about replacing same-sex union with same-sex marriage is on the table at present, but at the time of writing has not yet been decided. Finally, euthanasia remains firmly outside party competition and there is no sign that the UK is moving away from a restrictive regulation.

Policy processes concerning morality issues in Denmark and the UK resemble the expectations about the secular world and are distinctively different from those in the religious world. The colour of the government is not a central factor in terms of passing permissive legislation. When such legislation is passed, it is owing to issue-specific subsystem dynamics, especially the ability of interest groups to build coalitions with individual MPs rather than political parties. This first implies variation across issues. Pressure from women's groups and gay and lesbian groups has generated permissive regulation of abortion and same-sex marriage. Euthanasia lacks a natural constituency and pressure for permissive regulation has not emerged. Second, it implies variation for similar issues across the two countries. This is most obviously the case with regard to ART and stem cell regulation. Whereas scepticism towards technology from especially left-wing parties has been important for regulation of the issues in Denmark, the interests of the medical industry and doctors have played an important role in the UK. A third implication of issue-specific dynamics is that there is no general push towards more permissive regulation across all the issues in the two countries. They were early movers in terms of permissive regulation of abortion, but have done nothing on euthanasia and have been slow movers on same-sex marriage. In many ways, countries like the Netherlands and Spain have caught up with Denmark and the UK in terms of permissiveness, except perhaps for the very permissive British regulation on ART and stem cells.

CONCLUSION

The growing literature on cross-national difference in morality policy presents a rather unclear picture with respect to fundamental theoretical questions of whether or not politics matters, the role of religion and religious actors. This contribution argues that the problem emerges from lack of theoretical focus on the underlying policy process. Dividing countries into a religious and a secular world depending on whether or not they have a conflict between confessional and secular parties in their party system provides the key to understanding differences in policy processes. In the religious world, this brings these issues into 'macro politics' in the form of party competition and makes the colour of government a key determinant of policy development. In the secular world, these issues are far from macro politics and are driven by issue-specific dynamics.

Going back to the literature on cross-national policy differences, there are different answers to whether politics matters depending on which of the two worlds is discussed. In the religious world, government participation of confessional parties makes a great difference for policy development. Although one would perhaps expect very permissive policies in the secular world, the absence of a policy dynamic behind morality policy makes the end result less permissive. Secularization also matters in the religious world. This explains the difference between Spain and the Netherlands, but cannot explain comparative differences in the secular world, where Denmark is more secularized but UK is the more permissive on policy. Thus, the policy processes are structured differently in the two worlds, which determine what the key factors in the policy process are. It is further important to stress that one needs to focus on policy dynamics, which makes cross-national comparisons risky at a given time. For instance, a country like Spain has changed quite dramatically within the last seven to eight years in terms of morality policy. Also, the explanation for why the Netherlands appears as the most permissive country overall is the combination of early secularization and the presence of a conflict between secular and confessional parties in the party system.

The idea of the religious and the secular world and the focus on policy process suggest a number of further avenues of research. One avenue is extending the empirical scope beyond the countries studied here(cf., also Engeli, Green-Pedersen and Larsen 2012). In this regard, it is important to stress that what matters is the presence or absence of confessional forces in the party system, not the degree of religiosity or the particular denomination in a given country. This means that countries like Germany, Austria, Belgium, Switzerland and Portugal probably also belong to the religious world, whereas the Scandinavian countries and the UK together with France and Ireland belong to the secular world. Another avenue of future research is a more detailed understanding of the sub-system politics structuring morality issues in the secular world. With regard to ART and stem cells, for example, the roles of the medical communities in Denmark and the UK are strikingly different, but it is a more open question why they play different roles.

Biographical notes: Isabelle Engeli is assistant professor at the Graduate School of Public and International Affairs, University of Ottowa. Christoffer Green-Pedersen is professor at the Department of Political Science and Government, Aarhus University, Denmark. Lars Thorup Larsen is associate professor at the Department of Political Science and Government, Aarhus University, Denmark.

ACKNOWLEDGEMENTS

We would like to acknowledge the financial support from the Danish Social Science Research Council for the project 'Morality Politics in Comparative Perspective' and the support from the other members of the research group (Erik Albæk, Frédéric Varone, Donley Studlar, Arco Timmermans, Gerard Breeman, Laura Chaqués Bonafont and Anna M. Palau Roqué).

NOTES

1 Non-party, religious actors are not the main theoretical focus, but they will be included in the empirical analysis below. We expect their behaviour to be structured by the religious–secular conflict.

2 Our focus is on legislation at the national level, thus omitting court decisions, administrative decisions, and decisions at the subnational level.
3 See Engeli *et al.* (2012) for detailed documentation of the coding work. To give a better sense of the coding procedure, we present the indicators used for coding the policy decisions on ART. ART regulation contains two distinct dimensions (Bleiklie *et al.* 2004; Engeli 2010): the medical autonomy granted to physicians to practice ART; and the financial coverage for ART treatments. Each dimension was captured by a set of indicators. For medical autonomy, the seven indicators measured the autonomy granted to physicians to practice the three main ART techniques (artificial insemination, in vitro fertilization, intracytoplasmic sperm injection) and the four main related techniques (donation, cryopreservation, pre-implantation diagnosis, surrogacy). The seven indicators were coded from 0 (ban) to 3 (full autonomy) and were then aggregated into an additive index. The second dimension, financial coverage, captured the extent of public financial coverage for ART treatments and the regulation of the treatments rate, also from 0 (no public coverage and regulated rate) to 3 (full coverage and fully regulated rate). The two additive indexes were finally aggregated into a composite index that gives the overall measurement of the degree of permissiveness of the decision.
4 In terms of coding, we treat access to ART treatment for others than heterosexual couples as part of the same-sex marriage issue as the discussion has mainly related to homosexual (lesbian) couples.

REFERENCES

Albæk, E. (2003) 'Political ethics and public policy: homosexuals between moral dilemmas and political considerations in Danish parliamentary debates', *Scandinavian Political Studies* 26(3): 245–67.
Albæk, E., Green-Pedersen, C. and Larsen, L.T. (2012) 'Morality issues in Denmark: policies without politics', in I. Engeli, C. Green-Pedersen and L.T. Larsen (eds), *Morality Politics in Western Europe. Parties, Agendas and Policy Choices*, Basingstoke: Palgrave Macmillan, pp. 137–60.
Andeweg, R.B. and Irwin, G. (2009) *Governance and Politics of the Netherlands*, Basingstoke: Palgrave Macmillan.
Banchoff, T. (2011) *Embryo Politics. Ethics and Policy in Atlantic Democracies*, Ithaca, NY: Cornell University Press.
Baumgartner, F.R. and Jones, B.D. (1993) *Agendas and Instabilities in American Politics*, Chicago, IL: University of Chicago Press.
Bleiklie, I., Goggin, M. and Rothmayr, C. (eds) (2004) *Comparative Biomedical Policy: Governing Assisted Reproductive Technologies*, London: Routledge.
Blofield, M. (2006) *The Politics of Moral Sin*, London: Routledge.
Chaques, L. and Roqué, A.M.P. (2012) 'From prohibition to permissiveness: a two-wave change on morality issues in Spain', in I. Engeli, C. Green-Pedersen and L.T. Larsen (eds), *Morality Politics in Western Europe. Parties, Agendas and Policy Choices*, Basingstoke: Palgrave Macmillan, pp. 62–87.
Cowley, P. (ed.) (2000) *Conscience and Parliament*, London: Routledge.
Engeli, I. (2010) *Les politiques de la reproduction*, Paris: L'Harmattan.
Engeli, I., Green-Pedersen, C. and Larsen, L.T. (eds) (2012) *Morality Politics in Western Europe. Parties, Agendas and Policy Choices*, Basingstoke: Palgrave Macmillan.
Engeli, I. *et al.* (2012) *Morality Politics, Summary of Policy Coding*, Ottawa: University of Ottawa [available upon request].
Ertman, T. (2009) 'Western European party systems and the religious cleavage', in K. van Kersbergen and P. Manow (eds), *Religion, Class Coalitions, and Welfare States*, Cambridge: Cambridge University Press, pp. 56–90.

Fink, S. (2008) 'Politics as usual or bringing religion back in? The influence of parties, institutions, economic interests, and religion on embryo research laws', *Comparative Political Studies* 41(12): 1631–56.

Fink, S. (2009) 'Churches as societal veto players', *West European Politics* 32(1): 77–96.

Green-Pedersen, C. (2007) 'The conflict of conflicts in comparative perspective: euthanasia as a political issue in Denmark, Belgium, and the Netherlands', *Comparative Politics* 39(3): 273–91.

Kalyvas, S. and van Kersbergen, K. (2010) 'Christian democracy', *Annual Review of Political Science* 13: 183–209.

Kollman, K. (2007) 'Same sex unions: the globalization of an idea', *International Studies Quarterly* 51(2): 329–57.

Larsen, L.T., Studlar, D.T. and Green-Pedersen, C. (2012) 'Morality politics in the United Kingdom: trapped between left and right', in I. Engeli, C. Green-Pedersen and L.T. Larsen (eds), *Morality Politics in Western Europe. Parties, Agendas and Policy Choices*, Basingstoke: Palgrave Macmillan, pp. 114–36.

Lovenduski, J. (1986) 'Parliament, pressure groups, networks, and the women's movement: the politics of abortion law reform in Britain (1967–1983)', in J. Lovenduski and J. Outshoorn (eds), *The New Politics of Abortion*, London: Sage Publications, pp. 231–56.

Mazur, A. (2002) *Theorizing Feminist Policy*, New York: Oxford University Press.

Millns, S. and Sheldon, S. (1998) 'Abortion', in P. Cowley (ed.), *Conscience and Parliament*, London: Routledge, pp. 6–23.

Minkenberg, M. (2002) 'Religion and public policy. Institutional, cultural, and political impact on the shaping of abortion policies in Western democracies', *Comparative Political Studies* 35(2): 221–47.

Minkenberg, M. (2003) 'The policy impact of church-state relations: family policy and abortion in Britain, France and Germany', *West European Politics* 16(1): 195–217.

Monpetit, E., Rothmayr, C. and Varone, F. (2007) *The Politics of Biotechnology in North America and Europe*, Lanham, MD: Lexington Books.

Mooney, C.Z. (ed.) (2001) *The Public Clash of Private Values*, New York: Chatham House.

Norris, P. and Inglehart, R. (2004) *Sacred and Secular Religion and Politics Worldwide*, Cambridge: Cambridge University Press.

Outshoorn, J. (2001) 'Policy-making on abortion: arenas, actors and arguments in the Netherlands', in D.M. Stetson (ed.), *Abortion Politics, Women's Movements, and the State*, Oxford: Oxford University Press, pp. 205–58.

Platero, R. (2007) 'Love and the state. Gay marriage in Spain', *Feminist Legal Studies* 15: 329–40.

Rothmayr, C.F., Varone, U., Serdült, A., Timmermans, A. and Bleiklie, Y. (2004) 'Comparing policy design across countries. What accounts for variation in ART policy?', in I. Bleiklie, M. Goggin and C. Rothmayr (eds), *Comparative Biomedical Policy: Governing Assisted Reproductive Technologies*, London: Routledge, pp. 228–53.

Smith, T.A. and Tatalovich, R. (2003) *Cultures at War: Moral Conflicts in Western Democracies*, Peterborough, ON: Broadview Press.

Stetson, D.M. (ed.) (2001) *Abortion, Women's Movements and the Democratic State*, Oxford: Oxford University Press.

Tatalovich, R. and Daynes, B.W. (eds) (2011) *Moral Controversies in American Politics*, Armonk, NY: M.E. Sharpe.

Timmermans, A. and Breeman, G. (2012) 'Morality issues in the Netherlands: coalition politics under pressure', in I. Engeli, C. Green-Pedersen and L.T. Larsen (eds), *Morality Politics in Western Europe. Parties, Agendas and Policy Choices*, Basingstoke: Palgrave Macmillan, pp. 35–61.

van Kersbergen, K. (1999) 'Contemporary Christian democracy and the demise of the politics of mediation', in H. Kitschelt, P. Lange, G. Maarks and J.D. Stephens (eds), *Continuity and Change in Contemporary Capitalism*, Cambridge: Cambridge University Press.

van Kersbergen, K. and Manow, P. (2009) *Religion and Class Coalitions and Welfare States*, Cambridge: Cambridge University Press.

Varone, F., Rothmayr, C. and Montpetit, E. (2006) 'Regulating biomedicine in Europe and North America: a qualitative comparative analysis', *European Journal of Political Research* 45(3): 317–43.

Is morality policy different? Institutional explanations for post-war Western Europe

Donley T. Studlar, Alessandro Cagossi and Robert D. Duval

ABSTRACT Although there has been increasing recognition that morality policy in Western democracies is a distinctive field of study, many analyses are relatively narrow in issues and jurisdictions. This contribution examines broad empirical patterns for five morality policy issues across 18 West European democracies since World War II. The issues analysed are abortion, capital punishment, euthanasia, assisted reproductive technology (ART, including stem cell research) and same-sex marriage. Which of two prominent institutional theories of morality policy, policy type and two worlds, help explain morality policy processes? The results indicate that morality policy processes do differ from the usual ones of parliamentary government, and that important differences are captured by the religious/secular division of party systems, depending on which countries are considered for each category.

INTRODUCTION: POLICY PROCESSES FOR MORALITY ISSUES

Recently morality policy has been of increased interest to European politics scholars, moving beyond its normal realm of United States (US) politics (Albæk 2003; Engeli *et al.* 2012; Mooney 2001; Smith and Tatalovich 2003; Tatalovich and Daynes 2011). There has been increasing recognition that morality policy in Western democracies deserves special attention, but many analyses cover only one issue and/or a limited number of jurisdictions (Durham 2005; Engeli 2009; Engeli *et al.* 2012; Krabbendam and Ten Napel 2000; Mooney 2001; Smith and Tatalovich 2003).

This contribution is the first broadly comparative empirical study of morality policy across West European liberal democracies, taking account of multiple issues over a substantial time period. Based on the largest comparative data set to date, this contribution examines the institutional patterns of consideration for five morality policy issues across 18 advanced industrial democracies in post-World War II Europe.

Do morality issues constitute a distinctive category of policy by their content? While no definitive list of morality issues has been offered and there may be some variation across space and time, several studies (Engeli *et al.* 2012; Smith 2002; Studlar 2001) offer a suggestive list, including capital punishment (death penalty), abortion, alcohol consumption, euthanasia, homosexual rights, prostitution, gambling (gaming), assisted reproduction technology (ART), and stem cell research. With the exception of alcohol consumption and gambling, the six other issues are concerned with birth, sex and death, intimate physical experiences of human beings. All of these issues involve mass judgments of desirable policies not based primarily on socioeconomic advantage, but based on beliefs about right and wrong, which can trace their origins back to religious precepts. We shall examine five issues of common morality policy concern. These include one long-standing morality issue, capital punishment, and four of more recent vintage: abortion; euthanasia; assisted reproductive technology (ART)/stem cells; and same-sex domestic relations (often called 'gay marriage').

These kinds of intimate relations involving birth, sex and death are particularly susceptible to becoming politicized as morality issues. Even if the issues are complex and susceptible to scientific and economic influences, they deal with fundamental human concerns that most people in a society can readily grasp and on which they often become politically mobilized. This is especially true for groups concerned with religious or individual or group human rights principles; advocates from these groups wish to have their governments adopt policies in line with their often strongly value-based views, even if this conflicts with other groups in society and/or specialized professional opinion on the matter. Thus religiously affiliated groups generally favour more restrictive policies and secular groups support more permissive policies, although there are exceptions (Bleiklie *et al.* 2004; Montpetit *et al.* 2007).

Morality policies are of interest because of patterns and country variations in content, agenda-setting (duration) and the impact of institutions on policy adoptions. This contribution will concentrate on the latter problem through a comparative analysis of what three institutional theories reveal about these important dimensions of morality policy.

First we shall discuss the essentials of the party government model, the normal policy process in European democracies, followed by a review of two relevant institutional theories of morality policy, policy type and two worlds, with hypotheses from each. We shall then examine findings on the applicability of the two alternative institutional theories of morality policy processes. The conclusion will examine how well the existing institutional theories help our understanding of morality policy and suggest future directions for research.

LITERATURE REVIEW: PARTY GOVERNMENT MODEL AND MORALITY POLICY

The normal policy process for most Western democracies is 'parliamentary government', with the lower house of the legislature choosing the government based on party shares of the seats and ability to form any necessary coalitions for a workable governing agreement. Usually a government is based on a majority of seats, but the key point is to be able to sustain itself in office until the next scheduled general election. However, the government is subject to periodic votes of confidence from the legislature, which, if lost, compel the government to resign and allow formation of a new one, perhaps after an intervening general election. In order to make this 'fused' system of executive–legislative relations work, strong party cohesion among legislators is necessary to make credible policy commitments, both to voters in party manifestos, to governing coalition partners, and to interest groups and the public. The government controls the legislative agenda, and most policies debated are prepared, presented and defended by the cabinet, which normally expects legislative party unity in support. Although there are some variations in how dominant the executive is over the legislature and the scope given to individual legislators, this description of parliamentary government has been empirically validated for the countries considered here (Döring 1995; Laver and Shepsle 1994; Sieberer 2006).

Even in regimes utilizing the parliamentary model, however, other institutions may be involved in policy decisions. Political parties do not always display perfect party unity (Rasch and Tsebelis 2011; Sieberer 2006). Legislative parties exert different amounts of resistance against governments even of their own partisan persuasion. Questions involving human rights, and therefore sometime morality questions, are the province of the judiciary. Referendums are another possible venue for consideration of morality issues, especially in countries where they can be called through popular initiative (Butler and Ranney 1994). Constitutional decisions can be the results of action through the legislature, judiciary or referendums. While most European polities are unitary systems with weak second legislative chambers, some of them, such as Spain and the United Kingdom, have devolved authority in recent decades. Morality issues are still mainly a central-level state policy, however; the economically focused European Union (EU) occasionally has become involved in these disputes through: (1) endorsing the principle of the European Convention on Human Rights that countries should abolish the death penalty (Council of Europe 1999; Hood and Hoyle 2008); (2) specifying no discrimination against homosexuals as workers or customers (Eeckhout and Paternotte 2011); and (3) forbidding the patenting of stem cells from human embryos (O'Connell 2012). Although the European Parliament has tried to get the EU to adopt trans-border mobility laws more favourable to same-sex couples, thus far the EU Council has rejected them (Toggenburg 2008). More broadly, Kurzer (2001) argues that membership of the EU acts as a pressure for convergence of countries with policies deviant from the norm, including abortion in Ireland.

Overall, one would expect multiple arenas to be sites for morality policy disputes, more so than for issues that are more amenable to economic arguments over distribution, regulation or redistribution that are subject to the views of materially interested interest groups, economic sectors and social classes (Smith 1969; Tatalovich and Daynes 2011). The left–right social class division still dominates West European democracies and drives government formation and functioning through the party government model (Gallagher *et al.* 2011).

Observational studies for over a half century (Christoph 1962; Cohan 1986), most systematically developed by Smith (1969, 1975), Tatalovich and Daynes (2011) and Studlar (2001), indicate that there have been unusual policy processes on morality issues in Western democracies. Because the dominant model of party government obtains so broadly, the most likely deviation from established procedures occurs in executive–legislative relations. Opposition party and individual backbench Members of Parliament (MPs) often introduce morality measures in the legislature, and there are frequent splits in party voting on 'conscience' issues. Judicialization on a variety of issues has been spreading across Western democracies (Tate and Vallinder 1995); Majone (1997) suggests that this is at least partially because of the rise of the 'regulatory state' in Europe that needs the judiciary to adjudicate disputes. Morality policy has even been the subject of important court decisions even in countries where this rarely occurs (Austria, Sweden). Morality issues sometimes rise to the level of being subject to constitutional amendments. For instance, bans on capital punishment increasingly have been written into constitutions (Council of Europe 1999; Hood and Hoyle 2008). Butler and Ranney (1994; see also Gallagher *et al.* 2011) find morality to be one of the major issues in referendums. Where jurisdictions at different levels in federal, devolved or decentralized systems have legal authority to be involved in morality policy, this may occur, especially through implementation of decisions, as in Belgium, where Flemish regional authorities, lacking jurisdiction over homosexual rights, nevertheless have funded gay advocacy groups (Eeckhout and Paternotte 2011).

POLICY TYPE

Some commentators have argued that morality issues constitute a distinctive policy area not only by their content, but also by the processes used to decide them. Whether issues are examined individually (Christoph 1962; Cohan 1986) or as a group (Cowley 1998; Richards 1970; Smith 1969; Smith and Tatalovich 2003; Studlar 2001; Tatalovich and Daynes 2011), it has been claimed that morality issues constitute 'democratic', 'marginal', 'emotive-symbolic', 'morally redistributive', or 'social regulatory' policies, typically subject to institutional deviations from the normal policy process for other types of issues in a country. This question, whether policy content influences policy processes, was first raised by Lowi (1964) in US politics and has also been pursued in comparative politics by Smith (1969, 1975), Freeman (1986), Studlar (2001) and Smith and Tatalovich (2003). Recently, the policy type theory has been further tested in the study of European politics (Montpetit *et al.* 2007; Timmermans 2001) without definitive results.

On the basis of studies of the abortion issue, Studlar (2001) and Outshoorn (1996) argue that normal parliamentary government procedures rarely apply. The contentious value conflict involved in these policy deliberations make them difficult to contain within the normal institutional boundaries. In other words, morality policies lead to relaxation of usual institutional rules, spillover effects into other institutions as disaffected groups challenge decisions, extended debate and the revisiting of previously made decisions.

For the US, Tatalovich and Daynes (2011) contend that there are distinctive policy processes for morality issues, involving public opinion, interest groups, political parties and governmental institutions such as federalism, the executive, legislature and judiciary. Mooney (2001) and Donovan *et al.* (2010) argue that in the US morality issues typically arise from 'policy shocks' through judicial decisions, prompting popularly based reactions through multiple venues in the federal system, and are resolved through a variety of subcentral policies that are broadly responsive to constituency opinion in those jurisdictions. Smith (1969, 1975) and Smith and Tatalovich (2003) have extended this conception to comparative politics, arguing that while morality issues typically excite broad public involvement and divide parties through executive abdication of responsibility leading to free votes in the legislature, the resulting direction is likely to be along the lines preferred by a more post-material, permissive elite than generally more restrictive public opinion.

Thus, under the policy type model, one would expect the involvement of multiple institutions in this policy, including legislative initiatives on policy by opposition and backbench MPs, party divisions on legislative votes, constitutional disputes, participation of the judiciary at various levels, and, where available, decentralized institutions and referendums. Although we shall not directly compare morality issues to others, multiple deviations from the dominant parliamentary government model would be *prima facie* evidence that morality policy is different.

THE TWO WORLDS OF MORALITY POLICY

Recently another institutional explanation has been added to the study of morality issues in Western democracies, especially European parliamentary systems. Engeli *et al.* (2012; see also Fink 2008; Green-Pedersen 2007; Minkenberg 2002; van Kersbergen 2008) argue that debate over morality policy develops different patterns in party systems with a strongly Christian, especially Catholic-based, major party than in those in which parties are not closely tied to religious groups. Thus, there is a religious world of morality policy and a secular world of morality policy. In the former party systems, morality issues are more likely to be politicized by parties, and major change results from a change of government control from a coalition with a religiously based major party, usually the Christian Democrats, to a secularly based coalition of Socialist, Liberal and other centre-left parties lacking a religiously affiliated partner. Secularly based parties contain elements interested in advocating 'progressive' positions on issues, which can move the issue from one of parliamentary dissent to government-sponsored, or at least government-tolerated, bills. Even if party splits occurred in the voting, the secular parties normally largely have their MPs support more permissive legislation while members of religiously affiliated parties vote for more restrictive bills (Green-Pedersen 2007; Grießler and Hadolt 2006; Outshoorn 1996; Timmermans 2001). Thus, it would seem that the religious–secular dimension is an important determinant of the significance of party through government proposals, legislative votes and outcomes.

Once more permissive changes are instituted, that particular policy is likely to leave the political agenda, although the partisan morality policy alignments may reappear on related issues. Abortion becomes the 'master issue' for other conflicts. In other words, in religiously-based party systems, morality policy more closely resembles the normal party government model once a secular coalition gains control of government, even if there is not much explicit campaigning on it (Pennings 2010).

In contrast, in secular party systems, such issues are depoliticized and subject to change via free votes in parliament and judicial decisions rather than party competition. As an 'abnormal' issue for party government, however, it is revisited periodically if social forces can muster enough support in the legislature. Furthermore, somewhat different patterns of party voting on morality issues are more likely to appear in a secular party system than in a religious one, with more conservative party deputies often voting for permissive positions (Cowley 2001).

Although the two models can be considered complementary, the policy type model is based more on the nature of the issue and available venues while the two worlds model is based on political cleavages/politicization of issues. The following are hypotheses for the two worlds model, based on the assumption that resistance to change in religious party systems leads to more venues being involved in those countries. Which venues they utilize, of course, depends on availability, but all democratic political systems have institutional opportunities for conflict outside an executive-dominated parliament.

(1) Morality issues are more likely to be the subject of legislative party initiatives in the religious world than in the secular world;
(2) There is more unified party voting in the religious world than in the secular world;
(3) Judicial decision making on morality policy is more prevalent in the religious world.
(4) There is more constitutional debate on morality issues in the religious world.
(5) There is more decentralized consideration of morality issues in religious world.
(6) There are more referendums on morality issues in religious world.
(7) More venues are involved in morality policy in religious world.

As noted above, hypotheses from the two worlds model are partially derived from the policy type model, as modified by Engeli *et al.* (2012). While this contribution cannot resolve all of the differences among institutional explanations of morality policies, it can at least systematically address how well each accounts for patterns observable in a systematic data analysis.

DATA AND METHODS

Data were gathered through September 2012, from multiple secondary sources on the five policies to be examined here – the death penalty, abortion, euthanasia, same sex marriage and ART/stem cells (Albaek 2003; Bleiklie *et al.* 2004; Council of Europe 1999; Cowley 1998; Engeli 2009; Engeli *et al.* 2012; Evans 1996; Marsh and Read 1988; Montpetit *et al.* 2005, 2007; Outshoorn 1996; Richards 1970; Stetson 2001). Consideration of the policy by specific political institutions other than through party government processes at any time in a country is drawn from studies and news reports.

Not all countries have all of these institutional venues for policy debate. Of the six venues presented, all 18 of the countries, in principle, have four (legislative initiatives, party divisions, judicial involvement and constitutional conflict). Non-constitutional referendums on policy issues are readily available in only six (Denmark, Ireland, Italy, Luxembourg, Portugal and Switzerland), although the actual number of referendums conducted varies substantially across these countries (Gallagher *et al.* 2011). While it is not clear which countries could, in principle, allow morality issues to be decentralized, we identify nine countries as having significant decentralization of institutions (Austria, Belgium, Denmark, Germany, Italy, Netherlands, Spain, Switzerland and the United Kingdom) (Hooghe *et al.* 2010; Lijphart 1999).[1]

The role of different institutions in policy deliberations over morality policy constitutes a major basis for testing of the policy type and two worlds explanations. One instance of the policy being treated in other than the 'normal' executive-dominated process is enough to qualify; thus, Table 1 does not record frequency of occurrence of each process. A more refined study would consider a greater range of issues of different nominal types and the relative proportions that they are considered by different institutions.

There is not complete agreement about the two worlds, or even which countries have parties that could be labelled as 'Christian Democratic' in orientation (Engeli *et al.* 2012; Gallagher *et al.* 2011: 295).[2] For purposes of this contribution, we consider two versions of the religious/secular world party systems, with Ireland and Italy variously being religious, in addition to eight others: Austria; Belgium; Germany; Luxembourg; the Netherlands; Portugal; Spain; and Switzerland. The following eight countries consistently have secular world party systems: Denmark; Finland; France; Greece; Iceland; Norway; Sweden; and the United Kingdom.

Simple summary scores for each policy and country are compared in Table 1. All of the variables are measured through nominal categories. For statistical tests comparing group differences for religious and secular party systems in Table 2, therefore, the non-parametric Mann–Whitney U test was performed on these variables. The results are very similar, although overall somewhat stronger, than conventional difference of means t-tests of the same data (not shown).[3] Since the overall mean and median are close in value (columns 1 and 2 of Table 2), with the exception of total venues (expected, since some countries have more available venues than others), the distribution of scores is relatively symmetrical.

FINDINGS: GENERAL

Table 1 shows the overall scores for institutional dimensions of morality policy for the 18 West European countries. In contrast to the dominant European party government model for policy-making, the mean number of additional venues involved across all morality issues in these countries (column 1) is 1.9, ranging from 1.0 in Greece and Iceland to 3.0 in Germany and 3.2 in Switzerland. Column 2 shows the total number of venues used across all five morality issues in these countries (maximum possible 30, composed of 5 issues times 6 venues). The mean is 9.4, meaning that morality issue debate is normally confined to a few venues in each country, with some issues never reaching even all of those available.

Table 1 also shows, in more detail, institutional involvement in morality policy, both overall for each country and by specific issues. Overall, the most likely extra-party government venues for considering morality policy are the legislature, political parties and the judiciary, followed by constitution, decentralized venues and referendums. In general, where more venues are available for morality policy contention, more will be used. By issues, abortion easily is the most pervasive across all venues (51), followed by same-sex domestic relations (38), ART/stem cells (29), capital punishment (26) and euthanasia (25). Abortion is the leading issue in legislative, party and referendum venues, with euthanasia and same-sex domestic relations leading in the judiciary, and same-sex domestic relations in decentralization. Capital punishment is notable in having almost no judicial involvement but having the largest amount of constitutional amendments, as several European states have embedded this prohibition. ART/stem cells debate is centred in legislative initiatives, party votes and judicial deliberations. Abortion is primarily a legislative and party-centred issue, while same-sex marriage is prominent in judicial as well as legislative and party arenas. For euthanasia, the judiciary accounts for half of the extra-executive institutional involvement.

FINDINGS: POLICY TYPE

Table 1 indicates that across Western democracies there are not wide variations in the susceptibility of particular morality issues to unusual political processes, although it is noteworthy that abortion is the issue most subject to multiple arenas. However, there are specific variations by issue and political process. Overall, most procedural aberrations occur through legislatures and judiciaries. Judiciaries are rarely involved in capital punishment or ART, compared to the

Table 1 Institutional venues and morality policy

Country	M no. of venues (of 4–6)	Total venues (of 30)	Legislative party	Divided party	Judiciary	Constitution	Decentralization	Referendum
Austria	1.4	7	2	1	3	1	0	N/A
Belgium	1.6	8	3	1	2	1	1	N/A
Denmark	1.4	8	4	3	0	0	1	0
Finland	1.8	7	3	3	0	1	N/A	N/A
France	2.5	10	2	3	3	2	N/A	N/A
Germany	3.0	16	4	3	2	3	4	N/A
Greece	1.0	4	0	1	2	1	N/A	N/A
Iceland	1.0	4	0	2	1	1	N/A	N/A
Ireland	2.0	10	1	1	3	3	N/A	2
Italy	2.3	14	3	2	4	2	1	2
Luxembourg	1.2	6	4	0	0	2	N/A	0
Netherlands	1.4	7	2	1	3	1	0	N/A
Norway	1.8	7	3	3	1	0	N/A	N/A
Portugal	2.2	11	3	2	3	2	N/A	1
Spain	2.0	10	2	2	3	1	2	N/A
Sweden	1.8	7	2	2	2	1	N/A	N/A
Switzerland	3.2	19	4	4	2	2	3	4
UK	2.8	14	4	4	2	0	4	N/A

(Continued)

Table 1 Continued

Country	M no. of venues (of 4–6)	Total venues (of 30)	Legislative party	Divided party	Judiciary	Constitution	Decentralization	Referendum
Overall mean	1.9	9.4	2.6	2.1	2.0	1.3	1.8	1.5
Mean by issue	(of 4–6)	(of 435)				Total Issues		
Capital punishment	1.4	26	7	3	0	12	2	2
Abortion	2.8	51	14	17	8	4	4	4
Euthanasia	1.4	25	8	2	12	2	1	0
ART	1.6	29	6	8	6	3	4	2
Same-sex DR	2.1	38	11	8	10	3	5	1
			46	38	36	24	16	9
						Grand Total		

other three issues. Although unusual legislative procedures were first documented for capital punishment, in fact it is abortion that is the most common topic of these particular behaviours. Referendums are rare, but again abortion is the leading issue, largely due to the presence of this option in Catholic countries (Ireland, Italy, Portugal and Switzerland). Contestation at multiple levels of government is also a limited option, utilized in similar proportions for each issue. Attempts at constitutional changes are infrequent, but utilized the most for capital punishment, as expected, and secondarily abortion. This includes judicial decisions based on constitutional grounds.

Some countries are more susceptible to multiple venues on morality issues than others. These tend to be countries, with both secular and religious party systems, in continental Europe. While not all countries with extra venues (referendums and decentralization) use them for morality policy, for the most part those with these characteristics, as well as those with a powerful judiciary, do so. Overall, party government, even with legislative initiatives and divided party votes, is the most preferable model for dealing with morality policy mainly in Nordic countries.

Expectations from policy type theory on policy processes for morality issues, both overall and specific, are largely upheld. Once raised, issues have multiple institutional involvement, legislative initiatives are proposed, party divisions on floor votes occur, the judiciary is a significant actor (except on capital punishment), there is often constitutional debate, lower level institutions and referendums become involved where there are opportunities.

FINDINGS: TWO WORLDS

Data for the hypotheses from the two worlds model is presented in Table 2, with significance tests conducted utilizing the non-parametric Mann–Whitney U. Eighteen countries is a small number for such tests, but at least Table 2 indicates some preliminary findings for specific hypotheses. As noted above, the number of religious and secular countries varies depending on where Ireland and Italy are placed. Overall, we find the following generalizations:

(1) Table 2 summarizes all of the four iterations. They are ordered from the categorization with the most significant results on the left, in order, to the least number of significant findings on the right.
(2) With both the Irish and Italian party systems in the religious world, four of seven tests are significant: constitution is significant at 0.001; divided party and judiciary are significant at 0.05; the total venues variable is significant at 0.10. Legislative party, decentralization, and referendum are non-significant.
(3) With Italy secular and Ireland religious, there are three significant results: judiciary and constitution at 0.05; total venues at 0.1. Legislative party, decentralization and referendum continue to be non-significant.

Table 2 The two worlds of morality policy processes

	Mean	Median	It. Ir. (rel.) means		It. (Rel.), Ir. (sec.) means		It. (Rel.), Ir. (sec.) means		It. (sec.), Ir. (rel.) means		It. Ir. (sec.) means	
			Rel.	Sec.	Rel.	Sec.	Rel.	Sec.	Rel.	Sec.	Rel.	Sec.
Total venues	9.4	8.0	10.8+	7.6+	10.9+	7.9+	10.9+	7.9+	10.4	8.3	10.5	8.5
Legislative party	2.6	3.0	2.8	2.3	3.0	2.1	3.0	2.1	2.8	2.3	3.0	2.2
Divided party	2.1	2.0	1.7*	2.6*	1.8	2.4	1.8	2.4	1.7*	2.6*	1.8	2.4
Judiciary	2.0	2.0	2.5*	1.4*	2.4*	1.6*	2.4*	1.6*	2.3+	1.7+	2.3	1.8
Constitution	1.3	1.0	1.8**	0.8**	1.7*	1.0*	1.7*	1.0*	1.8*	0.9*	1.6	1.1
Decentralization (N = 9)	1.8	1.0	1.6	2.5	1.6	2.5	1.6	2.5	1.7	2.0	1.7	2.0
Referendum (N = 6)	1.5	1.5	1.8	0.0	1.8	1.0	1.8	1.0	1.8	1.0	1.7	1.3
Observations	N = 18		N = 10	N = 8	N = 9	N = 9	N = 9	N = 9	N = 9	N = 9	N = 8	N = 10

Note: +: > 0.1 level of significance; *: > 0.05 level of significance; **: > 0.01 level of significance.

(4) With Ireland secular and Italy religious, three significant results also emerge: divided party and constitution at 0.05; judiciary at 0.01. Legislative party, decentralization, referendum and total venues are non-significant.
(5) There are no significant results when both Italy and Ireland are in the secular world.
(6) In looking at the venues' difference of means tests, there is considerable consistency. Two variables – judiciary and constitution – are significant in three out of four tests although their levels marginally vary. Two variables – divided party and total venues – are significant twice, at the same levels. Three variables – legislative party, decentralization, and referendum – are never significant.
(7) Even those variables that are non-significant statistically are consistent in direction.

In terms of specific hypotheses, we find the following. Hypothesis 1 (legislative party) has no significant results although the numerical direction of the relationship is always correct. Hypothesis 2 (party division) is confirmed statistically in two of the four iterations. Divided party votes are more likely to occur on these policies in the secular world than in the religious world when Ireland is considered religious, either with or without Italy in that category. Hypothesis 3 (judiciary) has consistent results, with three of four tests statistically significant. In each instance, there is more frequent involvement of the judiciary in morality policy in the religious world than in the secular world, reflecting the intense commitment of both supporters and opponents of policy change to have their 'day in court' to resolve these issues if the legislature is not forthcoming. The fact that these issues can often be formulated in terms of 'human rights' may facilitate this process.

Hypothesis 4 (constitution) also has three statistically significant findings. Thus, there is evidence that debate on morality issues in the religious world, variously defined, is more likely to rise to the constitutional level. Hypothesis 5 (decentralization) has no significant results. Morality issues are not more likely to be considered at decentralized levels in the secular world than in the religious world. Hypothesis 6 (referendum) is not confirmed statistically. There are only six countries in which a referendum on morality issues is possible. The only clearly secular party system of these, Denmark, has never had a referendum on morality policy, while the two debatable party systems, Italy and Ireland, have had two each. Hypothesis 7 (multiple venues) is confirmed statistically twice in the four divisions of religious and secular worlds. In both cases, the religious world utilizes more venues, indicating that faith-based conflict over morality issues does lead to political controversy across institutions.

Although the data are fragile, overall the two worlds model aids explanation of morality policy institutional processes, although not always in expected ways. In most respects, the religious and secular worlds are similar, but policy controversy appears to be more intense and institutionally diverse in the religious world.

Whether Italy is considered part of the religious or the secular world affects several processes. These cases clearly need detailed investigation into the bases of the parties in these countries (Cagossi 2012; Engeli *et al.* 2012).

CONCLUSION AND FUTURE RESEARCH DIRECTIONS

This research broadly supports the views of previous students of particular issues in a limited number of countries. The diversity of institutions involved in morality policies in most of these 18 democracies indicates that the contentious value conflict involved in these deliberations makes them difficult to contain within normal party government boundaries. Consideration of morality policies leads to relaxation of normal institutional rules, spillover effects into other institutions as disaffected groups challenge decisions, and the revisiting of decisions. Nevertheless, most countries in Europe eventually are able to resolve these issues. There does not appear to be any general institutional configuration for quick, decisive settlement of morality policy; instead, the pertinent factors would appear to be a combination of cultural and institutional factors, namely Nordic countries operating on the usual parliamentary party government model.

This first extensive cross-country analysis of morality policy processes analysis has limits. It provides only a broad, largely descriptive analysis of the patterns of these five morality policy issues across Western Europe. Other morality issues may also be considered, case studies can be done on the specific dimensions of institutional political processing of them in particular countries, and improved metrics for these and other issues may be developed. There needs to be more direct comparison with institutional processes for other categories of policies, including frequencies of multiple venues. The findings here, however, can be considered baseline data on which others can build for a broader theory of morality policy, as well as extending the analysis to countries outside Europe.

Other possible explanations for morality policy similarities and differences may also be explored. Some of these may be cultural, such as family of nations (Castles 1993) and post- materialism (Norris and Inglehart 2004; Smith and Tatalovich 2003). Other institutional explanations may also be tested, such as punctuated equilibrium (Baumgartner and Jones 1993), veto groups (Tsebelis 2002), and majoritarian-consensus democracies (Lijphart 1999).

Timmermans (2001) proposes another variation of an institutional argument for explaining policy outcomes, involving both the number of institutional arenas in policy deliberation and the tightness of the rules governing the institutions. For morality issues, the number of institutions involved is likely to be higher than the norm for that country and may range from professional groups and expert executive committees to subcentral institutions and even the general public through referendums. As has been observed, normally tight rules of parliamentary government are often relaxed for morality policies. Decentralization as a variable affecting morality policy especially needs greater study, as the existent work tends to focus on single issues (Montpetit *et al.* 2005; Rothmayr *et al.* 2003). The role of international organizations may be important for some issues, as noted above for capital punishment and homosexual economic rights. In addition, the role of transnational advocacy organizations and diffusion may be important on some issues (Keck and Sikkink 1998; Nadelmann 1990; True and Mintrom 2001)

The two worlds model is a disaggregated version of the policy type model, emphasizing partisan ownership of issues rather than governmental institutions. Although both models seem to be promising explanations of morality policy processes, the two worlds model's additional explanatory value depends very much on how the worlds are divided. Depending on the venues available, morality policy is likely to be controversial across more venues in religious party systems than in secular ones. Further research into the linkage between dominant churches and parties in the problematically religious party systems (Ireland and Italy) is necessary to help resolve these questions.

Both models do demonstrate that there are at least nascent institutional patterns in morality policy that deviate from the normal party government model. While hardly definitive, these simple data explorations provide *prima facie* evidence for further testing of theories of morality policy content, duration and process. As in the US, the study of this policy needs to move from description towards explanation of differences. Morality policy does appear to be subject to policy processes that deviate in some ways from the European parliamentary party government model.

Biographical notes: Donley T. Studlar is Eberly Family Distinguished Professor at West Virginia University, USA. Alessandro Cagossi is a Ph.D. graduate student in Political Science at West Virginia University, USA. Robert D. Duval is Associate Professor of Political Science at West Virginia University, USA.

ACKNOWLEDGEMENTS

Thanks to William Harrison for research assistance. Earlier versions of this contribution were presented at the European Consortium of Political Research, Muenster, 2010, the Southwest Social Science Association, Las Vegas, 2011, and the International Political Science Association, Madrid, 2012.

NOTES

1 Although Hooghe *et al.* (2010) have several policy indicators for different levels of government, morality policy is not among them. Most discussions of morality policy at the level of individual countries focus on the central level, although variations by decentralized authorities are sometimes acknowledged (Engeli *et al.* 2012; Tremblay *et al.* 2011). For purposes of this paper, we consider Denmark to be a decentralized country because of the status of Greenland and the Faroe Islands, where exceptions to central Danish laws apply.
2 The Christian Democratic International became the Centrist Democrat International in 2001, thus confusing the formal distinction between Christian Democratic and other conservative parties. Similarly, the European People's Party in the European Parliament contains a broad array of centre-right parties. Italy and Ireland can be considered to have Christian Democratic parties in the same sense that the Conservatives in Spain are considered a highly religiously influenced party, through internal influence of church organizations and positions taken on morality issues rather than explicit connections between churches and parties. On the other hand, France and Greece also have parties in the Centrist Democrat International, but they do not have such religious ties.
3 The Mann–Whitney U typically provides comparable power to the standard two-sample t-test when the assumptions of the t-test are met, and is somewhat more robust when the assumptions are violated (e.g., normality). For an extended examination of the relative power of the two approaches, see Duval and Groeneveld (1987). While bootstrapped difference of mean (or median) scores could be provided in an attempt to increase robustness of the confidence intervals, the fact that the data is essentially a population, more than a random sample, the gain from using re-sampling methods on population data is not clear. Statistical inference on population data largely provides us with information on the strength of the relationship, since inference from a sample to a population is not at issue here.

REFERENCES

Albæk, E. (2003) 'Political ethics and public policy: homosexuals between moral dilemmas and political considerations in Danish parliamentary debates', *Scandinavian Political Studies* 26(2): 245–67.
Baumgartner, F.R. and Jones, B.D. (1993) *Agendas and Instability in American Politics*, Chicago, IL: University of Chicago Press.
Bleiklie, I., Goggin, M.L. and Rothmayr, C. (eds) (2004) *Comparative Biomedical Policy: Governing Assisted Reproductive Technologies*, London: Routledge.
Butler, D. and Ranney, A. (eds) (1994) *Referendums Around the World: The Growing Use of Direct Democracy*, Washington, CD: AEI Press.
Cagossi, A. (2012). 'Morality politics, Italian style: reluctant secularization in a religious world, or unsecular politics in a secularizing society'. Paper presented at International Political Science Association, Madrid, 8–12 July.
Castles, F.G. (ed.) (1993) *Families of Nations*, Brookfield, VT: Dartmouth.
Christoph, J.B. (1962) *Capital Punishment in British Politics*, Chicago, IL: University of Chicago Press.
Cohan, A.S. (1986) 'Abortion as a marginal issue: the use of peripheral mechanisms in Britain and the United States', in J. Lovenduski and J. Outshoorn (eds), *The New Politics of Abortion*, London: Sage, pp. 27–48.
Council of Europe (1999) *The Death Penalty Abolition in Europe*, Strasbourg: Council of Europe.
Cowley, P. (ed.) (1998) *Conscience and Parliament*, London: Frank Cass.

Cowley, P. (2001) 'Morality policy without politics? The case of Britain', in C.Z. Mooney (ed.), *The Public Clash of Private Values: The Politics of Morality Policy*, New York: Chatham House, pp. 213–26.

Döring, H. (ed.) (1995) *Parliaments and Majority Rule in Western Europe*, New York: St Martin's Press.

Donovan, T., Mooney, C.Z. and Smith, D.L. (2010) *State and Local Politics: Institutions and Reform*, Belmont, CA: Wadsworth.

Durham, M. (2005) 'Abortion, gay rights and politics in Britain and America: a comparison', *Parliamentary Affairs* 58(1): 89–103.

Duval, R.D. and Groeneveld, L. (1987) 'Hidden policies and hypothesis tests: the implications of type ii errors for environmental regulation', *American Journal of Political Science* 31(2): 423–47.

Eeckhout, B. and Paternotte, D. (2011) 'A paradise for LGBT rights? The paradox of Belgium', *Journal of Homosexuality* 58: 1058–84.

Engeli, I. (2009) 'The challenges of abortion and assisted reproductive technologies policies in Europe', *Comparative European Politics* 7(1): 56–74.

Engeli, I., Green-Pedersen, C. and Larsen, L. (eds) (2012) *Morality Politics in Western Europe: Parties, Agendas and Policy Choices*, London: Palgrave.

Evans, R.J. (1996) *Rituals of Retribution: Capital Punishment in Germany 1600–1987*, New York: Oxford University Press.

Fink, S. (2008) 'Politics as usual or bringing religion back in? The influence of parties, institutions, economic interests, and religion on embryo research laws', *Comparative Political Studies* 41(6): 1631–56.

Freeman, G.P. (1986) 'National styles and policy sectors: explaining structured variation', *Journal of Public Policy* 5(4): 467–96.

Gallagher, M., Laver, M. and Mair, P. (2011) *Representative Government in Modern Europe*. 5th ed. New York: McGraw-Hill.

Green-Pedersen, C. (2007) 'The conflict of conflicts in comparative perspective: euthanasia as a political issue in Denmark, Belgium, and the Netherlands', *Comparative Politics* 39(3): 273–91.

Grießler, E. and Hadolt, B. (2006) 'Policy learning in policy domains with value conflicts: the Austrian cases of abortion and assisted reproductive technologies', *German Policy Studies* 3(4): 698–746.

Hood, R. and Hoyle, C. (2008) *The Death Penalty: Worldwide Perspective*. 4th ed. New York: Oxford University Press.

Hooghe, L., Marks, G. and Schakel, A.H. (2010) *The Rise of Regional Authority: A Comparative Study of 42 Democracies*, London: Routledge.

Keck, M. and Sikkink, K. (1998) *Activists Beyond Borders: Advocacy Networks in International Politics*, Ithaca, NY: Cornell University Press.

Krabbendam, H. and Ten Napel, H.-M. (eds) (2000) *Regulating Morality: A Comparison of the Role of the State in Monitoring the Mores in the Netherlands and the United State*, Antwerpen-Apeldoom: Maklu.

Kurzer, P. (2001) *Markets and Moral Regulation: Cultural Change in the European Union*, Cambridge: Cambridge University Press.

Laver, M. and Shepsle, K.A. (1994) 'Cabinet government in theoretical perspective', in M. Laver and K.A. Shepsle (eds), *Cabinet Ministers and Parliamentary Government*, New York: Cambridge University Press.

Lijphart, A. (1999) *Patterns of Democracy: Government Institutions and Performance in Thirty-Six Countries*, New Havenm, CT: Yale University Press.

Lowi, T.J. (1964) 'American business, public policy, case studies, and political theory', *World Politics* 16(4): 677–715.

Majone, G. (1997) 'From the positive to the regulatory state: causes and consequences of changes in the mode of governance', *Journal of Public Policy* 17(2): 139–67.

Marsh, D. and Read, M. (1988) *Private Members' Bills*, Cambridge: Cambridge University Press.
Minkenberg, M. (2002) 'Religion and public policy: institutional, cultural, and political impact on the shaping of abortion policies in Western democracies', *Comparative Political Studies* 35(2): 221–47.
Montpetit, E., Rothmayr, C. and Varone, F. (2005) 'Institutional vulnerability to social constructions: federalism, target populations, and policy designs for assisted reproductive technology in six democracies', *Comparative Political Studies* 38(1): 119–42.
Montpetit, E., Rothmayr, C. and Varone, F. (eds) (2007) *The Politics of Biotechnology in North America and Europe: Policy Networks, Institutions, and Internationalization*, Lanham, MD: Lexington Books.
Mooney, C.Z. (ed.) (2001) *The Public Clash of Private Values: The Politics of Morality Policy*, New York: Chatham House.
Nadelmann, E.A. (1990) 'Global prohibition regimes: the evolution of norms in international society', *International Organization* 44(4): 479–526.
Norris, P. and Inglehart, R. (2004) *Sacred and Secular: Religion and Politics Worldwide*, New York: Cambridge University Press.
O'Connell, C. (2012) 'Stem cells – where are we now?', *Irish Times*, 27 January. Available at http://www.irishtimes.com/newspaper/innovation/2012/0127/1224310600371
Outshoorn, J. (1996) 'The stability of compromise: abortion politics in Western Europe', in M. Githens and D. Stetson (eds), *Abortion Politics: Public Policy in Cross-Cultural Perspective*, New York: Routledge, pp. 145–64.
Pennings, P. (2010). 'Exploring morality politics across space and time: does the "issue saliency theory"(still) hold?', Paper presented at European Consortium for Political Research, Muenster, Germany, 22–27 March.
Rasch, B.E. and Tsebelis, G. (eds) (2011) *The Role of Governments in Legislative Agenda Setting*, New York: Routledge.
Richards, P.G. (1970) *Parliament and Conscience*, London: George Allen and Unwin.
Rothmayr, C., Varone, F. and Montpetit, E. (2003) 'Does federalism matter for biopolitics? Switzerland in comparative perspective', *Swiss Political Science Review* 9(1): 109–36.
Sieberer, U. (2006) 'Party unity in parliamentary democracies: a comparative analysis', *Journal of Legislative Studies* 12(2): 150–78.
Smith, K. (2002) 'Typologies, taxonomies, and the benefits of policy classification', *Policy Studies Journal* 30(3): 379–92.
Smith, T.A. (1969) 'Toward a comparative theory of the policy process', *Comparative Politics* 1(4): 498–515.
Smith, T.A. (1975) *The Comparative Policy Process*, Santa Barbara, CA: ABC-Clio.
Smith, T.A. and Tatalovich, R. (2003) *Cultures at War: Moral Conflicts in Western Democracies*, Peterborough, ON: Broadview Press.
Stetson, D.M. (ed.) (2001) *Abortion Politics, Women's Movements, and the Democratic State: A Comparative Study of State Feminism*, New York: Oxford University Press.
Studlar, D.T. (2001) 'What constitutes morality policy? A cross-national analysis', in C.Z. Mooney (ed.), *The Public Clash of Private Values: the Politics of Morality Policy*, New York: Chatham House, pp. 32–51.
Toggenburg, G.N. (2008) '"LGBT" go Luxembourg: on the stance of lesbian gay bisexual and transgender rights before the European Court of Justice', *European Law Reporter* (May): 1–17. Available at http://www.ilga-europe.org/
Tatalovich, R. and Daynes, B. (eds) (2011) *Moral Controversies in American Politics*. 4th ed. Armonk, NY: M.E. Sharpe.

Tate, C.N. and Vallinder, T. (1995) *The Global Expansion of Judicial Power*, New York: New York University Press.

Timmermans, A. (2001) 'Arenas as institutional sites for policymaking: patterns and effects in comparative perspective', *Journal of Comparative Policy Analysis* 3(3): 311–37.

Tremblay, M., Paternotte, D. and Johnson, C. (eds) (2011) *The Lesbian and Gay Movement and the State: Comparative Insights into a Transformed Relationship*, Burlington, VT: Ashgate.

True, J. and Mintrom, M. (2001) 'Transnational networks and policy diffusion: the case of gender mainstreaming', *International Studies Quarterly* 45(1): 27–57.

Tsebelis, G. (2002) *Veto Players: How Political Institutions Work*, Princeton, NJ: Princeton University Press.

Van Kersbergen, K. (2008) 'The Christian Democratic phoenix and modern unsecular politics', *Party Politics* 14(2): 259–79.

From 'morality' policy to 'normal' policy: framing of drug consumption and gambling in Germany and the Netherlands and their regulatory consequences

Eva-Maria Euchner, Stephan Heichel, Kerstin Nebel and Andreas Raschzok

ABSTRACT Drug consumption and gambling are regarded as morality policies, especially in the American literature. Both are perceived as sinful and treated accordingly. This highly generalized assessment is rarely analysed systematically in a non-American context. Therefore, we investigate whether these policies are indeed framed morally and if this framing is stable over time in two European countries. Next, we analyse whether shifts in morality framing have consequences for regulation. In this way, we contribute to the literature on morality policies, particularly the ways in which these policies are defined and empirically identified. We identify morality policies based on how actors frame issues rather than by policies' substantive content. We show that the morality framing was once prominent but has lost its importance over time, and we find a close connection between frame shifts and policy output, although this is not a uniform development and does not characterize all cases.

INTRODUCTION

Recent years have seen the emergence of literature on morality policies that debates their main characteristics and investigates their consequences on the policy-making process (Engeli *et al.* 2012; Mooney 2001; Smith and Tatalovich 2003). Drug consumption and gambling have traditionally been located within the sphere of morality policies. Both were widely regarded as sinful and reprehensible and treated accordingly, especially with regard to the individual drug consumer or gambler, who was seen as an offender and whose crimes often entailed criminal prosecution (Kingma 2008; Reuband 2009). Both policy fields, drug consumption and gambling, are a good test case to compare if and to what extent classical morality policy issues experience noticeable changes in problem perceptions over time. We argue that framing is central for making a policy a morality policy in the first place and for establishing policy categories and classifications in general.

We concentrate on three research questions. First, have gambling and drug consumption predominantly been framed morally in the European context? If so, can we detect a general relocation from the morality frame to other frames over time? Finally, has such a shift away from morality framing entailed any consequences regarding the degree of regulatory intervention? Theoretically, we assume an on-going trend of issue reframing largely driven by the development of a secular society in Europe that fosters a decline in the perception of drug consumption and gambling as morally wrong. As a result of liberalization tendencies, we expect the emergence of new ideas, actors and scientific evidence that provide incentives to re-frame morality policies in non-moral terms. This change is presumably accompanied by a less restrictive regulatory and penal approach owing to altered problem perceptions.

The contribution adds to ongoing discussions in the field of morality policy over whether policies clearly and constantly belong to the category of morality policy, or if changes arise owing to modifications in the prominent framing. Additionally, we take a systematic and empirically based approach to examining framing that has rarely been utilized in previous studies (Mucciaroni 2011).

In the following section, we justify the policy and case selection. The next section presents the theoretical framework and the expectations derived from that framework. Then we address the method and data. The policy developments in the Netherlands and Germany will be discussed and empirically analysed in the following two sections. We conclude with a critical discussion and an outlook for further research.

POLICY AND CASE SELECTION

We examine drug and gambling policies in Germany and the Netherlands over six decades (1950–2010). The policies are chosen first because we aim to observe possible frame shifting over a long period, which would not be possible with 'younger' topics such as stem cell research or same-sex marriage. Second, both policies belong to the same subcategory of morality policies encompassing 'addictive behaviour or substances' (Heichel *et al.* 2013). Frame shifts are more likely in this subcategory than in others, for example, in the 'life and death category' (Knill 2013). Furthermore, non-morality frames are more similar and, hence, can be grouped and analysed in a coherent manner.

Germany[1] and the Netherlands represent two appropriate countries for our analysis. They are characterized by a similarly long history of regulating both fields under study. In addition, the parliamentary role of Christian Democratic parties has been of roughly equal importance during the observation period (Timmermans and Breeman 2012). Both countries also followed a similar process of secularization, with the number of Catholics shrinking from 40 per cent in the 1960s to 30 per cent in the 2000s (WVSA 2012: 1981 and 2006 wave). Following Engeli et al. (2012), the religious factor is crucial for morality policies. Morality framing is more likely in states where a pronounced religious party cleavage shapes the policy-making process.

Our focus is not on explaining but on tracing differences in framing and examining their regulatory consequences. We compare countries in which potential frame shifting is confronted with similar obstacles or accelerating factors, e.g., in terms of the openness of the political system to new actors, interests or ideas. For most of these relevant factors, the Netherlands and Germany are very similar.

THEORETICAL FRAMEWORK AND EXPECTATIONS

Our theoretical framework is threefold. First, it is derived from the general discussion around the definition of morality politics and policy. Second, it is based on common theories of value shifts, secularization, new ideas and actors. Third, we rely on the concept of policy framing mostly when elaborating on the link between frame shifts and policy choices.

Morality politics and policy: the framing aspect

We approach morality policy from the American research tradition, which emphasizes the politics dimension (see Knill [2013] for an overview of different concepts of morality policy). Policies are not *a priori* morality issues. Rather, morality policies result from the policy-making process, which makes the framing process crucial (Haider-Markel and Meier 1996; Mucciaroni 2011). Policies are considered morality issues if they are framed as such by at least one important advocacy group; however, the degree of morality framing that is required to label a policy a morality policy is still under debate. In a similar vein, authors outside morality policy research support the concept of 'blended issues'. They argue that policies can assume different dimensions, including those of economics, public health or morality. Depending on the framing of involved actors, one dimension prevails over the other at certain points of time, hence turning a non-morality issue into a morality policy (Studlar 2008: 394). On the basis of the theoretical discussion on morality policies and supporting evidence from American literature, our first expectation is as follows:

> Expectation 1a: Gambling and drug policy were once predominantly framed as morality policies.

Value shifting and secularization as background factors

Although we will not test any theories, we do have assumptions about the multiple avenues responsible for inducing frame shifts. The broader development relates to value change in society after the Second World War. Inglehart (1990) proposes a silent transformation of the Western value system from materialism to post-materialism; Flanagan and Lee (2003) investigate a shift from authoritarian to libertarian values; and Smith and Tatalovich (2003) even speak of a 'cultural theory' that encompasses forces of status differentiation and status equalization. Incorporated in these views of value change is the idea of secularization: Western, economically developed countries experience a declining influence of religion in society and state affairs (Pollack and Pickel 2007). This is suspected to contribute to the process of societal value change, which influences attitudes towards morality policies. We assume that the number of citizens conceiving of gambling or drug consumption as sinful has been decreasing. Consequently, value-based arguments are convincing for a much smaller group of citizens, leading opponents of more permissive regulation (such as Christian Democratic parties) to select other frames to persuade larger parts of the society (i.e., by using arguments related to health and public order) (Engeli *et al.* 2012).

New ideas, interests and actors

Broader societal developments are a necessary but no sufficient condition for frame shifts. We must also account for theories that explain frame shifting at the micro level. Theories such as the *punctuated-equilibrium theory* (Baumgartner and Jones 2009) provide factors that can explain this frame shifting. For example, changes in public opinion, scientific progress or the emergence of new actors with a specific set of ideas, beliefs and values lead to the development of 'policy monopolies' that enforce their interests and the framing of an issue in the political and public arenas. Therefore, the framing of issues can change over time. In connection with our assumption of secularization and a general value change in society, our next expectation is as follows:

> Expectation 1b: If a morality frame has been observed, it is losing importance in favour of other frames over the observation period.

Framing and policy choices

Finally, we are interested in the consequences of frame shifts for policy choices. Herein, we rely on a rationalist point of view, which conceives of politicians as office-seekers and assumes that their attitudes resemble those of their electorate owing to elections. Thus, secularization and value change intrude into the political sphere through re-election campaigns and the decision-making process. Issue framing moderates the interaction between a (secularized) society and policy change (see Hurka and Nebel [2013] for the interplay between external shocks, framing and policy change). If a group of actors is able to enforce its framing of a public issue within a policy subsystem, the existing policy monopoly is ruptured and replaced. The development of this process is strengthened by institutional venue shifts that allocate administrative and legislative responsibility to actors who were not formerly involved (Baumgartner and Jones

2009). The new policy monopoly shapes the process of problem definition by stressing one aspect and ignoring others, thereby illuminating a specific set of policy solutions (Larsen 2010; Studlar 2008). Meier (1999: 686) outlines this mechanism in more detail regarding alcohol policy: 'Viewing alcoholism as a disease suggests that treatment is the preferred policy option. Viewing alcoholism as a moral failing implies that law enforcement should be used to discipline the individual drinkers.'

Consequently, if we detect a shift from morality to non-morality frames, we expect at least incremental policy changes owing to new problem definitions and other sets of solutions. We rely on a conceptual measurement of policy change introduced in this collection (Heichel *et al.* 2013). The focus lies on the individual consumer, and we distinguish between criminalization and regulation of consumer behaviour. We expect that if consumption is seen as sinful, then criminalizing this behaviour seems necessary to stop the individual and to protect his or her environment. If consumption is seen as an individual right, however, then the behaviour should be legalized or permissively regulated. Consequently, we propose another expectation as follows:

> Expectation 2: The declining importance of the morality frame is accompanied by a more permissive regulation of gambling/drug policy with regard to the individual.

METHOD AND DATA

Our analysis of the framing and regulation of gambling and drugs applies a qualitative methodological approach that draws on primary and secondary sources. The framing analysis is based exclusively on the examination of governmental and parliamentary documents published between 1950 and 2010. We concentrate especially on the preambles or explanations of laws and on policy reports. Thus, we do not consider the entire politics sphere to be important for our purposes. Instead, we focus on the 'aggregated' policy framing by the legislative majority at a given time.

We conduct the framing analysis via an inductive procedure. First, we scan all documents to find those arguments justifying policy choices and describing the underlying problem. We find 31 relevant documents, 16 in the Dutch case and 15 in the German case.[2] Next, we sort the arguments and derive the frames from them. Where more than one frame is found in a document, we rank the frames according to their prominence, frequency and position in the text. Thus, our units of analysis are frames identified via thematic distinction (Krippendorff 2004: 107). We code only those syntactical entities that incorporate any statement on the motives and exclude purely neutral claims (i.e., technical comments on the legislative procedure). We are aware that the coding procedure is prone in terms of reliability. We tried to address this problem by performing the coding by ourselves and by discussing critical cases.

We identify four basic types of frames that appear in varying combinations or alone in the documents: the *morality frame*, the *health and social frame*, the *security and public order frame*, and the *economic and fiscal frame*. The frames are introduced briefly below (see also Table 1), while all other empirical results are presented in subsequent sections. Following Mucciaroni (2011), our distinction between morality and non-morality framing is based on the involvement of core values or 'first principles' in the arguments.

The *morality frame* judges drug use and gambling as a wrong and inherently bad behaviour. Morally framed justifications of policy choices are therefore value-based and target first principles. Drug consumption and gambling are regarded as generally contrary to (traditional) norms and values. Their spread is seen as a threat to society's value system that must be prevented. Additionally, it is argued that both behaviours endanger the individual in a fundamental and existential way because they curtail an individual's personality and human dignity. Protecting the individual from his or her own deeds becomes the central goal.[3]

In contrast to the morality frame, the other three frames identified are less value-based and are characterized by reasoning that refers to negative health and social consequences as well as to the effects of drugs and gambling on public security and on the national economy. Actors relying on the *health and social frame* stress the need to protect consumers' health and social conditions. The risk of addiction is emphasized, and the behaviour in general is considered to be a disease. Consumers are referred to as patients. Aspects such as misuse prevention and treatment are central. Drug consumption and gambling are both seen as having severe negative social consequences.

The *security and public order frame* summarizes arguments related to all kinds of threats from criminal activities in both fields. These are, in particular, the national and transnational drug trade, gambling fraud and money laundering. This frame also includes arguments referring to the aspect of public safety, aiming, for example, to prevent drug-related crime, ensure public safety and avoid public disturbances ('nuisances') caused by drug consumption and gambling.

The *economic and fiscal frame* is more relevant for gambling than for drug policy. According to this frame, gambling is accepted as a regular leisure and economic activity (albeit one requiring regulation). The state does not, however, surrender its claim for political steering. The fiscal side of the economic frame includes the aspects of licensing and taxation, and thus, the opportunity for the state to extract fiscal resources from gambling. Theoretically, this is also relevant for drug consumption, as the state could extract fiscal resources by taxing (certain) drugs after legalization.

In a second analytical step, we assess the degree of restrictiveness of a given regulatory provision. Here, we focus on the impact on the individual. We apply the following logic to measure the direction of change:

(1) The regulatory *status quo* becomes more restrictive if the new law limits the activities, freedom or behaviour of a person to a larger degree than before;

Table 1 Frame types, main features and examples

Frames		Features	Examples
Morality		Gambling/drug use as an inherently bad behaviour that (a) does not conform to societal norms and values, and (b) threatens the user in a fundamental and existential way	Drug use contrasts with a positive way of life and traditional norms and values; casinos are threatening the social order and deteriorate personality and character
Non-morality	Health and social	Gambling/drug use as threats to user's health and social conditions	The main task of drug policy is to control the negative consequences that affect the consumer's health; the main task of state gambling policy is to fight gambling addiction and to fight preconditions for addictive behaviour
	Security and public order	Gambling/drugs as threats to public security and order because of illegal activities or nuisance committed by (a) users/addicts, or (b) suppliers	The trade in illegal drugs and drug-related crime are a serious disturbance of public order and security; public order and security have to be defended; gambling is not a normal economic market; the protection of the consumer is of central concern
	Economic and fiscal	Gambling/drugs as damage (healthcare costs, missing workforce caused by addicts) or benefits (revenues through licensing, taxation) to national economy	Drug abuse and addiction cause significant economic damages; gambling laws should generate state income; illegal gambling should be restricted because it causes economic damages

Source: Authors' compilation.

this would include an increase in sanctions for prohibited actions. For example, we consider the enactment of a law that prohibits the consumption of a substance or increases the sentences for illegally dealing in certain drugs as making the country's drug regulation more restrictive.

(2) The regulation becomes more permissive if the new law removes or loosens restrictions concerning a specific behaviour or enhances a person's opportunity of action. An example from gambling policy is the legalization of games such as slot machines or profit-oriented lotteries.

EMPIRICAL ANALYSIS

Next, we analyse the framing of drug and gambling policy in the Netherlands and Germany over time to make assumptions regarding our expectations. If we do find a morality frame prevailing in one case, we will go one step further and investigate potential regulatory consequences.

Drug policy in the Netherlands

In the few documents found on illegal drugs published during the 1950s and 1960s, we could not detect any specific framing. The numerous documents found for the period after 1970 provide a clearer picture. Since that time, the health and social frame and the security and public order frame have prevailed. While the former played a dominant role in the 1970s and 1980s, the latter became central in the 1990s. In what follows, we describe the dominant arguments in more detail.

Since the 1970s, drug consumption has primarily been framed as a health and social problem. The permissive regulatory approach towards 'soft' drugs established in 1976 was justified with the varying dangerousness of drugs. The legislators distinguished between drugs with 'acceptable' and 'unacceptable' (Kamerstuk 13407, nr.3: 15[4]) risks to the health of the consumer and the society. The potential damages caused by 'soft' drugs (especially cannabis products) were considered less serious in contrast to risks related to the use of 'hard' drugs (e.g., heroin). The legislators also highlighted the threat to public health and security through increasing international trade in hard drugs and its links to organized crime (Kamerstukken 13407, nr.3: 13; 17975, nr.3: 4).

In 1985, the introduction of 'normalization' as a new principle in Dutch drug policy reinforced the dominant framing of drugs as being mainly a health and social problem. The central document opposed the moralization and mystification of hard drug use and proposed a "'cultural' integration' of addicts. Drug use was described as a '"normal" social phenomenon' that should be treated as an 'ordinary social problem' (ISAD 1985: 35ff.).

In the mid-1990s, the security and public order dimension gained prominence. In 1995, the government identified organized drug trafficking and especially 'nuisance' as the new main problems. Hard drug addicts and coffee shops were understood as causing such nuisance (Kamerstuk 24077, nr.3: 51,

9f.). Similar arguments were used to explain modifications to drug legislation enacted in the late 1990s and 2000s. The new regulations were intended to reduce and combat 'side effects of ... coffee shops' (Kamerstuk 25324, nr.3: 1), 'serious nuisance ... committed by drug addicts' (Kamerstuk 26023, nr.3: 1) and professional, large-scale cannabis cultivation and trafficking (Kamerstukken 25325, nr.3: 2; 30339: 7).

Only in 2009 was morally framed rhetoric used in an official document. In a letter by the Dutch Minister of Health, drug use was described as a behaviour that is 'not normal' (MvVWS 2009: 6). The letter referred to a report of the Advisory Committee on Drug Policy that demanded a 'more restrictive approach ... based on clearly defined social norms' and regarded drug use as a 'deviant lifestyle' (Adviescommissie 2009: 21f.).

Apart from this weak moral reasoning in the late 2000s, we could not find any evidence for a morality framing of Dutch drug policy during the period of analysis, either before the change towards the permissive drug regime in 1976 or afterwards. Consequently, we are unable to confirm Expectation 1a or to make assumptions regarding Expectations 1b and 2.

Drug policy in Germany

In Germany, the drug issue appeared on the political agenda in the late 1960s. The morality frame, the health and social frame and the security and public order frame were central during the 1970s and 1980s. Afterwards, the morality frame disappeared, while the other frames remained prominent. Although a largely restrictive regulatory regime towards both the demand and supply of drugs was established and expanded in the 1970s and 1980s, a moderate liberalization on the demand side followed in the 1990s and 2000s.

Until the early 1990s, drug policy was framed in three ways. First, moral arguments were used to justify a harsh approach against drugs. In 1971, the government explained that drug misuse would destroy not only the 'personality, freedom and existence' of consumers but also their families and the 'viability' of society as a whole (BT-Drs. 6/1877: 5[5]). According to the explanation of the drug law revision in 1981, only youths with a 'well-marked self-esteem' would be able to 'successfully resist the temptation to consume drugs'. Drug consumption was regarded as 'failing in life' (BT-Drs. 9/27: 26). In the National Plan on Combating Drugs (1990), the government judged drug use as being contrary to a 'positive way of life'. The plan identified individuals who followed a modern, individualized lifestyle characterized by the absence of 'traditional roles, norms and values' as potential drug consumers (Gesundheitsminister 1992: 15ff.).

Second, most policy modifications were justified by negative health effects for the consumer. Nearly all of the documents emphasized health damages as one of the main problems linked to drugs (e.g., BT-Drs. 6/1877: 5; BT-Drs. 9/27: 25). Since the 1980s, policy-makers have increasingly pointed to the negative social consequences of drug abuse but also of tough prison sentences for addicted offenders (BT-Drs. 9/27: 25ff.). In 1990, for the first time, addicts were officially characterized as 'sick persons' (Gesundheitsminister 1992: 23).

Third, arguments based on the disruption of security and public order have been present since the early decades under analysis. Political actors regularly emphasized the continuous increase in drug-related crime committed by addicts who were described as 'criminals' (e.g., BT-Drs. 9/27: 27) and as committing 'significant disturbance[s] of public security' (Gesundheitsminister 1992: 12). The government also stressed the expansion and transnational diffusion of drug trafficking, which was identified as the 'core' of organized crime (BT-Drs. 6/1877: 5; BT-Drs. 12/989: 1).

During the 1990s, the morality frame disappeared, whereas the security and public order and the health and social frames remained prominent. Legal amendments were justified with arguments such as the need to combat drug crime more effectively (BT-Drs. 12/989: 20) and to provide better medical assistance to addicts (BT-Drs. 12/934: 5). In the 2000s, arguments related to the poor health and social conditions of addicts remained crucial (BT-Drs. 16/11515: 9; Drogenbeauftragte 2003: 16ff.).

The shift from morality to non-morality framing is reflected in German regulatory development (Böllinger 2004). The disappearance of the morality frame during the 1990s was accompanied by a more permissive approach regarding drug consumers, including an expansion of treatment measures and the introduction of harm reduction elements (Kalke 2001: 30ff.). In 1992, amendments of the restrictive Narcotic Drugs Act facilitated the suspension of addicted offenders' sentences and a refrain from prosecution in cases of small amounts of drugs. Substitution treatment with methadone and the supply of syringes were legalized. Further amendments in 2000 and 2009 allowed the operation of drug consumption rooms and the use of diamorphine as a substitution substance. The new governmental strategy on drugs, published in 2003, incorporated harm reduction as the fourth pillar of German drug policy (in addition to law enforcement, prevention and treatment; Drogenbeauftragte [2003: 20]).

In conclusion, the empirical development largely confirms our expectations. While the morality frame was one of the three dominant frames in the 1970s and 1980s, it disappeared in the 1990s. This shift was accompanied by a gentle liberalization of regulation and penal provisions regarding the individual consumer.

Gambling policy in the Netherlands

Morality framing in Dutch gambling policy was prominent until the mid-1960s. Thereafter, the morality frame lost importance and finally disappeared in favour of the economic and fiscal, health and social, and security and public order frames. The shift from morality to non-morality frames coincided to a large degree with a more permissive regulatory regime with respect to the individual gambler.

During the 1950s, the morality frame prevailed in legislation, in combination with arguments related to security and public order. The lottery act of 1905 was still valid, and its understanding of gambling remained prominent. The act introduced the concept of 'Kanalisatie', which is based on three objectives: first, protecting the individual from fraudulent and misleading lotteries; second, protecting the individual from having his or her desire to gamble taken advantage of by fraudulent or misleading lotteries; and third, reducing the desire to gamble (Kamerstuk 213, nr.3: 2f.). The first two arguments are in line with our understanding of security and public order framing owing to the emphasis on the need to protect the consumer from fraud and other criminal activity. The last element coincides with our understanding of morality framing because the government aims to protect the individual from him or herself and his or her desire to gamble. Thus, gambling is considered to be an undesirable behaviour that has negative consequences for both the individual and society as a whole (Littler 2011: 109).

In the 1960s, the morality frame took a back seat in favour of the economic and fiscal frame. The Ministers of Justice, Agriculture and Fishery argued that the lottery branch was confronted with a turnover decrease of approximately 8 per cent in the first quarter of 1964 owing to increased gambling activities abroad. Furthermore, increasing the number of lottery draws would lead to new public revenues. Arguments such as reduced costs and workload were also decisive (Kamerstuk 7603, nr.3: 9f.). Morality reasoning surfaced again when the ministers discussed the regulatory approach of slot machines that would constitute a 'temptation', particularly for minors (*ibid.*: 8).

Economic and fiscal framing was further cultivated in the 1970s and 1980s, while the morality frame disappeared completely. The argument for reducing individuals' desire to gamble did not reappear. The Ministry of Economic Affairs and Finance gained importance as the Ministry of Justice initiated closed co-operation in the form of an inter-departmental working group (Kamerstuk 16481, nr.3: 1). In 1981, when the tax burden for casinos was first being discussed, one of the main arguments in favour of revision was that the current regulation reduced the gross profit to such an extent that the casinos in Zandvoort and in Valkenburg would have to be closed (Kamerstuk 15358, nr.3: 3). In the late 1990s, the health and social and security and public order frames gained prominence (Kamerstukken 25646, nr.3; 375).

The shift from morality to non-morality framing that began in the 1960s and was completed in the 1980s coincided, to a large degree, with more permissive regulatory changes. In the mid-1960s, the Dutch started to follow an approach overwhelmingly directed towards more permissive regulation handling of gambling, especially regarding the individual gambler. As the objective to reduce the individual's desire to gamble lost importance and other problem definitions, such as gambling abroad and public revenue deficits, became more prominent, different problem solutions arose. The Gambling Act of 1964 legalized, for example, the profit-oriented state lottery and opened up the opportunity for charity lotteries to award cash prizes. Only cash payout slot machines remained prohibited. Thus, the freedom of the individual gambler increased considerably. This regulatory trend was further cultivated during the 1970s and 1980s: in 1974, the government introduced Lotto as a monopoly and legalized casino games; a 1986 amendment allowed the commercial operation of cash payout slot machines in bars and arcades and of slot machines in casinos; and the 1981 tax reform levied a tax of 33.3 per cent on gross gaming revenues generated by casino gaming. Although this last reform also constituted a restrictive step for the individual gambler, it was of little importance in comparison to the path-breaking reforms implemented during earlier years.

In conclusion, the findings confirm our expectations. The morality frame was prominent in the early decades but lost importance and, thus, opened up new perspectives on gambling. This brought about new policy solutions that positively affected individual freedom in the gambling market.

Gambling policy in Germany

In Germany, although policy-makers relied on the morality frame when discussing the regulation of casinos in the 1950s, moral arguments were not dominant at any point during the whole period examined. The economic and fiscal frame and security and public order frame were central first, while the health and social frame arose later. Slightly more permissive regulation accompanied these frame changes over the decades.[6]

During the 1950s, the gambling acts of the 1920s, which were mainly justified by moral arguments, were still valid (Reichstag No.331.1919/20; Reichstag No.369.1920/24).[7] In 1952, the *Bundestag* had an intense debate over a proposed bill banning all casinos. The Christian Democrats argued that gambling would pose 'not only a threat to people's personality but also to their families and society as a whole' and that casinos would lead to a general 'moral decline' in society. Other parties' representatives refused the bill, arguing that 'casinos generate foreign currency' and that closing the casinos would lead to a 'decline in the employment rate' (BT-Drs. 1/2996: 8287ff.). Finally, the bill was rejected. Morality framing has not appeared in discussions about gambling regulation since that debate. Any remaining moral arguments, which were out of date even in 1952, were erased from state documents in the mid-1970s (Belz 1993: 9).

Until the 1980s, the economic and fiscal and security and public order frames dominated governmental reasoning. The governments stated that uncontrolled gambling halls could lead to an environment fostering criminal acts (BT-Drs. 3/318). Changes to the Criminal Code in 1998 were framed as essential for maintaining security and assuring state incomes from gambling (BR-Drs. 164/97). The modification of the horse betting and lottery laws in 1999 were justified as being fiscally necessary (BT-Drs. 14/2271).

The health and social frame first appeared in the mid-1980s and gathered increasing attention at the expense of other frames. For example, the Protection of Young Persons Act was justified by protecting youth from gambling offers

(BT-Drs. 14/243). In 2003, the governmental Action Plan on Drugs and Addiction defined individual pathological gambling as a discrete disease and warned against the dangerous consequences of gambling (Drogenbeauftragte 2003: 16ff.). The 2004 State Treaty on Lotteries and the 2008 State Treaty on Gambling aimed to protect gamblers, especially younger ones. Similar arguments were used in the preamble of the statutory order on gambling in 2005 (BR-Drs. 655/05).[8,9]

The decreasing persuasiveness of the morality frame in the 1950s coincided with the enactment of more permissive regulations. While the reform of the Industrial Code in 1960 led to an increase in the requirements necessary to obtain a license for gambling halls, the consolidation of non-morality frames in the 1970s occurred together with other liberalizing law amendments concerning the individual. The reform of the Criminal Code (1975) decreased sanctions for illegal slot machine gambling and erased punishment for regular gambling (Belz 1993: 8f.).

Overall, we did find evidence for a vanishing morality framing of gambling policy during the examination period. In the last six decades, Germany has followed a path towards more permissive gambling regulation in terms of the individual. Thus, we find empirical support for our hypotheses.[10]

INTEGRATED ANALYSIS

In this section, we present an integrated analysis of our results that addresses if and to what extent our expectations have been confirmed empirically. First, for three of the four cases analysed, we indeed did observe the initial dominance of a morality frame. Gambling and drug consumption were regarded as morally wrong and threatening traditional norms and values. Slot machines constituted a 'temptation', and drug abuse destroyed not only the 'personality, freedom and existence' of drug consumers but also their families and the 'viability' of society as a whole. The only exception is Dutch drug policy-making, which never used a morality framing.[11] Against this background, we interpret these findings as mostly confirming Expectation 1a.

Second, policy frame shifts for drug consumption and gambling were observed. We found a shift from a dominant or at least equally important morality frame towards non-morality frames in three cases. These frame shifts partly occurred early in our observation period (gambling in both countries during the 1950s and 1960s). German drug policy-making displayed the expected abandonment at a later point in time, during the 1990s. Frame shifting appears to be an incremental process rather than an abrupt change. First, moral arguments become less significant; then they disappear completely. Overall, the cases show that if a morality frame did exist, it has lost importance in favour of other frames. Thus, the developments largely confirm Expectation 1b. In other words, we can assume that, owing to secularization and value shifts in the society, policy-makers have decreasingly conceived of drug consumption and gambling as sinful behaviour and have therefore ceased relying on moral reasoning to justify the regulation of those activities. Country- and policy-specific sets of actors, ideas and interests ultimately seem to determine the precise moment of frame shift. For example, in the field of gambling, the trend towards legalization in several neighbouring countries of Germany and the Netherlands evoked the problem of losing potential tax revenue and control over gamblers and their behaviour (Kingma 2008). These changed circumstances yielded new ideas and interests that enlightened gambling from a different perspective and initiated the shift towards non-moral reasoning. The late disappearance of morality framing in German drug policy might have been caused by an extraordinary increase of drug consumers during the 1970s and a youth movement explicitly fighting against traditional norms and values (Reuband 2009). Although secularization was advancing, the movement provoked the maintenance of a morality-led perspective. Continuing problem pressure and newly involved actors during the 1980s and 1990s gave rise to the abandonment of moral arguments.

Finally, we investigate the connection between shifts towards non-morality framing and more permissive regulations. We can confirm this expectation for the three cases that feature a morality framing during the period analysed. In the Netherlands, for example, lottery gambling was discussed in relation to the problem of illegal gambling abroad and the loss of public revenues in the 1960s. The new problem definition led to a new set of potential policy choices and finally opened up the opportunity for charity lotteries to award cash prizes and for profit-oriented state lotteries. In general, policy change appears in the field of gambling in the form of legalized games, whereas in the field of drug consumption new forms of treatment and harm reduction are proposed as policy solutions. Thus, the shifts in problem definition

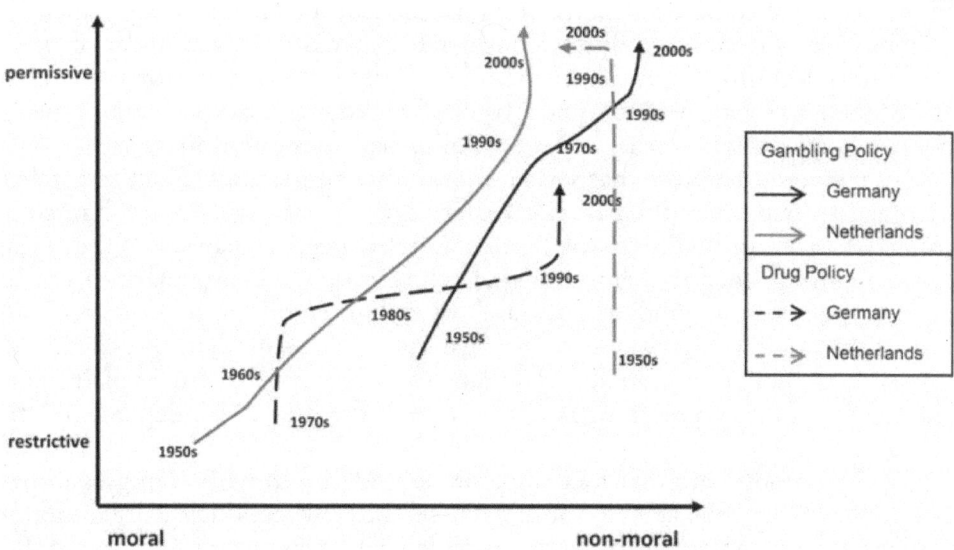

Figure 1 Frame and regulatory development (demand), 1950–2010

overwhelmingly and positively affect the demand side. Figure 1 summarizes the empirical findings, contrasting the regulatory development on a restrictive–permissive axis with the development of frames along a moral- to non-moral axis.

CONCLUSION

Our comparative analysis of the framing and the development of drug and gambling policy over six decades in the Netherlands and Germany provides several important insights. Frames matter for policies commonly assigned to the morality type. Morality frames are indeed observable here. Furthermore, shifts in the dominant frame are real and observable. Thus, we conclude that our assumptions concerning value changes in society, secularization and new interests and actors in the policy arena can provide a good explanation for these shifts. There is also a close connection between frame shifts and policy output. Shifts from morality to non-morality frames often lead to more permissive policy change. This seems closely related to new problem definitions, which bring about new policy solutions. Nevertheless, further examinations of these links should be performed because our analysis lacks a detailed investigation of country- and policy-specific sets of actors, ideas and interests, which ultimately determine the exact moment of change. Knill (2013) refers to this set as the 'cultural opportunity structure', which is one factor that determines the 'morality charge' of an issue.

In consequence, policies that are often labelled as 'moral' in the American literature are not coherently framed that way in the European countries we analysed. Drug and gambling policies shifted from morality policies to so-called 'normal' policies or – as in one case – were never discussed as morally wrong. Therefore, we argue that framing analysis is essential for the identification of morality policies, particularly in the European context, in which the religious–secular cleavage differs considerably across countries and over time. If morality framing is not dominant, not constantly observable or not present at all, then the very research endeavour of making the case for 'one type' of policy compared with 'other types' of policy becomes questionable.

Our research, therefore, has several important implications. First, researchers of morality issues should pay close attention to how policies are framed in countries over time. This is of particular relevance in analyses of European cases. Framing analysis helps the researcher grasp the particularities of this policy type and may guide the research by enlightening the role of important factors for policy change, such as structure (e.g., problem pressure) and agency (e.g., policy monopolies). Perhaps we are already able to explain many changes in morality policy with 'conventional' theories and independent variables.

We also recommend that such analyses be undertaken with even greater precision than we were able to provide here, i.e., by conducting quantitative content analysis across all parliamentary debates or by examining how policy frames differ for the demand and supply side. Another fruitful approach would be to emphasize the cross-sectional perspective and shed a more nuanced light on the set of actors, ideas and interests that bring about frame shifts and policy change.

Biographical notes: Stephan Heichel is Assistant Professor at the Chair of Comparative Public Policy and Administration, University of Konstanz, Germany. Eva-Maria Euchner, Kerstin Nebel, and Andreas Raschzok are Research Fellows in the Department of Politics and Public Administration, University of Konstanz, Germany.

ACKNOWLEDGEMENTS

We thank our three anonymous referees for their constructive comments. This contribution is based on the project MORAPOL (ERC Advanced Grant). We gratefully acknowledge the generous funding by the European Research Council.

NOTES

1. Until 1990, West Germany only.
2. Please see the website http://www.polver.uni-konstanz.de/knill/working-papers-downloads/ for a comprehensive overview.
3. We expected to find arguments emphasizing the fundamental right of individuals to decide on their own whether to gamble or to consume drugs. However, such arguments did not appear in the documents.
4. 'Kamerstukken': Dutch parliamentary documents, available from http://www.overheid.nl/ and http://www.statengeneraaldigitaal.nl/.
5. 'Bundestagsdrucksachen' (BT-Drs.): Documents of the German *Bundestag*; 'Bundesratsdrucksachen' (BR-Drs.): Documents of the German *Bundesrat*; both kinds of documents are available from http://www.dip.bundestag.de (1976 onwards).
6. We focus on national legislation; legislation of the *Bundesländer* was not analysed.
7. 'Reichstag' refers to the German parliament and its documents between 1918 and 1933, available at http://www.reichstagsprotokolle.de

8 See Note 5, above.
9 In light of European law, Germany tried to defend its state monopoly from the 2000s onwards by arguing that only nation states are able to control illegal gambling. This is one reason why the economic frame diminished in favour of the health and social frame.
10 We do not expect contradictory framing and regulation in the German *Länder* owing to vertical and horizontal linkages.
11 Dutch drug policy constitutes an extraordinary case; one might argue that the empirical finding was expectable in advance. However, the picture is much more complex because (1) the permissive regulations primarily refer to *soft* and not to *hard* drugs, and (2) the particular approach was not established before the mid-1970s.

REFERENCES

Adviescommissie (2009) *Geen deuren maar daden. Nieuwe accenten in het Nederlands drugsbeleid*, Den Haag: Adviescommissie Drugsbeleid, English version available at http://www.drugtext.org/table/new-emphasis-in-dutch-drugs-policy/ (accessed 15 March 2012).
Baumgartner, F.R. and Jones, B.D. (2009) *Agendas and Instability in American politics*, Chicago, IL: The University of Chicago Press.
Belz, A. (1993) *Das Glücksspiel im Strafrecht*, Kriminalwissenschaftliche Studien 17, Marburg: Elwert Verlag.
Böllinger, L. (2004) 'Drug law and policy in Germany and the European Community: recent developments', *Journal of Drug Issues* 34(3): 491–510.
Drogenbeauftragte (ed.) (2003) *Aktionsplan Drogen und Sucht*, Berlin: Die Drogenbeauftrage der Bundesregierung.
Engeli, I., Green-Pedersen, C. and Larsen, L.T. (eds) (2012) *Morality Politics in Western Europe. Parties, Agendas and Policy Choices*, Basingstoke: Palgrave Macmillan.
Flanagan, S.C. and Lee, A.-R. (2003) 'The new politics, culture wars, and the authoritarian-libertarian value change in advanced industrial democracies', *Comparative Political Studies* 36(3): 235–70.
Gesundheitsminister (ed.) (1992) *Nationaler Rauschgiftbekämpfungsplan. Maßnahmen derRauschgiftbekämpfung und der Hilfe für Gefährdete und Abhängige*, Bonn: Bundesminister für Gesundheit/Bundesminister des Innern.
Haider-Markel, D.P. and Meier, K.J. (1996) 'The politics of gay and lesbian rights: expanding the scope of the conflict', *The Journal of Politics* 58(2): 332–49.
Heichel, S., Knill, C. and Schmitt, S. (2013) 'Public policy meets morality: conceptual and theoretical challenges in the analysis of morality policy change', *Journal of European Public Policy* 20(3), doi: 10.1080/13501763.2013.761497
Hurka, S. and Nebel, K. (2013) 'Framing and policy change after shooting rampages: a comparative analysis of discourse networks', *Journal of European Public Policy* 20(3), doi: 10.1080/13501763.2013.761508
Inglehart, R. (1990) *Culture Shift in Advanced Industrial Society*, Princeton, NJ: Princeton University Press.
ISAD (1985) *Drugbeleid in beweging: naar een normalisering van de drugproblematiek*, Gravenhage: Interdepartementale Stuurgroep Alcohol- en Drugbeleid.
Kalke, J. (2001) *Innovative Landtage: Eine empirische Untersuchung am Beispiel der Drogenpolitik*, Wiesbaden: Westdeutscher Verlag.
Kingma, S.F. (2008) 'The liberalization and (re)regulation of Dutch gambling markets: national consequences of the changing European context', *Regulation & Governance* 2(4): 445–58.

Knill, C. (2013) 'The study of morality policy: analytical implications from a public policy perspective', *Journal of European Public Policy* 20(3), doi: 10.1080/13501763.2013.761494

Krippendorff, K. (2004) *Content Analysis: An Introduction to its Methodology*, Thousand Oaks, CA: Sage.

Larsen, L.T. (2010) 'Framing knowledge and innocent victims. Europe bans smoking in public places', *Critical Discourse Studies* 7(1): 1–17.

Littler, A. (2011) *Member States Versus the European Union. The Regulation of Gambling*, Leiden: Martinus Nijhoff.

Meier, K.J. (1999) 'Drugs, sex, rock, and roll: a theory of morality politics', *Policy Studies Journal* 27(4): 681–95.

Mooney, C.Z. (ed.) (2001) *Public Clash of Private Values: The Politics of Morality Policy*, New York: Chatham House.

Mucciaroni, G. (2011) 'Are debates about "morality policy" really about morality? Framing opposition to gay and lesbian rights', *Policy Studies Journal* 39(2): 187–216.

MvVWS (2009) *Hoofdlijnenbrief drugsbeleid. 11 september 2009*, Den Haag: Ministerie van Volksgezondheid, Welzijn en Sport.

Pollack, D. and Pickel, G. (2007) 'Religious individualization or secularization? Testing hypotheses of religious change – the case of Eastern and Western Germany', *The British Journal of Sociology* 58(4): 603–32.

Reuband, K.H. (2009) 'Entwicklung des Drogenkonsums in Deutschland und die begrenzte Wirksamkeit der Kriminalpolitik', *Zeitschrift für soziale Probleme und Kontrolle* 20(1/2): 182–206.

Smith, T.A. and Tatalovich, R. (2003) *Cultures at War. Moral Conflicts in Western Democracies*, Peterborough, ON: Broadview Press.

Studlar, D.T. (2008) 'US tobacco control: public health, political economy, or morality policy', *Review of Policy Research* 25(5): 393–410.

Timmermans, A. and Breeman, G. (2012) 'Morality issues in the Netherlands: coalition politics under pressure", in I. Engeli, C. Green-Pedersen and L., T. Larsen (eds), *Morality Politics in Western Europe. Parties, Agendas and Policy Choices*, Basingstoke: Palgrave Macmillan, pp. 35–62.

WVSA (World Values Survey Association) (2012) 'Publically available datasets', available at http://www.worldvaluessurvey.org (accessed 20 September 2012).

Framing and policy change after shooting rampages: a comparative analysis of discourse networks

Steffen Hurka and Kerstin Nebel

ABSTRACT In this contribution, we comparatively analyse the discourse networks generated by three shooting rampages. We formulate hypotheses on the extent to which (a) the framing cohesion of the *status quo* coalition and (b) the perceived causal complexity of the event are associated with varying degrees of subsequent gun policy change. Drawing on news reports in major newspapers, we collect information on actors and frames and systematically analyse those data with the tool *Discourse Network Analyzer*. The networks show that major gun policy change is possible if the *status quo* coalition is internally divided and the event's causal complexity is low. Incremental adjustments are also likely if the *status quo* coalition lacks cohesion, but if additionally causal complexity is high, i.e., the problem signified by the event is disputed. Finally, if the *status quo* coalition manages to retain its framing cohesion, deadlock is likely to occur regardless of the event's perceived causal complexity.

INTRODUCTION

As typical 'un-ness' events (Hewitt 1983: 10), shooting rampages are *un*expected, *un*scheduled and *un*pleasant. They quickly attract popular attention and instantly wipe any other issue from the political agenda. From a political science perspective, however, the question of how such shootings exert their impact on public policies has remained largely unaddressed. The few existing studies mainly focused on the most widely perceived shooting to date in Littleton (Colorado) in 1999, placing strong emphasis on the importance of media framing for the evolution of the public discourse and the political process (Birkland and Lawrence 2009; Haider-Markel and Joslyn 2001). Despite this overwhelming United States (US) focus of the relevant literature, shooting rampages occur across the globe at more or less regular intervals. In 2011, the devastating shooting on the Norwegian island Utøya reminded the world that the abuse of firearms is not a purely American phenomenon.

In the context of this collection, our contribution highlights the relevance of external shocks as a very specific aspect of morality policy-making and thereby complements other contributions which put their focus on the comparative analysis of long-term change processes (Euchner *et al.* 2013). While we focus on shooting rampages as one example of an external shock with particular significance for gun policy, other areas of morality policy are also susceptible to sudden events that have the potential to focus and accelerate public discourse (Heichel *et al.* 2013). The reactions that follow such types of events have been characterized as 'moral panics' (Cohen 2002), suggesting that the resulting discourse is often based on a perceived threat to core societal values.

We suggest in line with Knill (2013) that the regulation of firearms can best be described as a latent morality policy. Even though contestation around the issue is not purely value-based, values often become salient as a corollary of an external shock. In gun policy, similar to other areas of morality policy, this value conflict relates to a dimension between the poles of individual freedom and collective security. Can a society tolerate the possession of guns by individual citizens and, if so, to what extent should it be controlled? How many rights should the government enjoy *vis-à-vis* its citizens? How large is the residual risk a society can accept? All of these questions can hardly be answered in functionalist terms, as they require a judgment that boils down to basic values.

In this contribution, we examine the role discursive elements play in the process of crisis-induced policy change. We suggest that, in the aftermath of shooting rampages, framing assumes a central role for the setting of the political agenda and the possibility of subsequent changes in the affected country's firearm regime. Based on Kingdon's (2003) arguments on the agenda-setting potential of focusing events and inspired by recent contributions by Boin *et al.* (2009) on framing contests, we suggest that two discourse properties are particularly relevant: (a) the framing cohesion of the status quo coalition; and (b) the overall diversity of interpretative frames advanced in response to the events as an indicator of discursive complexity. We test our expectations against empirical evidence from three events: the shootings at Dunblane (United Kingdom, 1996); Erfurt (Germany, 2002); and Zug (Switzerland, 2001). While the shooting at Dunblane resulted in a prohibition of private handgun ownership in Great Britain, the Erfurt shooting led to a range of incremental adjustments in Germany's gun policies and the Zug shooting did not cause any change in the Swiss firearm regime. The respective data are the issue frames endorsed and refuted by the involved actors in two major, quality newspapers within the first month after the respective incident. We categorize and analyse those frames both descriptively and using a new network analytic tool called *Discourse Network Analyzer* (DNA) (Leifeld 2012).

The contribution is structured as follows: We first address the theoretical foundations of our study and present the three research hypotheses. Secondly, we describe and justify our case selection and provide information about our data and method. We then present the empirical evidence, both descriptively and analytically. The article concludes with a brief summary, some theoretical implications and guidance for future research.

EXTERNAL SHOCKS, FRAMING AND POLICY CHANGE

There is little scholarly dispute over the relevance of external shocks for the explanation of policy change and all major theoretical frameworks incorporate the concept, albeit with varying terminology and different connotations (Baumgartner and Jones 1993; Kingdon 2003; Sabatier 1998). In one way or the other, all of those frameworks acknowledge that policy change becomes more likely if certain events highlight (or are perceived to highlight) the need for reform. Yet, the frameworks differ with regard to their proposed causal mechanisms which link the external shock to policy change. We lack the space to review those theoretical arguments in detail, but argue that one of the most appealing has been advanced by Kingdon (2003) in his multiple streams approach. Following Kingdon's line of reasoning, the chance for policy change increases when a policy window opens and if this policy window is perceived by one or several policy entrepreneurs as an opportunity to push their cause. As a result, a previously neglected or even ignored issue can suddenly gain traction and access the public agenda. As Kingdon (2003: 98) notes, focusing events 'reinforce some preexisting perception of a problem, focus attention on a problem that was already "in the back of people's minds"'. Yet, focusing events are often highly complex and as such invite competing causal attributions. One and the same event can be interpreted through several lenses and thereby lead to interpretative conflict over the event's main underlying cause, and accordingly, over the lessons that should be drawn from it.

This latter argument has its roots in social constructivist approaches, which have taught us that social conditions are not automatically treated as social problems (Rochefort and Cobb 1993). In order to elevate an existing condition to a problem, a significant number of actors must perceive the condition as severe enough to demand political action. Corresponding shifts in problem perceptions become particularly likely when new information becomes available. Sometimes, this information comes in the form of focusing events (Birkland 2006; Kingdon 2003), which are 'sudden, relatively rare, can be reasonably defined as harmful [... and are] known to policymakers and the public virtually simultaneously' (Birkland 2006: 2). Such events lead to extreme increases of media attention and thereby often provide political decision-makers with the urge 'to do something' in order to fight a social problem which had largely gone unnoticed by the general population. Focusing events like shooting rampages can thereby serve as catalysts for policy change by highlighting previously neglected areas of public policy. Therefore, if we want to understand why and to what extent policies change after an external shock, we first need to understand how the external shock comes to be framed as an indicator of a social problem, and even more importantly which social problem. In other words, in order to gain a better understanding of the impact of external shocks, we need to pay close attention to the way the shock is perceived and its causes are portrayed (Boin *et al.* 2009; Haider-Markel and Joslyn 2001; Stone 1989).

A focusing event rarely ever passes without attempts to exploit the crisis (Boin *et al.* 2009). Despite initial claims from all sides that the event is incomprehensible and inexplicable, it rarely takes long until attempts at comprehension and explanation contribute to an opening of the corresponding policy window. As Birkland and Lawrence (2009) have demonstrated, shooting rampages are prime examples of such events that can be subjected to competing interpretative frames. But how do such framing contests unfold and what can we learn from them with regard to policy change?

In their model of the policy game, Boin *et al.* (2009) suggest that the framing strategies chosen by advocates of the *status quo* and advocates of change determine the occurrence and degree of policy change after an external shock. We endorse this argument, but go one step further and relax the assumption that the two coalitions are by definition unitary entities, both of which can only follow one of two strategies (Boin *et al.* 2009: 90). Instead, we argue in line with Schmitt *et al.* (2013) that what matters for the occurrence of policy change is the cohesiveness of the coalitions in terms of the frames endorsed and refuted by their members in the wake of a focusing event like a shooting rampage. Since shooting rampages are generally cohesively interpreted by gun policy change advocates as events that legitimize their policy goals, we suggest that the critical question is how the framing of the *status quo* coalition unfolds. If the advocates of the *status quo* continue to unequivocally resist gun-related policy change, we expect deadlock to occur because the original distribution of power essentially remains unchanged. If, however, a significant amount of actors from the *status quo* coalition defects as a result of the event, policy change will occur, because the *status quo* coalition will struggle to sustain its resistance in the face of declining cohesion.[1]

Yet, under the condition that the *status quo* coalition disintegrates, what determines the extent of policy change we should expect? We suggest that the degree of gun policy change after a shooting rampage should be strongly related to the event's perceived causal complexity. The more different causes can be brought to bear in order to explain the event, the harder it will get for the change advocates in the gun policy subsystem to convince the *status quo* coalition that the event has implications for gun policy arrangements. This is because more complex events enable the gun *status quo* advocates to divert attention to other policy areas in order to contain or prevent change on the gun issue. On the other hand, the more the debate is focused on one particular issue, e.g., guns, the more difficult it will get for an already fractionalized *status quo* coalition to prevent major policy change. We decided to pay particular attention to the gun issue, because it is the only issue that is invariably present after shooting rampages, compared to other issues which only occasionally become salient and are more context-specific. Despite this focus on one particular policy area, we think that our general arguments about coalition cohesion and discursive complexity can and should be transferred and tested with other types of external shocks and other areas of public policy.

Table 1 Hypotheses

Perceived causal complexity	Cohesion of SQ advocates	
	Low	High
Low	H1: Major change	H3: Deadlock
High	H2: Incremental change	H3: Deadlock

Based on our theoretical considerations, we expect the following relationships to hold after shooting rampages:

H1: If the *status quo* advocates are not cohesive and the perceived causal complexity is low (i.e., the discourse is focused on guns), *major gun policy* change becomes more likely.

H2: If the *status quo* advocates are not cohesive and the perceived causal complexity is high (i.e., the discourse is dispersed), *incremental gun policy* change becomes more likely.

H3: If the *status quo* advocates are cohesive, gun policy *deadlock* becomes more likely, regardless of perceived causal complexity.

Table 1 summarizes those expectations.

CASE SELECTION AND DESCRIPTION

So far, existing empirical research on the nexus between external shocks and policy change has mainly focused on technological failures like nuclear or natural disasters (e.g., Albright 2011; Birkland 2006; Nohrstedt 2008). Some studies also analysed regulatory responses to specific types of events like dog attacks (Lodge and Hood 2002), food scandals (Lodge 2011) or explosions in firework factories (de Vries 2004). Contributing to this line of inquiry, we selected three shooting rampages for comparative purposes based on their varying impacts on the gun policies of the countries in which they occurred:

Dunblane: On 13 March 1996, Thomas Hamilton (aged 43) entered a primary school in the Scottish town of Dunblane, shooting 16 children and one teacher before committing suicide. The perpetrator had been a member of the local gun club and therefore had had easy access to the weapon he used for the massacre. As a result of the shooting and the subsequent inquiry led by Lord Cullen, the Conservative government under John Major banned all private handguns with calibres above .22. After the elections in 1997, the new Labour government under Tony Blair extended the ban to all handguns.

Erfurt: Robert Steinhäuser (aged 19), a former student of the Gutenberg–Gymnasium in Erfurt, Germany, entered the school on 26 April 2002, shooting 13 faculty members, two students, one police officer and himself. Like

Thomas Hamilton, Steinhäuser had been a member of a gun club and used his sporting arms for the massacre. Ironically, the German Bundestag had tightened the national gun legislation on the same day the shooting took place. In the following debate, those changes were immediately questioned for their allegedly too limited magnitude and a consensus quickly emerged that some rules needed to be tightened even further. This led to a range of incremental adjustments including tighter age requirements, the prohibition of pumpguns with pistol grips and the introduction of compulsory medical-psychological tests for marksmen under the age of 25.

Zug: The third event occurred in the cantonal parliament of the Swiss town Zug on 27 September 2001. Friedrich Leibacher (aged 57) entered the plenary and shot 14 politicians before committing suicide. The perpetrator had had a long and ongoing dispute with the local administration. After several controversies which he had unsuccessfully taken to court, he was of the opinion that a conspiracy existed in Zug's administration and government. Leibacher had stored the weapons legally at home. However, the shooting did not lead to any changes in the Swiss firearm regime.

The most obvious difference between the three events is the venue in which they took place. One could argue that the simple fact that the Dunblane and Erfurt incidents were school shootings makes policy change more likely because of the particular gruesomeness associated with such shootings. However, this would not explain why other school shootings, like the one in Littleton (United States of America, 1999) did not lead to policy change (Birkland and Lawrence 2009) and why other, school-unrelated shootings, like the one in Port Arthur (Australia, 1996) did (Chapman *et al.* 2006). Therefore, we argue that the three cases are appropriate for our purpose, especially given the fact that all three were carried out with legal weapons and resulted in a comparable number of casualties.

METHOD AND DATA

DNA is a new tool in social network analysis, developed in order to enable researchers to identify discourse coalitions in a policy field via qualitative category-based content analysis (Leifeld 2012). The approach has two central features that make it the preferred option for our analysis. First, DNA allows us to identify actors and their most preferred frames and then convert these structured data into discourse networks.[2] This approach has both theoretical and methodological advantages *vis-à-vis* other approaches (see Leifeld [2012] for a more detailed discussion). Second, DNA is the first elaborate tool that allows for the quantitative analysis of discourse data and thereby opens venues for a structured comparative approach – a goal which had been elusive in discourse analysis for a long time. Thus, the innovation of DNA primarily lies in its potential to analyse actors and ideas simultaneously and thereby identify and compare discourse coalitions *empirically* instead of merely assuming their existence. This creates the possibility of pinpointing the extent of contestation around a given policy issue and visualizing the cohesion as well as the defection rates of different discourse coalitions.

Our analysis draws on data collected from newspapers in the three countries in which the massacres took place. We chose two quality daily newspapers for each country and collected all articles published within the first month after the incident that dealt with the respective event.[3] We chose this time period for two reasons. First, we are primarily interested in *initial* frames, that is, the direct reactions to the event. Second, we noticed that the decay of media attention followed similar patterns in all three cases (see Figure 1). After an initial spike in media attention, the number of articles devoted to the events declined and converged to zero within the first month.

After having collected the respective articles, we scanned them manually for event-related statements.[4] We ignored both comments from individual reporters and statements made in letters to the editor. We excluded the former owing to the possibility of bias arising through our newspaper selection and the latter primarily because of their arguably rather minor impact. Thus, our analytical focus lies primarily on representatives of political parties and interest groups, although we also collected statements from researchers and civil servants.

Four different features are coded for every statement: actor; organization; category; and agreement. If, for example, *The Independent* writes that 'The Labour leader said the review should consider tightening the law on hand guns in private possession' (Brown 1996), we code this as: Tony Blair (actor); Labour (organization); Guns (category); agreement (yes). With regard to gun policy,

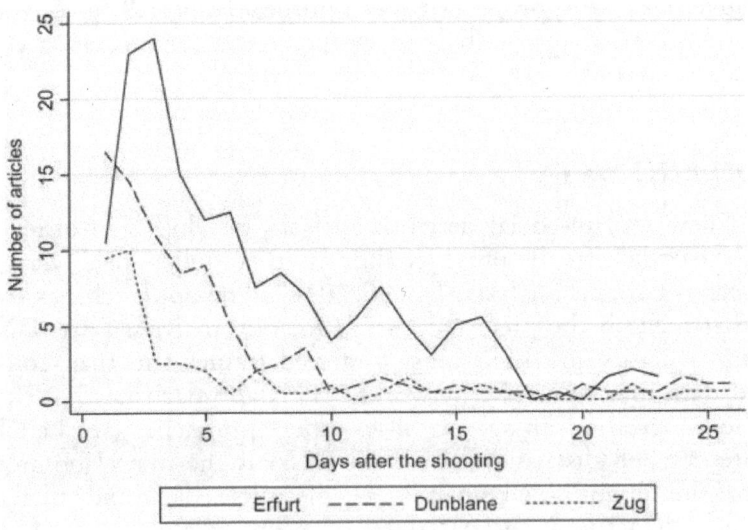

Figure 1 Decay of media attention after the shootings
Note: Average values for the two newspapers per country. National holidays and Sundays omitted.

we distinguished between statements demanding stricter measures (e.g., stricter age requirements, prohibition of certain weapons, etc.) and statements in favour of the *status quo* (e.g., opposition to 'knee-jerk' reactions). The same applies to demands for security measures (e.g., video surveillance, metal detectors, etc.) and corresponding rejection of such measures (e.g., public buildings should not become fortresses). The media category distinguishes statements which call for prohibitions and/or censorship in the media sector (violent films, video games, etc.) and statements which refuse such reactions. The society category incorporates statements that highlight societal neglect as a cause for the shooting and demand diffuse consequences like increased social cohesion and awareness. The politics category summarizes all positive and negative statements on general procedural consequences of the shooting, like calls for political inquiries. In the education category pros and cons about changes in the educational system of the country are summarized. The criminal justice category incorporates statements about increasing control and punishment of paedophiliacs (Dunblane specific). And finally, the lifting legal age category deals with claims about changing the legal age from 18 to 21 years (Erfurt specific).

We did not define the above mentioned categories *a priori*, but developed them in a check-and-revise style during the coding process. This is a common approach in discourse network analysis, since it is hardly possible to establish an exhaustive set of categories in a deductive way prior to the empirical research. It is very likely that sets of statements which had originally not been anticipated are found during the coding process (Leifeld 2012: 52). Thus, given the fact that we only had a preliminary idea about the emerging diversity of frames, this inductive proceeding proved to be the only alternative. The three cases were coded separately by the authors and the coding was continuously updated in the face of inconsistencies and contradictions. Although this procedure does not allow us to compute classical reliability scores, we are confident that our coding is consistent and complete.

We are aware of the potential validity problems caused by relying entirely on newspaper data. However, news media are the only source of information that provides us with a reasonably broad and comparable overview of the involved actors and their preferred issue frames. Other arenas of public debate like parliamentary hearings or plenary debates only give voice to a pre-selected pool of actors, sometimes focus exclusively on previously defined policy issues and, even more importantly, are handled very differently in different political systems.

DESCRIPTIVE STATISTICS – ACTORS AND FRAMES

The three events generated very different levels of discourse participation. While we counted 108 different actors after the Erfurt shooting, we only counted 48 in Dunblane and 40 in Zug. Several reasons could be responsible for this difference. As Jemphrey and Berrington (2000: 477) observed, the 'coverage of Dunblane was exceptional in terms of the level of restraint and sensitivity shown towards the bereaved, the survivors and the community', which was paralleled by an initial reluctance from many actors to politicize the event. Additionally, the lower number of political parties in Great Britain naturally focuses attention on a few key actors. With regard to Zug, it must be noted that the shooting took place only two weeks after the 9/11 attacks, which certainly had effects on the political agenda and, accordingly, the attention devoted to the Zug shooting. Nevertheless, all three events sparked a sharp increase in public attention. In all three cases, politicians were the origin of roughly two-thirds of all statements. In Erfurt and Dunblane, interest group representatives also participated in the political discourse to a relevant extent. The remaining statements came from diverse sources like administration officials, religious leaders or police representatives.

With regard to content, the dominant focus of the debate was quite different in the aftermath of the three shootings (see Figure 2). While the observers of the Dunblane shooting predominantly cited arguments referring to gun policy arrangements during the first month after the incident, the Zug debate exhibited a clear focus on matters of public security. The main focus in Erfurt was on the gun issue, but the debate was quite dispersed and also related to the question of whether the legal age should be lifted in general and issues of education. The focus on security matters in the aftermath of the Zug shooting deflected attention from the gun issue, and many of the gun-related statements made after the Zug shooting argued that the event did *not* highlight gun availability as a social problem – a feature that strongly distinguishes the Zug case from the other two cases.

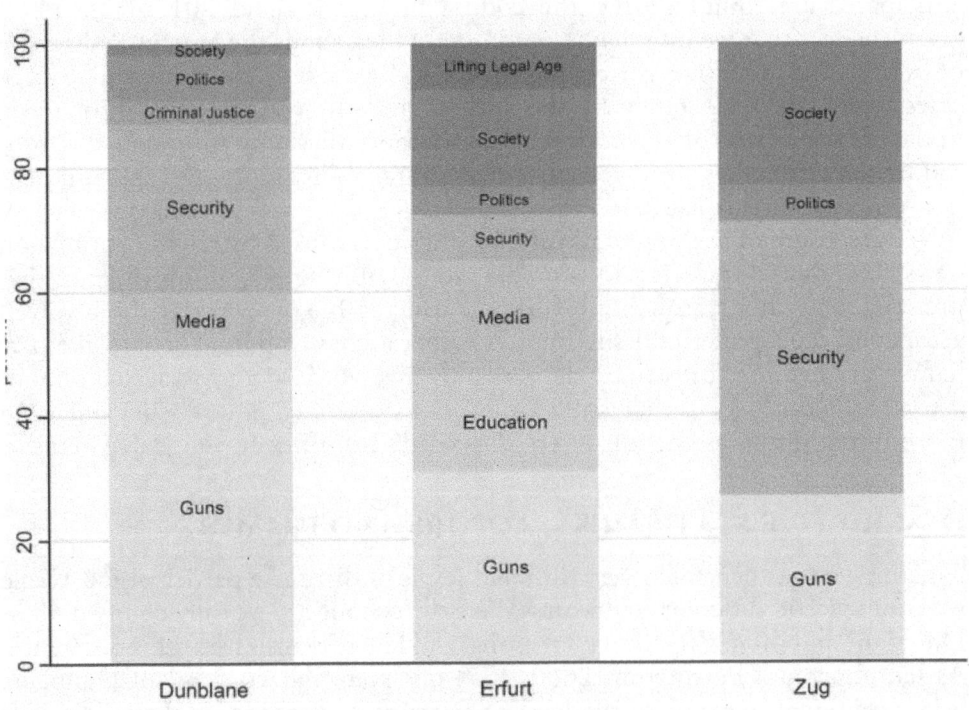

Figure 2 Statements per frame (percentages)

DISCOURSE NETWORK ANALYSIS – TRACING THE PATTERNS OF FRAMING CONTESTS

There are several ways to visualize discourse networks (Leifeld 2012). However, taking into account the problem that the depiction of discourse networks requires a lot of space, we must focus on one network type in this contribution. We decided to provide affiliation networks, because they allow us to compare the discursive relevance of different policy issues at the same time. Figures 3–5 display the results. The size of the rectangular frame nodes corresponds to the relative frequency of the respective frame. Solid lines indicate an actor's demand for change, dashed lines indicate that the actor refutes the need for change and dotted lines indicate that the actor made contradictory statements.

Dunblane – discursive foundations of major policy change

As the Dunblane affiliation network (Figure 3) shows, the discourse clearly focused on the gun issue, while other issues were only discussed to a much lesser extent.

Within the gun discourse, the most visible actors were politicians from the three major political parties in Great Britain: Conservatives; Labour politicians; and Liberal Democrats. The Labour party and the Liberal Democrats formed a cohesive coalition that demanded changes in gun policies, whereas the Conservative party was split between advocates of change and advocates

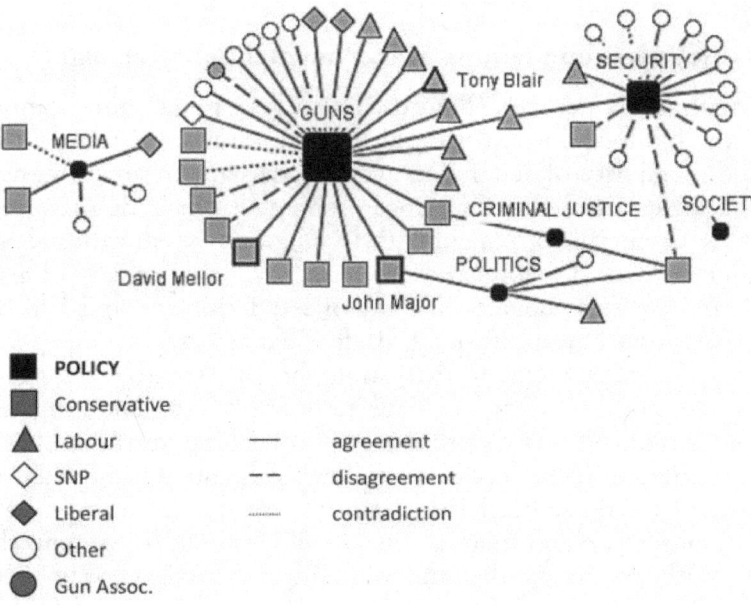

Figure 3 Dunblane discourse network

of the *status quo*. However, the majority of Conservative politicians in the discourse made positive statements on possible gun policy changes and, most importantly, Prime Minister John Major did not openly resist change and soon endorsed Labour's demands for a review of British firearm policies. In addition, the most visible Conservative actor in the immediate aftermath of the shooting, Member of Parliament (MP) David Mellor, advocated a total ban of private handguns early on. The Labour party, led by opposition leader Tony Blair, demonstrated exceptional cohesion in its demand for tighter gun controls.

Of course, the displayed network is only a snapshot of the immediate political reactions to the tragedy and many subsequent events contributed to the decision to ban handguns, most importantly the publication of the report of the Cullen inquiry and the formation of the Snowdrop Campaign, which managed to exert massive pressure on political decision-makers (Karp 2003). However it can be questioned whether both would have had a comparable impact if the Conservative party had cohesively opposed gun policy change in the immediate aftermath of the tragedy or if the *status quo* advocates would have been more successful in deflecting the public debate towards other policy issues. In addition, it is unlikely that a sweeping policy change would have been possible had the Labour side suffered any defections.

In sum, the Dunblane case supports H1 because the *status quo* coalition suffered at least two very important defections, the discourse was strongly focused on the gun issue and the event eventually led to a major policy change in Great Britain's gun policies.

Erfurt – discursive foundations of incremental policy change

The Erfurt affiliation network (Figure 4), displays a much more complex structure than the Dunblane network regarding the number of frames and actors. Although the majority of statements were made with regard to guns, a range of other relevant discourses developed, ranging from a debate over violent video games to specific arrangements in Germany's education system and general concern over developments in Germany's civil society. This resulted in a much more diffuse debate than the one at Dunblane and led to the discourse participation of a multitude of individual actors.

There was broad agreement that strengthening security arrangements in schools would not be an appropriate response to the shooting. A typical concern in this context was that schools could become 'fortresses', a metaphor we also encountered in the discourses following Dunblane and Zug. Likewise, the majority of discourse participants agreed that changes should be made in the education system and that access to violent media content should be restricted. With regard to the gun discourse, there is clear evidence of a highly cohesive change coalition consisting of members of the Social Democratic Party (SPD) and the Green Alliance. We observe opposition primarily

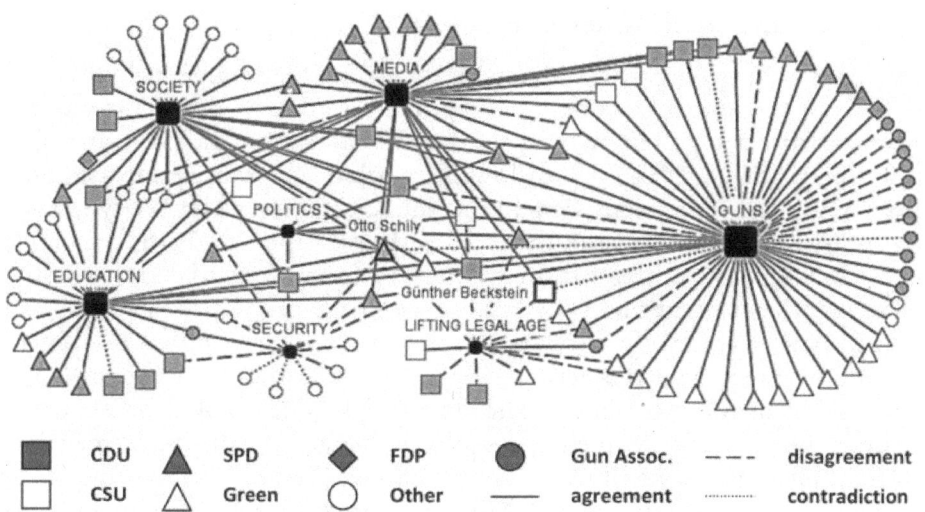

Figure 4 Erfurt discourse network

from the gun lobby or individual shooting clubs, but there is also evidence that even those actors were willing to concede to some gun policy changes, albeit to a much lesser extent than the Christian Democratic and Christian Social Union (CDU/CSU). After initial efforts to frame the Erfurt shooting as a societal failure and the result of the corrupting influence of violent video games, the opposition moved towards accepting the need to change certain gun policies, including (among others) a lifting of age requirements and a prohibition of pump guns. The major individual actors in the discourse were the Minister of the Interior Otto Schily (SPD) and Günther Beckstein (CSU), who was deemed to become Schily's successor in an eventual election victory in September of 2002. Both were initially sceptical about the need to tighten gun regulations, but changed their opinions as new information on the shooting's circumstances became available and their coalition colleagues started to endorse change.

The opposition thereby succumbed to mounting pressure to take a stance on guns and found it hard to deflect the debate on one single alternative issue. The special circumstance that the German Bundestag had just voted in favour of a tighter weapon law on the morning the shooting took place certainly accelerated the political process. It only took a few days until general agreement emerged over the need to further tighten some of the newly changed regulations, which was accomplished in the conciliation committee of the German Bundesrat.

Thus, the Erfurt case supports our H2 expectation as the *status quo* coalition was not particularly cohesive, the discourse following the incident was highly dispersed and, accordingly, the subsequent changes in Germany's gun policies were incremental in nature.

Zug - discursive foundations of deadlock

The Zug discourse (Figure 5), illustrates the strong focus on security matters in the wake of the massacre, compared with the lower relevance of the gun issue. The need for changes in security measures was quite contested among the various participants. Many saw the Swiss tradition of a transparent relationship between political representatives and the public endangered by overly restrictive new security arrangements and therefore withheld support. Yet, as the graph in Figure 5 shows, several actors from different backgrounds also endorsed calls for tighter security measures and the lines between the camps are blurry.

With regard to guns, the network shows strong cohesion within the Socialdemocratic Party (SP) on the need for tighter rules in the Swiss firearm regime, which is one of the most liberal ones in Europe. The graph suggests that the Christian Democratic People's Party (CVP) belongs to the same coalition as the SP. However, all of the CVP statements we counted as agreeing to gun policy changes were extremely diffuse and unspecific when compared to the very focused consequences demanded by the SP.[5] Such unspecific statements like assurances to 'review' the current laws imply ostensible concessions and are likely to be made primarily in an attempt to win time. Therefore, we conclude that both change and *status quo* advocates exhibited high cohesion in their support and their rejection of gun policy changes. As a result, and in addition to the already low magnitude of the gun discourse, it hardly comes as a surprise that deadlock occurred and no gun policy changes were implemented in Switzerland in the wake of the Zug massacre. Yet, security measures in public buildings were bolstered in many parts of the country as a response to the

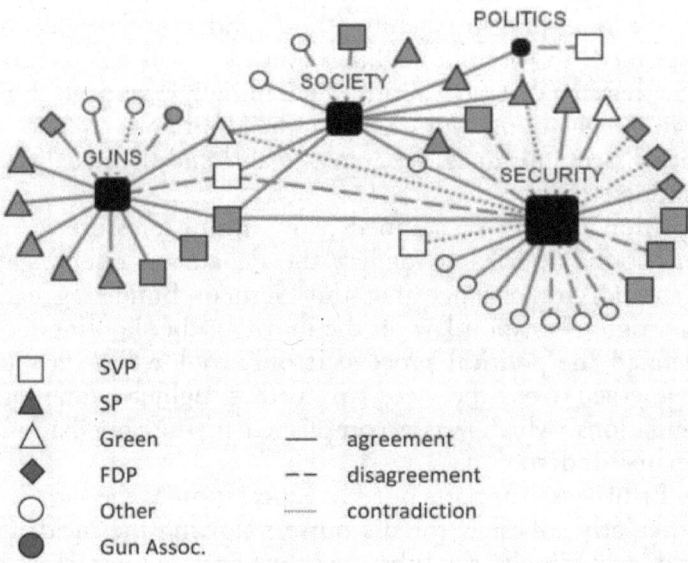

Figure 5 Zug discourse network

shooting (Raaflaub 2011), which lends some support to our general argument on the relevance of discursive complexity. In sum, the empirical evidence suggests that the Zug case supports H3.

CONCLUSION

Drawing on theoretical frameworks that emphasize the relevance of focusing events as catalysts for policy change (Birkland 2006; Boin *et al.* 2009; Kingdon 2003), this contribution tested the extent to which the varying occurrence and degree of gun-related policy change after shooting rampages can be traced back to the cohesion of the *status quo* coalition on the issue of gun control and the general variance of interpretative frames brought forward by different actors in the immediate aftermath of the events. We based our empirical analysis upon statements made by different actors in the news media following the first month after the shooting rampages at Erfurt (Germany), Dunblane (United Kingdom) and Zug (Switzerland), which all led to different levels of change in the three countries' gun policies.

The extent to which the discourses were dispersed among different issues varied strongly. In Dunblane, guns were the dominant issue, which made it hard for advocates of the *status quo* to deflect popular attention to other policy issues or dilute the debate by pointing to threats of general societal norms. At the same time, several prominent Conservatives either voiced their willingness for concessions early on (as in the case of Prime Minister Major) or even played a central role in the change movement (as in the case of MP David Mellor). Also in Erfurt, gun control was the major issue, but much more than in Dunblane the discourse also extended to several other policy areas. However, the gun *status quo* advocates not only failed to make those competing issues dominant, they also failed to keep their cohesion with regard to the gun issue. This resulted in a range of incremental changes, but it did not result in a large-scale change like in Dunblane. This difference was certainly also owing to the lack of a dedicated pro-change social movement in Erfurt and the later emergence of such a group, the Snowdrop Campaign, in Dunblane (Karp 2003). Finally, in contrast to the shootings in Dunblane and Erfurt, the shooting in Zug resulted in a discourse that primarily focused on matters of security, whereas gun control was a side issue. Within the gun control debate, however, we observed a *status quo* coalition which collectively watered down the gun debate by making only diffuse and unspecific pledges. As a result, the Zug debate petered out without any concrete changes as the momentum for policy change faded.

On a theoretical level, the contribution has several implications. First, discursive elements are worth exploring as pieces of the larger puzzle of policy change. Shifts in problem perceptions and corresponding volatility of competing discourse coalitions are interesting phenomena that should be incorporated more systematically in event-based explanations of policy change. Such an approach could further improve our understanding of the emergence and exploitation of policy windows in the aftermath of focusing events (Boin *et al.* 2009; Kingdon 2003). This is because statements made in response to external shocks can be interpreted as manifestations of actor preferences and the resulting discourse networks are indicative of the actual size of the policy window. Second, our contribution suggests that a more profound micro-foundation of existing theoretical frameworks is imperative. Locating the analytical focus on the frames advanced by individual actors could inform us more deeply about their motivations and strategies in order to prevent or facilitate policy change. Finally, we claim that the processes we highlighted in this contribution should be particularly relevant if the respective event has the potential to be framed as a threat to basic moral values. The resulting clash of frames and counter-frames after events which are based on human failure can be expected to be of higher intensity than after focusing events that are based on technical deficiencies (e.g., plane crashes) or events of non-human, or at least only indirect human, causation (e.g., natural disasters). The involvement of private human failure or misconduct is particularly prevalent in morality policies and makes related events susceptible to moral exploitation, especially if the conflict of values is usually latent and only erupts as a result of the event (Heichel *et al.* 2013; Knill 2013).

We have demonstrated that framing and policy change are two sides of the same coin in the aftermath of external shocks like shooting rampages. However, whether or not gun policies change as a result of such events hinges on many additional factors and the processes discussed in this contribution are not sufficient explanations. In addition to imminent elections (Boin *et al.* 2009), also national gun traditions, competing focusing events and prior policy configurations can also have an impact on whether or not gun policies change. Most importantly, institutional variables on the level of the political systems certainly constrain or facilitate policy change to varying extents in the further political process. However, we would like to point out that the emergence of the political discourse after an external shock precedes this process and is therefore worth exploring in its own right. After all, in order to understand why a problem is dealt with politically and subjected to the decision-making process, we must first understand why it is actually seen as a problem.

Finally, future research endeavours should broaden the empirical focus. For instance, distinguishing between actors in terms of their procedural power could lead to additional insights about which group of actors dominates the discourse. Moreover, we suggest that our hypotheses are transferable to other empirical contexts and would therefore like to encourage scholars to take up our line of inquiry by examining other types of external shocks and areas of public policy. Such a research programme could eventually lead to a more thorough understanding of how different societies process sudden and disruptive events politically.

Biographical notes: Steffen Hurka and Kerstin Nebel are PhD candidates and research assistants at the University of Konstanz, Germany.

ACKNOWLEDGEMENTS

We thank our three anonymous referees for their constructive comments. This contribution is based on the project MORAPOL (ERC Advanced Grant). We gratefully acknowledge the generous funding by the European Research Council.

NOTES

1 Note that this argument is also closely linked to the Advocacy Coalition Framework (Sabatier 1998). However, Sabitier's framework explicitly requires the researcher to look at a decade or more, while our focus lies on rapid policy change after an external shock.
2 These networks can be visualized by other software packages such as *visone* or *UCINET*.
3 Germany: *Frankfurter Allgemeine Zeitung* and *Süddeutsche Zeitung*; United Kingdom: *The Guardian* and *The Independent*; Switzerland: *Neue Zürcher Zeitung* and *Der Tagesanzeiger*.
4 Dunblane: 171 articles, 106 statements; Erfurt: 408 articles, 311 statements; Zug: 76 articles, 84 statements. A list of the analysed articles can be made available upon request.
5 We decided not to differentiate between diffuse and focused statements in our networks, because this would have made them more confusing and harder to interpret. In Erfurt and Dunblane, we observed that diffuse statements generally spread across different types of actors, but not so much in Zug.

REFERENCES

Albright, E.A. (2011) 'Policy change and learning in response to extreme flood events in Hungary: an advocacy coalition approach', *Policy Studies Journal* 39(3): 485–511.
Baumgartner, F.R. and Jones, B.D. (1993) *Agendas and Instability in American Politics*, Chicago, IL: The University of Chicago Press.
Birkland, T.A. (2006) *Lessons of Disaster: Policy Change after Catastrophic Events*, Washington, DC: Georgetown University Press.
Birkland, T.A. and Lawrence, R.G. (2009) 'Media framing and policy change after Columbine', *American Behavioral Scientist* 52(10): 1405–25.
Boin, A., t'Hart, P. and McConnell, A. (2009) 'Crisis exploitation: political and policy impacts of framing contests', *Journal of European Public Policy* 16(1): 81–106.
Brown, C. (1996) 'Government orders review of gun laws', *The Independent*, 20 March 1996.
Chapman, S., Alpers, P., Agho, K. and Jones, M. (2006) 'Australia's 1996 gun law reforms: faster falls in firearm deaths, firearm suicides, and a decade without mass shootings', *Injury Prevention* 12(6): 365–72.

Cohen, S. (2002) *Folk Devils and Moral Panics*, 3rd edn, London: Routledge.
De Vries, M.S. (2004) 'Framing crises: response patterns to explosions in firework factories', *Administration & Society* 36(5): 594–614.
Euchner, E-M., Heichel, S., Nebel, K. and Raschzok, A. (2013) 'From "morality" policy to "normal" policy: framing of drug consumption and gambling in Germany and the Netherlands and their regulatory consequences', *Journal of European Public Policy* 20(3), doi: 10.1080/13501763.2013.761506
Haider-Markel, D.P. and Joslyn, M.R. (2001) 'Gun policy, opinion, tragedy, and blame attribution: the conditional influence of issue frames', *The Journal of Politics* 63(2): 520–43.
Heichel, S., Knill, C. and Schmitt, S. (2013) 'Public policy meets morality: conceptual and theoretical challenges in the analysis of morality policy change', *Journal of European Public Policy* 20(3), doi: 10.1080/13501763.2013.761497
Hewitt, K. (1983) 'The idea of calamity in a technocratic age', in K. Hewitt (ed.), *Interpretations of Calamity*, London: Allen and Unwin, pp. 3–32.
Jemphrey, A. and Berrington, E. (2000) 'Surviving the media: Hillsborough, Dunblane, and the press', *Journalism Studies* 1(3): 469–83.
Karp, A. (2003) 'Dunblane and the international politics of gun control', in S. Nagel (ed.), *Policymaking and Peace – A Multinational Anthology*, Boston, MA: Lexington Books, pp. 193–211.
Kingdon, J.W. (2003) *'Agendas, Alternatives and Public Policies'*, 2nd edn, New York: Longman.
Knill, C. (2013) 'The study of morality policy: analytical implications from a public policy perspective', *Journal of European Public Policy* 20(3), doi: 10.1080/13501763.2013.761494
Leifeld, P. (2012) 'Discourse networks and German pension politics', Ph.D. thesis, University of Konstanz.
Lodge, M. (2011) 'Risk, regulation and crisis: comparing national responses in food safety regulation', *Journal of Public Policy* 31(1): 25–50.
Lodge, M. and Hood, C. (2002) 'Pavlovian policy responses to media feeding frenzies? Dangerous dogs regulation in comparative perspective', *Journal of Contingencies and Crisis Management* 10(1): 1–13.
Nohrstedt, D. (2008) 'The politics of crisis policymaking: Chernobyl and Swedish nuclear energy policy', *Policy Studies Journal* 36(2): 257–78.
Raaflaub, C. (2011) 'Balancing security with freedom', available at http://www.swissinfo.ch/eng/politics/internal_affairs/Balancing_security_with_freedom_.html?cid=31183432 (accessed 12 July 2012).
Rochefort, D.A. and Cobb, R.W. (1993) 'Problem definition, agenda access, and policy choice', *Policy Studies Journal* 21(1): 56–71.
Sabatier, P.A. (1998) 'The advocacy coalition framework: revisions and relevance for Europe', *Journal of European Public Policy* 5(1): 98–130.
Schmitt, S., Euchner, E.-M. and Preidel, C. (2013) 'Regulating prostitution and same-sex marriage in Italy and Spain: the interplay of political and societal veto players in two Catholic societies', *Journal of European Public Policy* 20(3), doi: 10.1080/13501763.2013.761512
Stone, D. (1989) 'Causal stories and the formation of policy agendas', *Political Science Quarterly* 104(2): 281–300.

Diverging against all odds? Regulatory paths in embryonic stem cell research across Western Europe

Isabelle Engeli and Christine Rothmayr Allison

ABSTRACT An interest-driven account of embryonic stem cell research would, given the considerable financial and scientific concerns, likely predict regulations to converge towards permissive policies. However, across Western Europe, national regulations of embryonic stem cell research vary considerably, from general bans to permissive policies. There is a lack of systematic accounting for the non-convergence, and the sparse attempts at explanation are contradictory. Drawing on qualitative comparative analysis and configurational causality, we assess the interaction of a number of explanatory factors. Our empirical analysis reveals the importance of one factor in particular, path-dependence, insofar as prior policies on assisted reproduction exert a strong and systematic effect on the subsequent regulation of embryonic stem cell research.

INTRODUCTION

Since the early stages in the development of human biotechnology, the differences in regulations across Western Europe intrigued and puzzled comparative public policy scholars. Regulatory paths on human biotechnology diverge substantially and this is also the case for regulating embryonic stem cell research (ESCR).[1] Given the economic and scientific potential of human biotechnology and the increased international competition in research and development (R&D) activities (Ernest & Young 2011; National Science Board 2012), purely economic and interest-driven accounts of policy trajectory would predict minimal state regulation combined with strong promotional activities (Banchoff 2005: 204; Tiberghien 2009). However, while some countries – in Asia (e,g., India, Singapore, South Korea) and Europe (Belgium, the United Kingdom) – as well as some American states have adopted minimal regulations, other countries, such as France, Germany and Italy, have opted for a highly restrictive regulatory framework to govern ESCR. The convergence hypothesis arguing that the increased international scientific and economic competition would make state regulations converge towards minimal regulation has therefore proven to be wrong with respect to ESCR in Western Europe. The question then arises as to how to explain that policies have not converged across countries after two decades of ECRS research.

Our contribution sheds some light, not on why policies converge but on why policies don't converge when one would expect them to do so. The literature on policy diffusion has spent a great deal of time on showing and explaining why policies converge. It has only recently moved toward investigating why policy diffusion does not necessarily result into policy convergence (Brooks 2007; Knill 2005; Radaelli 2005). For biomedical policies, Banchoff (2005) and Jasanoff (2005) have argued that previous policies on embryo research and assisted reproduction explain the lack of convergence. Banchoff (2005), through small-N case study comparison, has shown that negative policy feedback leads to policy stability or only incremental change. Other comparative studies have resulted in competing explanations for the variation in embryo research or ECRS, such as actor networks, political cleavages, religious values or attitudes towards science (Bleiklie *et al.* 2004; Engeli 2009, 2012; Fink 2008; Gottweis 2002; Gottweis *et al.* 2009; Montpetit *et al.* 2007; Rothmayr *et al.* 2004).

These contradictory results reveal the need for systematic, comparative research that attempts to explain the lack of convergence in regulatory approaches for ESCR (see Engeli, Rothmayr and Varone 2012). In most studies, the hypotheses are not tested systematically, beyond the comparison of a limited number of qualitative case studies and cover too short a period in order to actually investigate policy trajectory (see Banchoff 2005). This contribution contributes to a systematic analysis of how the principal explanatory factors evoked in the literature jointly lead to diverging regulations. Drawing on comparative qualitative analysis methodology (QCA; Ragin 2000, 2008), we cover 22 *regulations* of ESCR in Western Europe between 1998 and 2011. Taking the regulation as the unit of analysis, we investigate how value-driven path dependence in combination with party politics and public opinion, two other prominent factors evoked in the literature, lead to diverging regulatory paths in the case of ESCR.

THEORETICAL FRAMEWORK: PARTY POLITICS, PUBLIC OPINION OR PATH DEPENDENCY?

Comparative studies on human biotechnology have relied on the policy process theories, historical institutionalism, religion and politics and morality politics literatures. Given the variety of theoretical approaches used in the research, the findings have been contradictory and many explanations have proven to be, at best, weak. Among the various factors evoked in the literature, our analysis focuses on the three approaches that have been most prominent to explain the regulation of human biotechnology in Western Europe: path dependency; party politics; and public opinion.

Path dependency explanation

A first path to explaining current ESCR policies looks at past policy experiences. Path dependency (Pierson 2000, 2006) or policy heritage (Rose and Davis 1993) approaches are thus of particular relevance. More 'advanced' techniques such as ESCR can easily be assimilated to earlier debates and policies on assisted reproductive technologies (ART) and embryo research (Banchoff 2005; Jasanoff 2005). Banchoff's work has successfully demonstrated that past policies on embryo research impacted ESCR policies in Germany and the United Kingdom (UK). They influenced not only the actor constellation, but also the 'terms of policy controversy' (Banchoff 2005: 211). In line with his findings, first we argue that there is a lock-in effect related to the considerable cost of debating 'moral' policy issues. Debating over ESCR strongly polarizes political actors, and also potentially divides political parties and governmental coalitions. Thus, sticking to an already established consensus prevents reopening any policy debate and reduces the odds of severe internal divide within political parties or governmental coalitions (Banchoff 2005: 209–11). Furthermore, policies already in place have an impact on actor constellations. They give a comparative advantage to those defending the *status quo* in comparison to forces seeking fundamental policy change (Banchoff 2005: 208–9; Pierson 2000). If, during the process of regulating assisted reproductive technologies, medical and research interests have established privileged networks with key administrative political actors resulting in policies favouring, instead of limiting, assisted reproductive technologies, these policies strengthen the already established privileged relationship and give research and medical interests an important say in further developing ART-related policies. To the contrary, if medical and research interests had to accept more restrictions on assisted reproductive technology than they would have wished for, their adversaries who 'won' the first round of policy-making will be able to mobilize additional resources in the form of the already established norms – i.e., constitutional values or policy frames (see Banchoff 2005: 208–9). Our first hypothesis, therefore, uses past policies as explanatory variable:

> H1: The more severely prior policies restricted assisted reproductive technologies, the more likely are severe restrictions on embryonic stem cell research.

Party politics explanation

Qualitative case studies on the impact of past policy frames on ECRS or other biomedical issues focus exclusively on cases where a strong politicization of the issue can be observed. However, as the most recent research on morality policy demonstrates, the degree of politicization varies considerably depending on the political cleavages characterizing a political system. First, the comparative literature on biomedicine pointed to the importance of partisan politics, but argued that there is no clear-cut connection between the composition of the government and the policy outcome (Varone *et al.* 2006). The most recent research on morality policy successfully revisited this argument. Engeli, Green-Pedersen and Larsen (2012) show that because morality issues touch upon basic questions of the beginning and the end of life, whether the religious cleavage structures a party system or not, is an important factor for understanding the 'conflict definition' of morality policy issues. In other words, the presence of Christian Democratic parties or a Conservative party with religious ties is crucial for understanding policy-making processes for morality policies. Indeed, the secular versus the religious world, as the authors demonstrate, generate different agenda-setting patterns and conflict definitions. In the religious world compared to the secular world, as Engeli Green-Pedersen and Larsen (2012) demonstrate, embryo and ESCR are more likely to be politicized. We argue that Christian Democrats in particular are likely to have an interest in the politicization of ESCR. In order to broaden their electoral appeal in a strongly secularized environment, for many issues parties with religious ties would opt for policy solutions that are not necessarily based on religious values; however, for the issue of ESCR, it is more likely that they adopt an non-secular strategy, trying to appeal to their core religious voters. Given the challenge of adapting to the process of secularization without losing their religious identity and core electoral base, the issue of ESCR is an opportunity to reassert their religious identity and recapture attention to religious themes. Christian Democratic parties would not, however, opt for a strategy of politicization in order to strengthen their profile, if such a strategy might put in peril a governmental coalition in which they presently participate. If in the religious world the politicization is more likely, we can also speculate about how the presence of Christian Democrats and the composition of government might influence policy outcomes. Given the religious dimension of the issue, once ESCR has emerged onto the political agenda, Christian Democrats have little choice but to mobilize for policies that protect 'the beginning of life'. Hence, they will advocate restrictive policies or perhaps even total bans. Drawing on the recent literature on morality issues, we thus formulate a first hypothesis regarding the impact of party politics:

> H2: If religious cleavages characterize the party system, policies are more likely to turn out restrictive.

The left–right cleavage is also of relevance for understanding policy outcomes for ESCR (Fink 2008: 1635).[2] While, at the beginning of the biotechnology revolution, biomedical issues were sometimes associated with biotechnology and its impact on the environment in general (Rothmayr and Ramjoué 2004; Rothmayr and Serdült 2004), political debates over the last two decades have followed separate paths. Hence, in its early stages of policy-making in the 1980s, a resistance to biomedical developments by leftist parties could be observed. However, because of the connection of ESCR to the abortion issue and leftist parties, generally having a secular character, advocating for pro-choice positions in the case of abortion (McBride Stetson 2001), leftist parties will tend to seek policies that are friendly towards scientific research. As Fink's analysis shows, after the ECSR research breakthrough leftist parties tended to adopt liberal laws on embryo research, while prior to the breakthrough their policy record was more mixed (Fink 2008: 1641–2). In the case of ESCR, we would accordingly expect them to advocate for less restrictive policies than Conservative or Christian Democratic parties.

H3: The stronger left-wing parties, the more likely are permissive policies.

Public opinion explanation

There is a long tradition in democratic theory that emphasizes the impact of public opinion (Berry *et al.* 1998; Dahl 1989; Page and Shapiro 1983) and recent research on policy change has shown that political leaders are influenced by public majority while making policy choices (Burstein and Lincoln 2002; Soroka and Wlezien 2010). Within the comparative literature on biomedicine and biotechnology, besides institutional factors in terms of past policy choices and partisan explanations, public opinion broadly defined as attitudes, beliefs and opinions on political and social issues has also emerged as a prominent explanation for policy outcomes (Bernauer 2003; Fink 2008; Jasanoff 2005, Gottweis 1998; Jasanoff 2005). The findings on the importance of public opinion for biomedical policies are in line with recent research results on the public opinion – public policy nexus over the last decades: public opinion does matter for explaining policy outcomes and policy change (Burstein 1998; Burstein and Linton 2002; Soroka and Wlezien 2010; Soule 2004; Stimson *et al.* 1995).

In the case of biomedicine, two types of values or attitudes have been identified as having an impact: religious values and attitudes towards science. Namely, Fink's comparative quantitative analysis of embryo research laws points out the importance of religious values for explaining embryo research laws together with partisan explanations (Fink 2008). While his theoretical argument is based on the influence of the Catholic Church as an interest group, the literature on morality policy more largely suggests that religious values have an impact on policy debates and policy outcomes (Mooney 2001). As has been demonstrated for abortion, citizens who cherish religious values are more likely to adhere to a pro-life than a pro-choice position (Weisberg 2005). Equally for embryonic stem cell research, we can expect that secular citizens will be more in favour of permissive solutions, while religious citizens prefer more restrictive policies that guarantee a stronger protection of what they see to be the beginning of life.

H4: The more the general public cherishes religious values, the more likely is the adoption of policies imposing severe restrictions on ESCR.

In terms of attitudes towards science, Nielsen *et al.* (2002) have argued that there are two types of resistance towards biotechnology, traditional blue (religious) and modern green (environmental) forms of resistance. As various case studies reveal (see discussion of H3), green resistance towards biotechnology applications is often based on a critical attitude towards science and technological progress in general (Brossard and Nisbet 2007). And, in fact, independently of the concrete biotechnology application on the political agenda, low trust in scientific experts and scepticism of the benefits of technological progress help to explain the more critical evaluation of the potential benefits of ESCR versus the potential risks of the new technology (Ho *et al.* 2008). Science and technology studies also point to the fact that attitudes change over time, initial negative evaluations or resistance can fade over time as the benefits of new technology become more evident or the science better and more widely understood (Nisbet 2005). Hence, we propose to test a fifth and last hypothesis:

H5: The more positively public opinion evaluates scientific progress, the more likely are policies without any severe restrictions.

DATA AND METHODS

In this section, we first present our dependent variable, the policy decisions on ESCR, and then discuss the independent variables and the fuzzy-set qualitative comparative analysis (FsQCA) methodology. Owing to space constraints, all the detailed information regarding the coding, the FsQCA calibration and data sources is provided in the Appendix.[3]

The diverging paths in regulating embryonic stem cell research across Western Europe

In this analysis, our dependent variable, the *outcome* in FsQCA terminology, is the policies on ESCR adopted in the major Western European Countries (Portugal, Spain, France, Italy, Belgium, the Netherlands, Germany, Switzerland, the United Kingdom, Denmark, Sweden, Norway, Finland, Iceland, Greece). We are considering all the legally binding and explicit policy decisions that have been made on ESCR in these countries since the first successful derivation of embryonic stem cells in 1998.[4] We conceptualize medical and scientific autonomy as the degree of freedom granted to doctors and researchers to conduct ESCR and the conditions under which research should be conducted (Engeli, Rothmayr and Varone 2012). Three regulatory components are taken into account. First, different types of embryo can be used for ESCR. Permissive regulation allows for creating embryos for research purposes, while restrictive policies only allow for research on imported stem cell lines from other countries. The grounds for research are the second regulatory component. Permissive regulations do not constrain research on specific grounds, whereas restrictive regulations ban research with the exception of a limited number of therapeutic and observational research. Finally, permissive regulatory frameworks require a general authorization for being allowed to conduct ESCR, but do not impose an approval procedure specific to each research project as restrictive regulatory frameworks require.

We have coded the policies according to an additive index of the three regulatory components (equal weighting). The calibration into fuzzy-set scores goes from 0 (ban), 0.33 (restrictive regulation), 0.67 (intermediate regulation) to 1 (permissive regulation); see the Appendix for the detailed presentation. Figure 1 plots the regulatory trajectories for ESCR from 1998 to 2011 across Western Europe.

There is a clear pattern of policy diffusion. All but two Western European countries – Austria and Ireland – have designed policies to address regulatory issues in the field of ESCR over the last 15 years. Nevertheless, across Western Europe the policy diffusion has not resulted in convergence towards a generally permissive regulation. On the contrary, confronted with rapid and cutting-edge developments in human biotechnology, governments have adopted strongly diverging policies, ranging from fully prohibiting ESCR to broad permissiveness. In addition, most countries have not radically changed their policies over time. Three clusters of countries can be distinguished. The United Kingdom, Belgium, Iceland and Sweden form the *permissive cluster*. All these countries have adopted very permissive policies that allow for the creation of embryos for research purposes under the condition of a general permit to conduct ESCR granted to the research team or the research center. The *restrictive cluster* covers the countries that have imposed a general ban on ESCR or severe restrictions. In Italy, the current legislation explicitly bans embryo research and does not allow for any exception, even for non-harmful research.

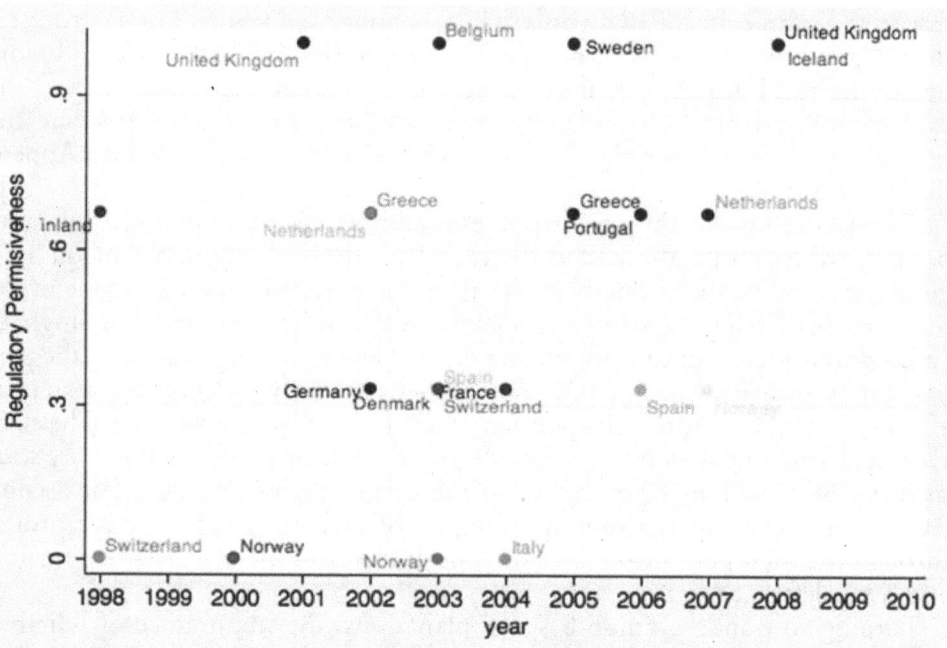

Figure 1 Regulatory divergences on ESCR across Western Europe

Switzerland and Norway initially banned ESCR and then later moved towards a less restrictive regulation and adopted a regulation similar to Spain, France, Denmark and Germany, whereby the creation of embryos for research purposes is banned and severe restrictions are imposed on the use of leftover or imported embryos for ESCR, which has to be systematically approved. Finally, the third cluster of countries has adopted an *intermediate* approach. Finland, Greece and Portugal have banned the creation of embryos soley for research purposes, but do not impose severe restrictions on the use of leftover embryos. The Netherlands constitutes a particular case – although the 2002 Embryo Act allowed for the creation of embryos, in 2007 a temporary ban was imposed that remains in force.

Accounting for the diverging parths

Accounting for this divergence in a systematic way poses two main methodological challenges: first, the number of policies is limited and the size of the N (=22) does not allow for robust regression analysis; second, the literature emphasizes different explanations, and this suggests that the analysis should move beyond monocausality and instead investigate the patterns in the configurational impact of different combinations of factors that may lead to a similar outcome. To this end, we draw on configurational comparative methods, and in particular fuzzy-set qualitative comparative analysis, which is increasingly used in comparative public policy research (for a review, see Rihoux *et al.* [2011]). Configurational comparative methods allow for simultaneously benefitting from the complexity of each case, while helping to identify causal processes that could lead to middle-range generalization (Ragin 2000, 2008). Before describing the FsQCA procedure applied to this analysis, we first discuss the explanatory variables. Owing to space constraints, we can only describe the general principles of operationalization and refer to the methodological Appendix for details.

To test the first of the two hypotheses addressing the importance of party politics, we have operationalized the causal condition 'importance of the religious cleavage' as the strength of the religious parties in the party system. In most systems, religious parties are, most of the time, not strong enough to access government but can still impact on the policy-making process in the parliament (Green-Pedersen 2007). Accordingly, to fully capture any potential effect of Christian Democrats politics, instead of measuring whether Christian Democrats are in government, we use the total percentage of parliamentary seats held by the Christian Democrats and the other religious parties. The second party politics hypothesis assuming an impact of a left-wing executive is captured through the total percentage of cabinet positions held by the Social Democrats and other left-wing parties.

Turning to public opinion-based explanations, the importance of religious values within the society is measured by the classic survey question measuring the moral attitude towards the justifiability of abortion together with the aggregate level of religiosity of the society. The public's opinion on science is captured through the public's attitude on scientific advances. Finally, the impact of prior ART regulation is measured through the medical autonomy granted to physicians to decide upon both the technology to be used and the conditions to be applied to treatment (Varone *et al.* 2006: 319–20). ART techniques are *permissively* regulated (score 3) if they are not subjected to any substantial restriction (that is, are generally permitted) but might be conditioned by licensing/reporting procedures. The regulation is qualified as *intermediate* (score 2) if some light restrictions are imposed. ART techniques are *restrictively* regulated (score 1) if their use is severely constrained. Finally, they could be *banned* outright (score 0).

The FsQCA procedure applied in this analysis implies two steps: the construction of the truth table and the analysis in itself.[5] The first step consists in constructing the so-called truth table, mapping out the logically possible combinations of conditions; that is, the multidimensional vector space encompassing all the combinations among the different fuzzy-sets. In this analysis, six conditions are included, so the vector space has 64 corners (2^6), meaning that there are 64 logically possible combinations of conditions.

The truth table (Table 1) presents the distribution of the membership scores across the 22 empirical cases – the entire set of policies on ESCR adopted in Western Europe.[6] The empirical cases included in our analysis cover for only 14 of 64 logically possible combinations (rows 1 to 14). The 50 other combinations (rows 15 to 64) are called 'logical remainders' in FsQCA terminology. There are logically possible combinations not supported by any of the empirical cases. Once the truth table is constructed, the empirical relevance of the causal configurations must be assessed according to the number of cases with fuzzy-set memberships greater than 0.5 (column 'N') that each configuration of causes displays and then by the level of consistency (column 'consistency'); that is, the degree to which a causal combination of condition is a subset of the outcome.[7] As we aim to analyse permissive and restrictive policies, the classification of configurations will be explained when presenting the results for the two outcomes. The second step of the FsQCA procedure analyses the truth table and reduces the logical complexity. Drawing on the Quine–McClusky algorithm (Ragin 2008), the aim of the second step is to identify the sufficient path(s) leading to the outcome (here, permissive policies) and to the negation of the outcome (here, restrictive policies).[8]

Explaining the diverging regulatory paths over ESCR

Table 2 presents the results of the minimization of the causal conditions leading to permissive and restrictive policies on ESCR. The N being relatively small, a frequency cut-off of 1 was adopted and every configuration has been taken into account in the analysis of the permissive regulatory paths. To compensate, a consistency value of 1.00 was set as benchmark criterion to distinguish between positive and negative outcomes in our 22 empirical cases. The

Table 1 Truth table for positive outcomes

Causal conditions						Outcome		
Religious	Left	Abortion	Science	Church	Path_ART	Outcome	Consist.	N
1	0	1	0	0	1	1	1	2
0	1	1	1	0	1	1	1	3
0	1	1	0	0	1	1	1	1
0	1	0	0	0	1	1	1	1
0	1	1	1	1	1	1	1	2
1	1	1	1	0	1	1	1	1
0	0	1	1	1	1	0	0.88	1
0	0	0	1	0	0	0	0.52	2
1	1	1	0	1	0	0	0.47	1
0	0	1	1	1	0	0	0.46	2
1	0	0	1	0	0	0	0.45	1
0	1	0	1	0	0	0	0.43	2
1	0	1	0	0	0	0	0.28	2
1	1	0	1	0	0	0	0	1

Table 2 Sufficient paths towards permissive and restrictive policies

Paths	Consistency	Coverage	N	Case
Permissive policies: parsimonious solution PATH_ART	0.81	0.93	11	All cases containing at least PATH_ART
Permissive policies: complex solution church*science*PATH_ART*LEFT +	1.00	0.28	2	Sweden 2005; Finland 2008
CHURCH*ABORTION*SCIENCE*religious* PATH_ART +	0.87	0.38	3	Portugal 2006; Greece 2002; Greece 2005
church*LEFT*religious* PATH_ART +	1.00	0.35	4	Belgium 2003; United Kingdom 2001; United Kingdom 2008; Iceland 2008
church*ABORTION*left*RELIGIOUS* PATH_ART	1	0.14	2	Netherlands 2002; Netherlands 2007
Restrictive policies: parsimonious solution path_art	0.89	0.74	11	All cases containing path_art
Restrictive Policies: Complex solution church*abortion*path_art*SCIENCE	1.00	0.37	6	France 2004; Denmark 2003; Norway 2007; Spain 2006; Norway 2003; Norway 2000
CHURCH*ABORTION*path_art*left*religious*SCIENCE	1.00	0.14	2	Italy 2004; Spain 2003
CHURCH*ABORTION*path_art*LEFT*RELIGIOUS*science	1.00	0.05	1	Germany 2002
church*ABORTION*path_art*left*RELIGIOUS*science	1.00	0.11	2	Switzerland 1998; Switzerland 2003

Notes: Restrictive solutions: frequency cut-off: 1.00, consistency cut-off: 1.00; solution coverage: 0.62, solution consistency: 1.00. Permissive solutions: frequency cut-off: 1.00, consistency cut-off: 0.88; solution coverage: 0.70, solution consistency: 0.93.

FsQCA minimization procedure computes at least two different solutions. The parsimonious solution includes both the empirical cases and the logical remainders, while the complex solution is computed on the basis of the empirical cases only. As our N is relatively small, the complex solution based on the empirical cases displays more robust results and we will concentrate the discussion of the findings on this solution exclusively.

The complex solution reveals that four different paths result into permissive policies. As the paths display a great deal of similarity in the causal combinations, we focus the discussion on our series of three competing explanations. The major finding resulting from the analysis of the causal configuration triggering permissive policies is the strong and systematic effect of the value-based path dependence of the ART regulation over ESCR policies. This holds true for both the parsimonious and the complex solutions. Indeed, the causal condition PATH_ART is systematically present in all the five paths leading to permissive outcomes and across very different national contexts. If the religious factors are included in the different paths, they nevertheless do not tend to prove decisive. Indeed, a high or low level of religiosity ('church' condition), the presence or absence of religious parties in parliament ('religious') or a public opinion more or less conservative towards abortion ('abortion') all do not modify the systematic impact of value-based path dependence on the outcome of permissive regulations for ESCR. Even in societies still strongly attached to religious norms, such as Portugal and Greece, the very permissive regulation of the ART sector has strongly impacted the way these two countries have approached the regulation of embryo research. The same holds true for the 'Social Democratic politics' explanation ('left') and the public's attitude towards science ('science'). While leftist governments have enacted permissive policies, as is the case in Belgium and the United Kingdom, in the Netherlands a coalition government has followed the same regulatory path.

Owing to space constraints, we cannot develop the qualitative explanation for all the cases with permissive outcomes and have to focus instead on one empirical case in order to illustrate our main finding on the importance of value-based path dependence. In the Netherlands, ART treatments has benefited from strong public support since the beginning of the 1980s and the number of ART centres has increased rapidly (Timmermans 2007; Timmermans and Scholten 2006). During the 1980s and '90s, the government refrained from any restrictive intervention in the field of ART and instead only issued procedural decrees. When the technological breakthroughs in embryo-related research during the 1990s put the issue back on the political agenda, the large coalition government adopted a similar regulatory approach. The resulting 2002 Embryo Act is one of the most permissive regulations in Europe regarding embryo-related research. While it imposes a temporary ban on embryo creation for research purposes and therapeutic cloning, the Act provides the science community with a great deal of autonomy in conducting research on embryonic stem cells derived from leftover in vitro fertilization (IVF) embryos. The reintegration of Christian Democrats in the government coalition in 2002 has not resulted in any major revision of the initial regulation (Timmermans 2007).

The analysis of the *restrictive* regulatory paths in the field of ESCR across Western Europe largely confirms our main findings for permissive outcomes. For the minimization of the configuration of conditions leading to restrictive policies, as before, the frequency cut-off is set to 1 and the consistency cut-off to 0.88. Here again, the systematic effect of value-based path dependence is striking. Both the parsimonious and complex solutions stress the importance of the absence of a permissive ART regulation to account for restrictive ESCR policies, the negated condition 'path_art' being present in all the restrictive paths. Nevertheless, the restrictive regulatory paths allows for a more fine-grained understanding of the contribution of religious factors to human biotechnology policies. Among the countries that have adopted restrictive regulations, Christian Democrats and more generally religious-based parties have been traditionally weak in France and Denmark, while they have been stronger in Germany, Switzerland, Italy and also in Norway. In Norway, the Christian Democrats were not institutionally strong enough to exert any decisive impact on the regulation and that is why this condition is absent of the path. On the contrary, in Germany and Switzerland, Christian Democrats have successfully pressed for restricting embryo-related research more severely than ART in general. The German and Swiss cases are both characterized by an early and broad mobilization against ART and biotechnology more generally (see Engeli and Varone 2011; Rothmayr and Ramjoué 2004; Rothmayr and Serdült 2004). In neither case did the debate focus on whether to adopt intermediary or restrictive solutions, but on whether it would not be preferable to prohibit outright ART treatments. The German case illustrates particularly well the interaction of value-based path dependence and religious factors.

The German Embryo Protection law was adopted in 1992 under a coalition government of Christian Democrats (the Christian Democratic Union and Christian Social Union; CDU/CSU) and Liberals (Free Democratic Party; FDP). Based on the 1975 decision of the German Federal Constitutional Court (Bundesverfassungsgericht) to strike down the abortion law, the Christian Democrats advocated for strong protection of the embryo. Furthermore, mobilization against ART was also motivated by distrust of the scientific and political elite that characterized the strong German social movements of the 1980s. Against this constellation of actors seeking very restrictive policies, the German Research Council, together with other research interests, did not succeed in defending their position that embryo research should be permitted under certain conditions based on the constitutionally guaranteed freedom of science. They were somewhat more successful with ESCR in the late 1990s because they had a strong ally in Chancellor Schröder. The derivation of stem cells in Germany would have demanded a change to the existing legal framework, but the governing Social Democrats and Greens were divided over the issue, and so were the other parties. Hence, parliament struck a compromise between the advocates of ESCR and their opponents. Parliament did not revise the 1992 Embryo Protection law, but allowed only for the *import* of stem cell lines from abroad under specific conditions.

CONCLUSION

All but two West European countries have designed ESCR regulations since 1998. Nevertheless policy diffusion has not resulted in any major convergence of policies throughout Western Europe (Knill 2005). Our empirical analysis confirms that domestic factors do matter. Domestic constraints and opportunities still exert a strong impact on how the policies are fostered even as biotechnology is becoming a key field of economic competition. Because human biotechnology also touches upon moral and social norms, economic competition and technological development are not the principal drivers of policy change. The domestic arena still plays an important role, and regulatory paths in ESCR across Western Europe are still diverging against all odds.

Through fuzzy-set qualitative comparative analysis we were able to analyse how different, competing explanations jointly cause diverging regulatory paths. The results show that *no one single regulatory path* leads to permissive or restrictive frameworks for ESCR, but in any of these trajectories, whether in the secular or the religous world (Engeli, Green-Pedersen and Larsen 2012), earlier policies on ART are an indispensable explanation. Prior research suggested that path-dependent mechanisms were at work. For the first time, this hypothesis has been tested in a systematic manner for Western Europe. And, indeed, the results of the analysis highlight the importance of prior policies regulating assisted reproduction for later adopted regulations for ESCR. Value-driven path dependency is at work, and while breakthroughs in IVF were a necessary but not sufficient condition for breakthroughs in ESCR, the reasons for a path-dependent effect are not of technical nature, but essentially political, the result of lock-in effects related to the considerable costs of debating 'moral' policy issues and because of the comparative advantage existing norms give to the defenders of the *status quo*. In short, on the one hand, our analysis confirms the findings of Banchoff (2005). But, on the other hand, it also reveals the importance of the moral dimension of ESCR policies, by pointing to the influence of religious cleavages in party systems, as well as the public's religious attitudes. There again, our findings align with results of prior research, by Fink (2008) emphasizing religious values, and more recently by Engeli, Green-Pedersen and Larsen (2012) on the importance of religious cleavages in party systems. However, in contrast to these prior studies, through the systematic comparison of 22 regulatory frameworks over 13 years, we were able to show the configurational impact of different combinations of factors that may lead to a similar outcome. The fuzzy-set qualitative comparative analysis allowed the combination of 'a-historical and historical modes of inquiry' and to taking into account structure and agency in explaining patterns of change through including past policies and partisan cleavages as fairly stable factors together with others, more variable over time, such as public opinion and party strength (Capano and Howlett 2009: 2–3).

The principal purpose of this contribution is to discuss why there has been no convergence for ECSR. However, one might ask to what extent the explanatory factors we evoked were also responsible for assisted reproductive technology policies in the first place.[9] Economic and research competition do not play the same important role for regulating ART in general that they do for ECRS. Hence, for ART policies, there is no expectation of convergence in the literature. As we pointed out in the introduction and the theoretical framework, we find various competing explanations in past research. Indirectly, our results confirm the importance of religious cleavages structuring party systems and public opinion. At the same time, because there are various paths leading to permissive or restrictive policies, clearly these factors alone are not sufficient to explain policy outcomes. This explains, at least partly, why case study-based research has resulted in competing explanations, because, indeed, in function of the countries studied a different combination of factors accounts for policy outcomes.

Finally, the interpretation of our results should not be understood as an argument that ESCR regulation will not change fundamentally in the near- or long-term future, and policy stability and incremental changes will continue to dominate regulatory paths. As we well know from the policy process literature in general, and agenda-setting literature more specifically, patterns of stability and change can alter dramatically in very short periods of time. While we think it is rather unlikely that convergence will result from the adoption of new international norms, tangible results or new breakthroughs could contribute to trigger more fundamental change that might lead to converging patterns of regulation, under the condition that domestic actors in countries with restrictive policies mobilize in order to seize this opportunity for challenging the *status quo*.

Biographical notes: Isabelle Engeli is Assistant professor, Graduate School of Public and International Affairs, University of Ottawa. Christine Rothmayr Allison is Associate professor, Département de science politique, Université de Montréal

ACKNOWLEDGEMENTS

We would like to thank Donley Studlar, Christoph Knill, Frédéric Varone and the three anonymous reviewers for their helpful suggestions and comments.

NOTES

1 Embryonic stem cells are capable of self-renewal and differentiation into various types of cells. For the time being, the derivation of embryonic stem cells implies the destruction of the embryo.
2 The literature cited points towards the importance of the presence and strengths of Green parties for biomedical policies. However, Green parties are only present in some countries, and we therefore have captured the influence of the Green movement in Europe by including the cleavage over science–nature in the following section on public opinion.
3 See Appendix at http://www.mwpweb.eu/IsabelleEngeli/ or http://pol.umontreal.ca/repertoire-departement/vue/rothmayr-allison-christine/.
4 We have excluded two major European countries – Austria and Ireland. In these countries, no binding and explicit regulations on ESCR have been elaborated so far. See the Appendix for a detailed justification (see Note 3).
5 The software fs/QCA 2.0 has been used for the analysis (Ragin *et al.* 2006). The description of the procedure is based on Ragin (2000, 2006).
6 See Note 4.
7 Formula (Ragin 2006: 7): Consistency $(X_i \leq Y_i) = \sum (min (X_i, Y_i)) / \sum (X_i)$, 'where "min" indicates the selection of the lower of the two values, X_i represents membership scores in a combination of conditions, and Y_i represents membership scores in the outcome'.
8 Where the negated outcome is: $\sim O = 1 - O$.
9 Banchoff's (2005) and Fink's (2008) work explain ECRS respectively embryo research policies and not policies for assisted reproduction.

REFERENCES

Banchoff, T. (2005) 'Path dependence and value-driven issues. The comparative politics of stem cell research', *World Politics* 57(2): 200–30.
Bernauer., T. (2003) *Genes, Trade and Regulation*, Princeton, NJ: Princeton University Press.
Berry, W.D., Rinquist, E.J., Fording, R.C. and Hanson, R.L. (1998) 'Measuring citizen and government ideology in the American states, 1960–1993', *American Journal of Political Science* 42(1): 327–48.
Bleiklie, I., Goggin, M.L. and Rothmayr, C. (eds) (2004) *Comparative Biomedical Policy*, London: Routledge.
Brooks, S. (2007) 'When does diffusion matter? Explaining the spread of structural pension reforms across nations', *The Journal of Politics* 69(3): 701–15.
Brossard, D. and Nisbet, C. (2007) 'Deference to scientific authority among a low information public: understanding US opinion on agricultural biotechnology', *International Journal of Public Opinion Research* 19(1): 24–52.
Burstein, P. (1998) 'Bringing the public back in: should sociologists consider the impact of public opinion on public policy?' *Social Forces* 77(1): 27–62.
Burstein, P. and Linton, A. (2002) 'The impact of political parties, interest groups, and social movement organizations on public policy: some recent evidence and theoretical concerns', *Social Forces* 81(2): 380–408.
Capano, G. and Howlett, M. (2009) 'Introduction: the determinants of policy change: advancing the debate', *Journal of Comparative Policy Analysis: Research and Practice* 11(1): 1–5.
Dahl, R. (1989) *Democracy and its Critics*, New Haven, CT: Yale University Press.
Engeli, I. (2009) 'The challenges of abortion and assisted reproductive technologies policies in Europe', *Comparative European Politics* 7(1): 56–74.

Engeli, I. (2012) 'Policy struggle on reproduction: doctors, women, and Christians', *Political Research Quarterly* 65(2): 330–45.

Engeli, I. and Varone, F. (2011) 'Governing morality issues through procedural policies', *Swiss Political Science Review* 17(3): 239–58.

Engeli, I., Green-Pedersen, C. and Larsen, L.T. (eds) (2012) *Morality Politics in Western Europe. Parties, Agenda and Policy Choices*, London: Palgrave.

Engeli, I., Rothmayr, C. and Varone, F. (2012) 'Lessons from bio-medical technology regulation: North-American and European comparison', in M. Howlett and D. Laycok (eds), *Regulating Next Generation Agri-Food Bio-Technologies*, London: Routledge, pp. 164–81.

Ernst & Young (2011) *beyond Borders: Global Biotechnology Report 2011*, available at http://www.ey.com/GL/en/Industries/Life-Sciences/Beyond-borders–global-biotechnology-report-2011, accessed: 20 July 2012.

Fink, S. (2008) 'Politics as Usual or bringing religion back in? The influence of parties, institutions, economic interests, and religion on embryo research laws', *Comparative Political Studies* 41(12): 1631–56.

Gottweis, H. (1998) *Governing Molecules*, Cambridge, MA: MIT Press.

Gottweis, H. (2002) 'Stem cell policies in the United States and in Germany: between bioethics and regulation', *Policy Studies Journal* 30(4): 444–69.

Gottweis, H., Salter, B. and Waldby, C. (2009) *The Global Politics of Human Embryonic Stem Cell Science*, Houndsmille: McMillan.

Green-Pedersen, Ch. (2007) 'The conflict of conflicts in comparative perspective. Euthanasia as a political issue in Denmark, Belgium, and the Netherlands', *Comparative Politics* 39(3): 273–91.

Ho, S.S., Brossard, D. and Scheufele, D.A. (2008) 'Effects of value predispositions, mass media use, and knowledge on public attitudes toward embryonic stem cell research', *International Journal of Public Opinion Research* 20(2): 171–92.

Jasanoff, S. (2005) *Designs on Nature*, Princeton, NJ: Princeton University Press.

Knill, Ch. (2005) 'Introduction: cross-national policy convergence: concepts, approaches and explanatory factors', *Journal of European Public Policy* 12(5): 764–74.

McBride Stetson, D. (ed.) (2001) *Abortion Politics, Women's Movements, and the Democratic State*, Oxford: Oxford University Press.

Montpetit, E., Rothmayr, C. and Varone, F. (eds) (2007) *The Politics of Biotechnology in North America and Europe: Policy Networks, Institutions, and Internationalization*, Lanham, MD: Lexington Books.

Mooney, C.Z. (ed) (2001) *The Public Clash of Private Values: The Politics of Morality Policy*, Chatham, NJ: Chatham House.

National Science Board (2012) *Science and Engineering Indicators 2012*, Chapter 4 and 5, available at http://www.nsf.gov/statistics/seind12/start.htm (accessed August 2012).

Nielsen, H.T., Jelsoe, E. and Öhman, S. (2002) 'Traditional Blue and modern Green resistance', in M. W. Bauer and G. Gaskell (eds), *Biotechnology*, Cambridge: Cambridge University Press, pp. 179–223.

Nisbet, M.C. (2005) 'The competition for worldviews: values, information, and public support for stem cell research', *International Journal of Public Opinion Research* 17(1): 90–112.

Page, B.I. and Shapiro, R.Y. (1983) 'Effects of public opinion on policy', *American Political Science Review* 77(1): 175–90.

Pierson, P. (2000) 'Increasing returns, path dependence, and the study of politics', *American Political Science Review* 94(2): 251–67.

Pierson, P. (2006) 'Public policies as institutions', in I. Shapiro, S. Skowronek and D. Galvin (eds), *Rethinking Political Institutions: The Art of the State*, New York: New York University Press, pp. 114–31.

Radaelli, C. (2005) 'Diffusion without convergence: how political context shapes the adoption of regulatory impact assessment', *European Journal of Public Policy* 12(5): 924–43.
Ragin, Ch. (2000) *Fuzzy-Set Social Science*, Chicago, IL: University of Chicago Press.
Ragin, Ch. (2006) *User's Guide to Fuzzy-Set/Qualitative Comparative Analysis 2.0*, Tucson, AZ: Department of Sociology, University of Arizona.
Ragin, Ch. (2008) *Redesigning Social Inquiry: Fuzzy Sets and Beyond*, Chicago, IL: University of Chicago Press.
Ragin, C.C., Drass, K.A. and Davey, S. (2006) *Fuzzy-Set/Qualitative Comparative Analysis 2.0*, Tucson, AZ: Department of Sociology, University of Arizona.
Rihoux, B., Rezsöhazy, I. and Bol, D. (2011) 'Qualitative comparative analysis (QCA) in public policy analysis: an extensive review', *German Policy Studies* 7(3): 9–82.
Rose, R. and Davies, P.L. (1993) *Inheritance in Public Policy. Change without Choice in Britain*, New Haven, CT: Yale University Press.
Rothmayr, C. and Ramjoué, C. (2004) 'Germany: ART policy as embryo protection', in I. Bleiklie, M. Goggin and C. Rothmayr (eds), *Comparative Biomedical Policy*, London: Routledge, pp. 174–90.
Rothmayr, C. and Serdült, U. (2004) 'Switzerland: policy design and direct democracy', in I. Bleiklie, M. Goggin and C. Rothmayr (eds), *Comparative Biomedical Policy*, London: Routledge, pp. 191–208.
Rothmayr, C. et al. (2004) 'Comparing policy design across countries: what accounts for variation in art policy?', in I. Bleiklie, M. Goggin and C. Rothmayr (eds), *Comparative Biomedical Policy: Governing Assisted Reproductive Technologies*, London: Routledge, pp. 228–53.
Soroka, S.N. and Wlezien, Ch. (2010) *Degrees of Democracy: Politics, Public Opinion, and Policy*, New York: Cambridge University Press.
Soule, S.A. (2004) 'Going to the chapel? Same-sex marriage bans in the United States', *Social Problems* 51(4): 453–77.
Stimson, J.A., MacKuen, M.B. and Erikson, R.S. (1995) 'Dynamic representation', *American Political Science Review* 89(3): 543–65.
Tiberghien, Y. (2009) 'Competitive governance and the quest for legitimacy in the EU: the battle over the regulation of GMOs since the mid-1990s', *Journal of European Integration* 31(3): 389–408.
Timmermans, A. (2007) 'Accomodation, bureaucratic politics, and supranational leviathan: ART and GMO policy-making in the Netherlands', in E. Montpetit, C. Rothmayr and F. Varone (eds), *The Politics of Biotechnology in North America and Europe*, Lanham, MD: Lexington Books, pp. 169–92.
Timmermans, A. and Scholten, P. (2006) 'The political flow of wisdom: science institutions ad policy venues in the Netherlands', *Journal of European Public Policy* 13(7): 1104–18.
Varone, F., Rothmayr, C. and Monptetit, E. (2006) 'Regulating biomedicine in Europe and North America: a qualitative comparative analysis', *European Journal of Political Research* 45(2): 317–43.
Weisberg, H.F. (2005) 'The structure and effects of moral predispositions in contemporary American politics', *The Journal of Politics* 67(3): 646–68.

Regulating prostitution and same-sex marriage in Italy and Spain: the interplay of political and societal veto players in two catholic societies

Sophie Schmitt, Eva-Maria Euchner and Caroline Preidel

ABSTRACT This contribution adds to the scholarship on morality politics. It addresses the conditions of morality policy change by comparing the decision-making dynamics in the regulation of prostitution and same-sex partnerships in Italy and Spain over two decades. We seek to explain why and under what circumstances some political actors are successful in reforming morality policies. For this purpose, we develop a four-fold typology of morality policy change. Our findings highlight that the different regulatory dynamics in both Catholic nation-states depend on the balance of power among the change and blocking coalitions and their degree of congruence. We show that governments succeed in realizing their morality policy goals only if they are able to form a coalition with the relevant political and societal actors. Furthermore, the Catholic Church, not least owing to its historical ties with both nation-states (Italy and Spain), plays a particular but context-specific role.

INTRODUCTION

This contribution presents an in-depth comparative analysis of the evolvement of two morality policies in two countries. By systematically contrasting policy-making concerning the regulation of prostitution and processes of institutionalizing same-sex partnerships in Italy and Spain, we provide empirical evidence on the determinants of morality policy change. Spain has liberalized prostitution and same-sex partnerships during the last two decades, whereas Italy has retained its strict regulation since the late 1950s because initiatives for adapting sexuality policies repeatedly resulted in non-decisions.

We ask: what determines the success of governmental initiatives for changing sexual policy across countries and policy fields? While recent research on morality policy emphasizes the role of religious denomination in society, this factor hardly explains the puzzle observed here. In order to refine existing theoretical approaches, this comparative case study provides in-depth analyses of the decision-making process on two sexual policies over the last 20 years. By explaining the different dynamics in both countries, and given that international influences can be held constant, we draw on Tsebelis's (2002) veto player theory, namely actor constellation and institutional hurdles.

Our findings highlight that the different regulatory dynamics in both Catholic nation-states depend on the balance of power among the change and blocking coalitions as well as on the degree of congruence. Based on the constellation of these two explanatory factors, we develop a four-fold typology of policy change processes. Our findings show that governments succeed in realizing their morality policy goals only if they are able to form a coalition with the relevant veto players that pursue congruent policy agendas.

The contribution is structured as follows. Next, we introduce our empirical puzzle along with the current state of affairs. In the third section we present our theoretical argument and expectations, followed by the empirical application in the fourth section. Finally, we offer some conclusions along with an outlook for future research.

EMPIRICAL PUZZLE, RESEARCH QUESTION AND METHODOLOGICAL APPROACH

This contribution addresses the question: what explains the policy-making dynamics in the fields of prostitution policy and the regulation of same-sex partnerships in two Catholic societies during the last 20 years? In so doing, this empirical study adds to the emerging literature on morality policy. In this context, we follow a broad *a priori* definition of morality policies as addressing core values and questions of self-determination (cf. Heichel *et al.* 2013).

As illustrated by Table 1, Italy has been characterized by the failure to change existing regulatory regimes with respect to both issues, while Spain has experienced a number of reform laws during the two decades.

Prostitution in Italy is still regulated on the basis of the 1958 prostitution law. The act as such is legal, and the criminalization of street prostitutes, for instance, mainly takes an indirect form (e.g., by sentencing side-activities, such as

Table 1 Regulatory reforms in morality politics

	Prostitution	Same-sex partnership
Italy	Restrictive regulation reform failure (2007)	Restrictive regulation reform failures (2003, 2008)
Spain	Permissive regulation reforms (1995, 2003, 2009)	Permissive regulation reforms (1995, 2005)

Note: As we focus on policy outputs, we include the year of decision-making instead of its entering into force.

loitering). There is also a ban on most forms of assistance to prostitutes by third persons, including both profit and non-profit facilitation or procuring prostitution (cf. Danna 2001). In the absence of a comprehensive regulatory framework, there are currently few restrictions to regulate prostitution as such.

Similarly to the issue of prostitution, the Italian Civil and Criminal Codes do not take a position with regard to issues of sexual orientation and identity. While homosexuality has never been explicitly criminalized, family laws traditionally excluded homosexual couples from the possibility of starting a family or forming a civil union.

Spain's prostitution regime is more permissive than the Italian one. Three reforms in the last two decades[1] account for the current *status quo*. Adult, voluntary prostitution is tolerated and related infrastructure is mostly permitted. Third parties are criminalized only if they endanger the health or life of prostitutes. However, the state does not recognize prostitution as a regular profession with social insurance coverage or legal contracting rights (Consejo de Estado 2010).

Similarly, the legal approach towards same-sex partnerships is more permissive in Spain than in Italy owing to a comprehensive reform in 2005, following the election victory of the Spanish Socialist Workers Party (PSOE). This law grants equal rights to registered same-sex couples and heterosexual couples with respect to inheritance, residence, adoption of the spouse's children, tax benefits and divorce.

The literature on morality policy change in general, and prostitution politics or same-sex partnerships in particular, does not explain these divergent trajectories in morality policy-making. While single case studies on the respective policy processes abound (see Danna [2004] and Valiente Fernández [2004] for analyses on prostitution politics; cf. Calvo [2007] or Platero [2007] on the institutionalization of same-sex marriages in Spain), comparative approaches are still the exception. Only in the last decade have scholars of prostitution policy adopted a comparative perspective primarily based on actor-centred explanations (see Kilvington *et al.* [2001], Outshoorn [2004] and West [2000] on prostitution politics; cf. Paternotte [2008] for a comparative analysis of same-sex unions in three European countries).

Moreover, theoretical approaches towards morality policy change are unable to account for these divergent regulatory trajectories (see Heichel *et al.* 2013). While some scholars of morality policy-making expect the level of religiosity in society to constitute the decisive factor (Fink 2008), they fail to explain the differences between morality policy choices in Italy and Spain. Similarly, studies that highlight the importance of institutional criteria and political actors, including Christian Churches or other interest groups, in moderating the religion effect (cf. Schwartz and Tatalovich 2009) do not provide explanations to our puzzle. Further, Engeli *et al.* (2012) argue that the cleavage structure of the national party system determines the politicization of morality issues. The authors focus on the impact of a nation-state's party system on agenda-setting and policy formation processes in morality policy-making by analysing the underlying degree of political conflict. Our approach adds to Engeli *et al.* (2012) by analysing how these lines of conflict influence the formation and power of influential actor coalitions.

The present analysis approximates a most similar system design enabling us to focus on institutional and actor-centred factors which determine the dynamics of the decision-making processes on the national level and, thereby, the success or failure of governmental initiatives for change. In so doing, we analyse two culturally similar Mediterranean nation-states with comparable proportion of Catholics in society.

THEORETICAL APPROACH

For explaining the empirical puzzle, we assume that political actors act strategically based on associated trade-offs when initiating and supporting policy proposals. However, institutional factors constrain their leeway for political action (Hall and Taylor 1996). Furthermore, we suppose that actor coalitions constitute the central units for decision-making. They include executive and legislative players as well as societal actors who share a general policy goal. For putting a policy proposal into effect, not only parliamentary but also non-parliamentary support is needed. Interest groups may not have a vote, but they have a voice and the resources to both mobilize the electorate and lobby parliamentary representatives. In the political arena we differentiate between two actor coalitions: firstly, the change coalition, subsuming the actors who prefer the policy proposal over the *status quo*; and secondly, the blocking coalition, covering all actors who – in light of the policy initiative – aim to maintain the *status quo*.

Based on these assumptions, we argue that the success of governmental initiatives and the extent of projected policy change in the field of sexual policies largely depend on the congruence within the change coalition and the balance of political power among the change and the blocking coalitions in the legislative arena.

Partisan and societal veto players in morality politics

This argumentation follows Tsebelis's (2002) veto player theory. Veto players are actors, whose support is required to enforce policy change. Besides partisan and institutional veto players, we take societal veto players into account. The consideration of societal veto players may be debatable, as they have no direct influence on the formation of majority coalitions in parliament. However, regarding the specific constitution of morality politics, interest groups can become veto players depending on their mobilization capacity, preferences and political access (cf. Fink 2009). As morality politics imply political conflicts on first principles and technically simple issues, debates are of greater public interest than in non-morality politics. Consequently, societal actors have a higher potential to mobilize the public for their purpose (cf. Mooney 2001).

As vote- and office-seekers, politicians bear the citizens' interests in mind when they take political decisions (cf. Strøm 1990: 566 ff.; cf. Mooney 2001).

In addition to mobilization capacity, the preference constellation within the group is decisive. Following Tsebelis's (2002) absorption rule, it has to take up an extreme position which is not absorbed by other veto players – a task, that may be easier in morality than in non-morality policy owing to the value-driven conflicts. Moreover, the internal cohesion and discipline of adherents is crucial. The more the internal opinions coincide and the more members are willing to follow common goals, the more they can signal a unified position. The veto power of interest groups also varies with their institutional ties to the state. The more the organization is coupled to the political structures by formal or informal participation rights, the more likely it gains veto power (cf. Fink 2009).

However, societal veto players differentiate from their partisan and institutional counterparts in a central aspect. While parties as well as institutional actors use their veto power based on their political responsibility, interest groups make strategic use of their potential veto power.

Coalitions' size and congruence

According to Tsebelis's (2002) approach, we expect firstly that governmental initiatives are successful if they can build a change coalition subsuming all veto players. In contrast, the probability for policy stability increases if at least one veto player accommodates with the blocking coalition. Hence, the more veto players a coalition subsumes, the more political power it has in enforcing its goals. A second factor is the congruence of veto players within the change coalition. The more the actors' positions lay apart from each other, the smaller is the set of possible deviations from the *status quo* and the more incremental the intended change will be. Consequently, if the government wants to realize its proposal it has to adjust its initiative to the positions of the different veto players.

Nevertheless, institutional settings play a decisive role in determining the conditions for coalition building. By specifying, for example, the electoral system and decision rights for second chambers or presidents, they define to a large extent the number of veto players. The more they increase the number of actors with veto power and the wider the distance among their preferences, the more difficult is the formation of a coalition (cf. Tsebelis 2002).

Four types of policy change dynamics

Hence, the balance of political power between the change and blocking coalitions as well as the congruence of actors within the change coalition determine the policy change dynamics. We derive four different scenarios, describing the political process of governmental initiatives. In the first scenario we find a strong change coalition, subsuming all veto players, whose positions do not lie far apart from each other. Consequently, the government does not struggle to enforce successfully a far reaching reform. In the second scenario the congruence among the veto players decreases, while they still build a common coalition, cohering in their willingness to change the *status quo*. Consequently, the set of possible modifications of the *status quo* shrinks. In order to be successful, the government must propose incremental changes to *the status quo*. In the third scenario, the balance of power among the change and blocking coalitions is reversed. Owing to the far distance of veto players in the political arena, the blocking coalition incorporates veto players. As long as the smaller change coalition follows congruent policy goals, the government struggles in finding a majority in parliament and, hence, fails in changing the *status quo*. If the congruence within the change coalition decreases, the government is capable of entering into negotiations with the blocking actors allowing for at least minimal policy change via co-operation. This last case presents the fourth scenario.

MORALITY POLICY-MAKING IN ITALY AND SPAIN

The following subsections illustrate the formation of actor coalitions in homosexuality and prostitution politics in Italy and Spain since the mid-1990s. In so doing, we identify the relevant partisan and societal veto players and their strategic positioning.

Actors, coalitions and morality politics in Italy

Italy: multiple access points for morality policy-making
Italy is a multi-party system with considerable fragmentation among its political parties, which follows, however, a bipolar trend. Legislative initiatives can be introduced by the government or by members of parliament. Parliamentary committees are responsible for evaluating and – if necessary – modifying the bill. In order to become a law, the final draft must be approved by both chambers before it can be signed by the president. In practice, these processes are far less straightforward. In the majority of the cases legislative initiatives dry up in parliament as the commissions usually struggle with an overload of simultaneous proposals on the same issues. Thus, the main task of the commissions is to craft compromises, which do not usually return from the commission to the assembly for final voting. The picture becomes even more complex when considering the strong fragmentation among Italy's interest groups. Ideologically similar groups often compete over access to the political arena through *ad hoc* intervention with single political actors or members of parliament (Constantelos 2001). These dynamics, which are also a consequence of the realignment of the Italian party system since the early 1990s, are not least owing to the absence of a regulatory framework to co-ordinate access of organized interest to political decision-making. The Vatican as a specific interest group in Italy, however, has traditionally played an important role in Italian policy-making.

Since the dissolution of the Italian Catholic party, the Vatican and the Italian Catholic Church have continuously sought to rebuild their ties with newly emerging political parties and Catholic politicians on all administrative levels (Mudu 2002).

These highly interwoven processes require strong actor coalitions in order for a legislative proposal to be successful. In sum, the fragmentation of political parties prevents most parliamentary initiatives or policy proposals from entering the voting stage in parliament. Therefore, institutional veto players can be considered less pivotal than partisan or societal veto players when it comes to morality policy-making in Italy.

Patterns of morality policy-making in Italy

Figure 1 summarizes parliamentary activity with regard to the regulation of prostitution and same-sex partnerships in Italy. The bars indicate the absolute number of parliamentary initiatives by government and opposition parties. This way, they illustrate how competitively these issues have been debated over the course of the recent legislatures.

Figure 1 illustrates the situation the centre-left government (Prodi II) faced when it tried to institutionalize same-sex partnerships in Italy in 2007. While the political left managed to dominate the agenda-setting in parliament regarding the issue of sexual orientation and civil unions, throughout the 15th legislature (2006 to 2008), the government's initiative was also accompanied by one legislative proposal and five motions from the conservative political opposition seeking to reverse the government's goal to regulate same-sex partnerships. These patterns illustrate the dynamics in parliamentary debate. On the one hand, the political left was unable to agree on one bill on same-sex partnerships with the number of alternative policy proposals by members of the government

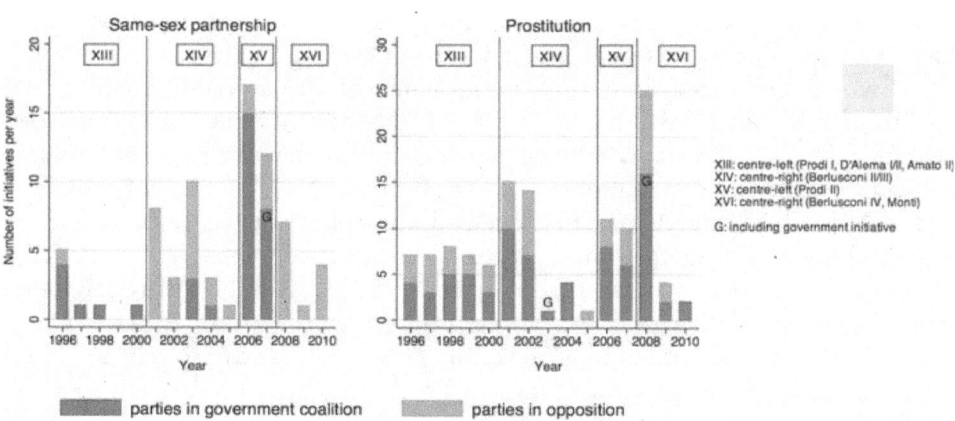

Figure 1 Number of parliamentary initiatives in morality politics in Italy
Source: Authors' compilation based on http://www.senato.it and http://www.parlamento.it.

coalition amounting to 17 in 2006 and 2007. On the other hand, the opposition made use of its ability to slow down decision-making on this matter by way of several parliamentary motions.

With respect to the issue of prostitution politics, the 2003 bill (14th legislature, governments Berlusconi II and III) was accompanied by 10 alternative proposals on the issue of voluntary prostitution by the political opposition, while in the 2008 case the number of opposing proposals amounted to nine. In addition, the two conservative governments (led both times by Prime Minister Berlusconi) also had to cope with considerable internal opposition in parliament, with 22 or 15 alternative conservative policy proposals respectively.

Homosexuality policies and actor coalitions in Italy
These figures illustrate that the issues of same-sex partnerships and prostitution have been highly contested in parliament in Italy. We argue that these dynamics in parliament reflect the underlying veto player positions on the two morality issues.

The government's 2007 initiative on same-sex partnerships was a response to increased parliamentary and societal pressure. As a consequence, Prodi's centre-left alliance favoured the institutionalization of same-sex partnerships in its manifesto prior to the 2006 elections. However, the subsequent formulation of the 2007 bill on civil unions already showed that the change coalition was rather small. Yet, the conflict on this issue only openly emerged with the presentation of the bill in parliament, when all policy actors had to take a stand on the issue.[2] With respect to the partisan veto players, the centre-left coalition (Prodi II) had to cope with the challenge to reconcile different party ideologies. While the strongest government party (the Democrats of the Left) was in favour of the initiative, representatives of the Christian Democratic party continued to argue against the institutionalization of same-sex partnerships. In contrast, members of the left-leaned socialist government parties argued for more far-reaching measures by introducing competing policy proposals themselves. However, the Democrats of the Left were not willing to negotiate a compromise, which illustrates the strong congruence of the arguably small change coalition. This internal fragmentation of the government created partisan veto players that threatened the success of the bill on same-sex partnerships by joining the blocking coalition.

The Catholic Church as a first societal veto player acted both inside and outside parliament against the institutionalization of same-sex partnerships. Since the 1990s, the Church gradually abandoned 'its policy of relative non-involvement in Italian and Roman political issues' (Mudu 2002: 190; cf. CDF 1986). On the issue of homosexuality policy the Vatican sought to directly influence parliamentarians and voters. In 1992, the Vatican published an appeal to the electorate to not vote for politicians propagating the equal treatment of same-sex partners, while in 2003 the Church directed another paper towards Catholic politicians themselves (CDF 2003). Finally, at the end of March 2007 and as a response to the Prodi initiative, the Italian Episcopal Conference explicitly rejected the recognition of any kind of (homosexual) relationship that is different to the concept of a family (CCI 2008). In sum, the Catholic Church acted mainly by directly interacting with the members of parliament on the Prodi proposal – in support of the blocking coalition.

In this context, the gay movement as a second potential veto player was very committed to the official recognition of same-sex partnerships in Italy. As a number of organizations preferred farther-reaching measures than the government coalition, they did not actively support the 2007 bill. Rather, a number of deputies with ties to the gay movement or gay organizations made use of their mandate to claim farther-reaching policy change (Mancuso 2008). This strategy of direct interaction with members of parliament had also paved the way for the very first initiatives in parliament on this issue in the beginning of the 1990s (Rossi Barilli 1999: 215). This commitment of certain members of parliament was formalized by the conclusion of a symbolic treaty between select deputies and Arcigay, the most influential gay rights organization in Italy in 2008.

These dynamics show that the change coalition on same-sex partnerships for the Prodi initiative – despite its internal congruence – was rather small. While Catholic deputies intentionally joined the blocking coalition, left-leaned deputies did so indirectly by presenting their own initiatives. The two deviationist veto players were supported by different interest groups (i.e., the Catholic Church in the former and gay organizations in the latter case) that followed a targeted strategy of direct interaction with policy actors (i.e., members of parliament in this context). As a consequence of this veto player constellation, the proposal has never been voted on in parliament and the policy initiative eventually failed. Therefore, the 2007 initiative on same-sex partnerships constitutes an example of scenario three.

Prostitution policies and actor coalitions in Italy
With respect to prostitution politics, the change coalition faced challenges similar to those surrounding the regulation of same-sex partnerships. In both instances (2003 and 2008) the conservative Berlusconi government tried to pass laws to ban street prostitution. While the 2003 initiative sought in the first place to criminalize the clients of prostitutes, the 2008 bill went even beyond that goal, banning both the offering and the demand of prostitution in public places.

The high number of concurring initiatives from the government coalition during both the 14th and the 16th legislatures indicates that support for the policy proposals – and hence the change coalition – was rather limited. The work of the inter-ministerial commission that drafted the 2003 proposal was accompanied by strong opposition also from the government parties (e.g., the strongest Christian Democratic party).[3] This lack of support markedly increased the number of partisan veto players in the blocking coalition.

In this context, the Catholic Church also played an active role by spearheading two popular initiatives that were presented in parliament in 2004. As such it became an active societal veto player that was not willing to support the change coalition in parliament. More precisely, the Church could not agree with the conservative governments' stance that sought to regulate (or criminalize) prostitution instead of offering support to women in order to overcome their dependence on prostitution.

This reasoning was shared by most (religious and secular) non-governmental organizations (e.g., Caritas Italy or On the Road) with regard to both initiatives (of 2003 and 2008). In this context, the Catholic association Community of Pope John XXIII, which carries out anti-trafficking initiatives, constitutes an exception in that it was explicitly in favour of the restrictive policy proposals of 2003 and 2008 (Caiffa 2005). Nevertheless, these organizations did not actively try to shape the policy-making process, which is why they cannot be regarded as societal veto players with regard to the issue of prostitution politics. Societal influence of the women's movement was even weaker – with the exception of the Committee for the Civil Rights of Prostitutes (which has, however, only limited access to national decision-making; Longo and Vianello [2008: 36]). In both instances (2003 and 2008), the feminist movement failed to exhibit commitment for the issue, which was mainly owing to the internal and regional fragmentation of the movement.

This actor behaviour illustrates the weaknesses of the change coalition on the regulation of prostitution. The change coalition – despite its internal congruence – failed to gain the necessary partisan support. Instead, partisan veto players (subsuming left-leaned and Christian Democratic parties) joined the blocking coalition. In this context, the Catholic Church constituted an important ally. Through its activism it was a very strong societal veto player that made use of a number of different venues of influence. Thus, the change coalition did not only fail to convince the Catholic Church but was also unable to gain support from the feminist movement. These actor constellations account for the failure of both initiatives in parliament, hence representing scenario three.

Actors, coalitions and morality politics in Spain

Spain: channelled access to morality policy-making
In Spain, the executive–legislative dimension is predominantly majoritarian, with the national executive generally consisting of single-party governments with either absolute majorities in parliament or the support of regional parties. Party discipline is strong owing to closed election lists and the concentration of power and resources in the hands of the parliamentary group leaders. While executive bills are rarely modified through votes in committee or plenary sessions, the government rather negotiates proposals with the opposition in early stages (cf. Gunther and Montero 2009). Institutional veto players are less decisive as their power is either limited (i.e., Senate) or they are not able to intervene during the policy-making process (i.e., Constitutional Court). Thus, the institutional setting facilitates the formation of strong and congruent change coalitions.

The plural interest group system supports these processes. After the transition, multiple small interest groups channelling public opinion emerged. They lack formalized ties with political parties or the executive. Approaching political parties is a more promising strategy than the direct lobbying of individual deputies owing to strong party discipline (cf. Hamann 2001). Hence, the willingness to participate, the size and cohesiveness of interest groups are important features of interest groups.

Patterns of morality policy-making in Spain
Figure 2 summarizes parliamentary activity concerning prostitution and same-sex partnerships in Spain. Three aspects are particularly striking. First, the total number of bills and motions is much lower than in Italy. This is probably the result of stricter legislative requirements and a limited number of parliamentary parties. Second, opposition parties seem to be less willing to make use of these instruments, which might be a product of regular negotiations across parties behind closed doors. Third, the number of parliamentary initiatives put forward on prostitution policy is lower than the one on same-sex marriage, pointing towards a less controversial debate.

Homosexuality policies and actor coalitions in Spain
The law on same-sex marriage in 2005 initiated radical policy change in Spain. It granted rights to registered same-sex couples with respect to inheritance, residence, adoption of the spouse's children, etc. A closer look at the actor constellation reveals that the power of the change coalition and its high degree in congruence paved the way for comprehensive reform. Main partisan veto players were the small left-wing parties (Izquierda Unida [IU], Esquerra Republicana de Catalunya [ERC] and Iniciativa per Catalunya Verds [ICV]) and the moderate Catalan party Convergència i Unió (CiU). They put forward most of the opposing initiatives (cf. Figure 2). In this context, the socialists were able to

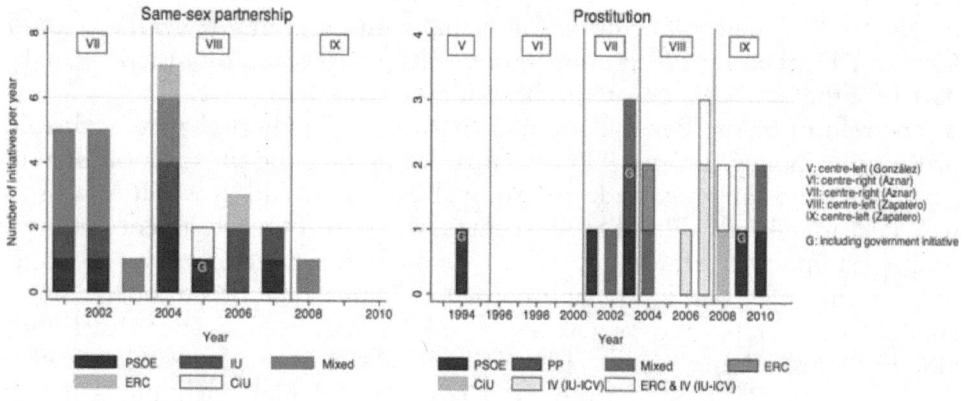

Figure 2 Number of parliamentary initiatives in morality politics in Spain
Source: Authors' compilation based on http://www.congreso.es.

form a powerful change coalition with the left-wing parties and to deprive the CiU of its veto power. The congruence of the coalition increased as soon as the PSOE adjusted its legislative proposal and extended adoption rights of same-sex couples (cf. Chaqués and Palau 2012). The coalition was accompanied by the active and cohesive interest group of gay and lesbian rights, the Federación Estatal de Lesbianas, Gais, Transexuales y Bisexuales (FELGTB). The FELGTB spoke with one voice in 2004, equally approaching left-leaned and centre-left parties (López et al. 2007). Their lobbying activity at the subnational level led to far-reaching rights for same-sex couples in single regions and increased public mobilization.

In contrast, the blocking coalition formed by the right-wing party Partido Popular (PP), the CiU and the Catholic Church was less cohesive. Although the Catholic Church might have acted as a veto player with high mobilization capacity,[4] it was not able to enforce its preferences in the decision-making arena. This behaviour is partially owing to its long tradition of partisan neutrality and given the silent blocking strategy of the PP. In sum, the favourable power structure and the high degree of congruence of the change coalition finally smoothed the way towards for radical reform, which hence constitutes an example of the first scenario.

Prostitution policies and actor coalitions in Spain
It is more challenging to draw the line between change and blocking coalition and to identify veto players in the field of prostitution policy, since various actors were involved in the policy-making process. In general, there are two central actor groups – one known as a pro-regulatory coalition accepting prostitution as a form of work and composed by the leftist parties IU and ICV and several interest groups. The other 'pro-abolitionist' group aims to fight the phenomenon of prostitution altogether. This coalition is relatively large but its degree of congruence low because its proponents follow two different lines of arguments. While some members disapprove of prostitution as an extreme form of women's exploitation (e.g., Institute of Women), some actors consider it as inherently immoral (e.g., the Catholic Church). Depending on the direction of change, the abolitionist group takes part of either the change or the blocking coalition.

The reform of the Penal Code in 1995 caused a radical change of Spanish prostitution policy. From 1995 onwards, facilitating the prostitution of third persons was no longer considered criminal behaviour and prostitution as such was decriminalized. The PSOE formed a minority government and was seeking support of either one of the main partisan veto players (i.e., the CiU or the IU). The PSOE approached the issue of prostitution mainly in connection to rape and sexual abuse, which has been a consensual topic amongst most of the parties. Consequently, both veto players were willing to support the PSOE in a strong and congruent change coalition. Although some members of the pro-abolitionist group were active as societal veto player, their mobilization capacity was not sufficient and the Catholic

Church remained rather inactive (Valiente Fernández 2004: 110). This led in combination to a weak blocking coalition that was unable to prevent major policy change. Therefore, the case provides evidence for the first scenario.

The second reform in 2003 introduced a more restrictive regime in criminalizing any activity related to the exploitation of third persons. In other words, any type of procurement was banned, including cases of mutual consent. As other aspects, such as the role of clients and the location of prostitution, were left untouched, the reform put forward an incremental alteration. PP represented a majority government and was not forced to approach other political parties. Moreover, the mobilization capacity of societal veto players (i.e., Hetaira) was low (cf. López et al. 2007: 118). This is partially owing to the fact that the issue of domestic violence overshadowed the debate and occupied many resources of feminist organizations. Furthermore, the debate was framed mainly in relation to the less controversial issue of sex-trafficking. The Catholic Church, in contrast, supporting the change coalition, stands out for its intense activity in favour of a restrictive regulation of both the offering and the demand of prostitution. In 2001, the Episcopal Conference presented a directive dealing with the link between organized human trafficking and prostitution (cf. López et al. 2007: 116). Other supporters of the pro-abolitionist approach, however, that blamed predominantly clients and procurers, argued for different policy solutions (cf. Outshoorn 2004). The growing heterogeneity in turn reduced the congruence of the change coalition. In a nutshell, the change coalition was large and powerful but less congruent, which prevented a radical change. Hence, the case characteristics fit nicely with our second scenario.

Six years later in 2009, the PSOE liberalized prostitution policy. The act stopped the general criminalization of any type of procurement. The socialists were leading a minority government, obliging them to approach partisan veto players either from the left (IU, ERC, IV) or from the moderate-right (CiU). The incorporation of left-wing parties proved difficult, since prostitution policy divides the leftist party spectrum (cf. Outshoorn 2004). In the end, the PSOE and the CiU built a large change coalition. Its degree of congruence was rather low. The small left-wing parties formed a strong and active blocking coalition with the help of societal actors. They lobbied intensively at the regional level, which facilitated far-reaching law proposals in the Catalan parliament and increased public mobilization. These circumstances opened up the possibility of entering into negotiations with the change coalition and of co-operating in incrementally adjusting the regulatory status. In sum, the change coalition was less congruent owing to diverging positions of the members. Moreover, it was confronted with a large and cohesive blocking coalition mobilizing various new actors. The PSOE profited from its centre-left position in the party spectrum, enabling co-operation not only with the small left-wing but also with moderate right-wing parties. This flexibility paved the way for the incremental adjustment of the Spanish prostitution policy towards a more permissive regulatory regime. Therefore, the 2009 reform constitutes an example for the fourth scenario.

Summary: actors, coalitions and morality policy change

In conclusion, we find empirical examples for all four scenarios (see Figure 3).

Spanish prostitution reform in 1995 and the institutionalization of same-sex marriage in 2005 fall into Scenario 1. In both moments, the change coalition was powerful and its preferences rather homogeneous allowing for radical policy change. The act on prostitution policy in Spain in 2003 provides evidence for the second scenario. A powerful and large change coalition formed by the PP and other pro-abolitionist supporters had to cope with weak internal congruence between the Catholic Church and feminist groups. The Italian reform attempts in the fields of prostitution policy and same-sex partnership come close to Scenario 3. While the change coalitions as such appear congruent and determined to carry out their policy proposals, important partisan and societal veto players left the change coalition. As a consequence, the reform proposals lacked the necessary support in parliament. Finally, the 2009 reform of prostitution policy in Spain lends evidence to Scenario 4. A low degree in congruence and a rather weak power structure opened up the opportunity for the blocking coalition to negotiate with the change coalition and, hence, to agree on incremental regulatory adjustments. In sum, the findings for all cases and across both countries support the expectation that the balance of political power among the change and blocking coalitions, as well as the congruence among the actors within the change coalition, are important determinants for policy change.

		Congruence among actors within change coalition			
		High		Low	
Balance of political power	change coalition > blocking coalition	Scenario 1 radical change		Scenario 2 incremental change I	
		SPAIN	Same-sex marriage 2005 Prostitution 1995	SPAIN	Prostitution 2003
	change coalition ≤ blocking coalition	Scenario 3 failure		Scenario 4 incremental change II via cooperation	
		ITALY	Same-sex marriage 2007 Prostitution 2003, 2008	SPAIN	Prostitution 2009

Figure 3 Actor coalitions and regulatory change in Spain and Italy

CONCLUSION

Our empirical analysis of the regulation of prostitution and the institutionalization of same-sex partnerships in two Catholic societies allows for some conclusions that might be of interest to the scholarship on comparative morality policy analysis.

On the one hand, we find evidence for the expectation that morality policy change is subject to the political and societal actors' strategic positioning as veto players. Given that morality policies deal with fundamental principles, policy change requires broad political and societal support for the government initiative. If the change coalition is challenged by the majority of veto players, the success of the policy proposal depends on the flexibility of the change coalition to negotiate a compromise with its opponents. While the Italian decision-makers lacked the necessary willingness to adjust initial policy plans, Spanish politicians were able to realign crucial veto players in the bargaining process not least owing to institutional conditions. These findings highlight the contingent influence of the legislature for morality policy change (cf. Heichel *et al.* 2013).

Our comparative analyses of the political processes also illustrate the role of the Catholic Church and the religious denomination in society on morality policy-making. In Italy, the Catholic Church is a powerful and active societal veto player having direct access to the decision-making process. Its mobilization capacity is very high owing to the geographical proximity of the Vatican and an extremely religious population. About 24 per cent of Italians attend religious services once a week whereas only 14 per cent of the Spanish population claims to do so, and this number is steadily decreasing owing to a notable secularization process (WVSA 2012: 2005 wave). Until the 2000s, the Catholic Church in Spain followed a strategy of partisan neutrality, avoiding any political involvement and thus restraining itself from being a strong societal veto player (cf. Montero 1999). As a consequence, religious factors do play an important role when it comes to explaining morality policy change in the two Catholic countries. However, it is necessary to shed a nuanced light on the cultural and institutional Church–state relations, the Church's situational preferences and behaviour, as well as its mobilization capacity.

These findings suggest venues for future research. In the first place, we highlighted the impact of partisan and societal veto players and the ability of the change coalition to incorporate them. Yet, we lack systematic understanding and detailed empirical information of the exact causal mechanisms enabling societal actors to access the change coalition. Future research might also address the following questions. In what way does the regulatory *status quo* matter in regard to the extent of morality policy change? Do these findings hold true in corporatist systems equipping some interest groups with more power in the decision-making process?

Biographical notes: Sophie Schmitt is a Postdoctoral Research Fellow at the Institute for Research Information and Quality Assurance, Berlin, Germany. Eva-Maria Euchner and Caroline Preidel are Junior Researchers Fellow in the Department of Politics and Public Administration, University of Konstanz, Germany.

ACKNOWLEDGMENTS

This article is based on the project MORAPOL (ERC Advanced Grant). Generous funding by the European Research Council is gratefully acknowledged.

NOTES

1 Owing to the focus on voluntary prostitution, we do not include the Immigration Act of 2000 and the Penal Code reform of 1999.
2 See 'Unioni di fatto, Dl divisi Poi passa la linea Bindi', *La Repubblica*, 7 February 2007: 1.
3 See 'Il Polo litiga anche sulla prostituzione', *L'Unità*, 4 August 2002: 7.
4 The Catholic Church campaigned yet in the mid-1990s against homosexuals and argued in its Episcopal Conference that homosexuality is a result of bad habits, bad companies and negative early experiences. It even intensified its activity from the 2000s onwards (i.e., publishing several officials press statements, presenting a pastoral directory for the family in 2003).

REFERENCES

Caiffa, P. (2005) 'Approvato dal governo il ddl contro la prostituzione', *Chiesa Cattolica Italiana*, 19 September.
Calvo, K. (2007) 'Sacrifices that pay: polity membership, political opportunities and the recognition of same-sex marriage in Spain', *South European Society and Politics* 12(3): 295–314.
Chaqués, L. and Palau, A.M. (2012) 'From prohibition to permissiveness: a two waves change on morality issues in Spain', in I. Engeli, C. Green-Pedersen and L. Thorup Larsen (eds), *Morality Politics in Western Europe*, Basingstoke: Palgrave Macmillan, pp. 62–87.
Chiesa Cattolica Italiana (CCI) (2008) *Nota a riguardo della famiglia fondata sul matrimonio e di iniziative legislative in materia di unioni di fatto*, 28 March.
Congregation for the Doctrine of the Faith (CDF) (1986) *Letter on the Pastoral Care of Homosexual Persons*, 1 October.
Congregation for the Doctrine of the Faith (CDF) (2003) *Considerations Regarding Proposals to give Legal Recognition to Unions between Homosexual Persons*, 3 June.
Consejo de Estado (2010) 'Informe sobre anuncios de contenido sexual y prostitución en prensa', *Comisión de estudies del Consejo de estado*, E 1.
Constantelos, J. (2001) 'Italy: the erosion and demise of party dominance', in C.S. Thomas (ed.), *Political Parties & Interest Groups*, London: Lynne Rienner Publishers, pp. 119–37.
Danna, D. (2001) 'Cattivi costumi: Le politiche sulla prostituzione nell'Unione Europea negli anni Novanta', *Quaderni del Dipartimento di Sociologia e Ricerca Sociale, Università di Trento* (25).
Danna, D. (2004) 'Italy: the never-ending debate', in J. Outshoorn (ed.), *The Politics of Prostitution*, Cambridge, New York: Cambridge University Press, pp. 165–84.

Engeli, I., Green-Pedersen, C. and Larsen, L.T. (eds) (2012) *Morality Politics in Western Europe*, Basingstoke: Palgrave Macmillan.

Fink, S. (2008) 'Politics as usual or bringing religion back in? The influence of parties, institutions, economic interests, and religion on embryo research laws', *Comparative Political Studies* 41(12): 1631–56.

Fink, S. (2009) 'Churches as societal veto players', *West European Politics* 32(1): 77–96.

Gunther, R. and Montero, J. (2009) *The Politics of Spain*, Cambridge: Cambridge University Press.

Hall, P. and Taylor, R. (1996) 'Political science and the three new institutionalisms'. *MPIFG Discussion Paper 96*, 1–32.

Hamann, K. (2001) 'Spain: changing party-group relations in a new democracy', in C.S. Thomas (ed.), *Political Parties & Interest Groups*, London: Lynne Rienner, pp. 175–92.

Heichel, S., Knill, C. and Schmitt, S. (2013) 'Policy analysis meets morality policy: theoretical aspects, concepts and explanatory factors of policy change', *Journal of European Public Policy* 20(3), doi: 10.1080/13501763.2013.761497

Kilvington, J., Day, S. and Ward, H. (2001) 'Prostitution policy in Europe: a time of change?' *Feminist Review* 67: 78–93.

Longo, V. and Vianello, F. (2008) 'Context study Italy', *QUING Project*, Vienna: Institute for Human Sciences (IWM), available at http://www.quing.eu/files/results/cs_italy.pdf, accessed 22 April 2012.

López, S., Peterson, E. and Platero, R. (2007) 'Issue histories Spain: series of timelines of policy debates', *QUING Project*, Vienna: Institute for Human Sciences (IWM), available at http://www.quing.eu/files/results/ih_spain.pdf, accessed 15 February 2012.

Mancuso, A. (2008) 'Bertinotti, Boselli, Ferrero primi firmatari Patto con Arcigay', *Arcigay*, 4 April.

Montero, J. (1999) 'Religión y política en España: los nuevos contornos del cleavage religioso', *Revista Mexicana de Sociología* 61(1): 39–65.

Mooney, C.Z. (2001) 'The public clash of private values', in C.Z. Mooney (ed.), *The Public Clash of Private Values. The Politics of Morality Policy*, New York: Chatham House, pp. 3–18.

Mudu, P. (2002) 'Repressive tolerance: the gay movement and the Vatican in Rome', *GeoJournal* 58(2–3): 189–96.

Outshoorn, J. (ed.) (2004) *The Politics of Prostitution*, Cambridge: Cambridge University Press.

Paternotte, D. (2008) 'Les lieux d'activisme : le «mariage gai» en Belgique, en France et en Espagne', *Canadian Journal of Political Science* 41(4): 935–52.

Platero, R. (2007) 'Love and the state: gay marriage in Spain', *Feminist Legal Studies* 15(3): 329–40.

Rossi Barilli, G. (1999) *Il Movimento Gay in Italia*, Milan: Feltrinelli Editore.

Schwartz, M.A. and Tatalovich, R. (2009) 'Cultural and institutional factors affecting political contention over moral issues', *Comparative Sociology* 8(1): 76–104.

Strøm, K. (1990) 'A behavioural theory of competitive political parties', *American Journal of Political Science* 34(2): 565–98.

Tsebelis, G. (2002) *Veto Players. How Political Institutions Work*, New York: Princeton University Press.

Valiente Fernández, C. (2004) 'La política de la prostitución: el papel del movimiento de mujeres y los organismos de igualdad en España', *Reis* 105: 103–32.

West, J. (2000) 'Prostitution: collectives and the politics of regulation', *Gender, Work and Organisation* 7(2): 106–18.

World Values Survey (WVS) Association (2012) 'Publically available datasets', available at http://www.worldvaluessurvey.org (accessed 15 June 2012).

Policy entrepreneurs and controversial science: governing human embryonic stem cell research

Michael Mintrom

ABSTRACT   Policy entrepreneurs are political actors who seek policy changes that shift the *status quo* in given areas of public policy. This contribution examines the actions of policy entrepreneurs who have sought government funding and favourable regulation to advance human embryonic stem cell research. Those policy entrepreneurs have faced significant opposition owing to the morality issues at stake. Placing the actions of those policy entrepreneurs in a broader context makes two contributions. First, it explores how policy entrepreneurs pursue their goals in the face of intense morality politics. Second, it illustrates how the work of policy entrepreneurs can be both supported and inhibited by ideas, institutions and interest-group politics.

INTRODUCTION

The history of Western civilization has been punctuated by controversies between scientific communities, governments and religious entities. Those controversies have centred on issues of knowledge, power and control. To people of faith, knowledge claims disrupting the perceived natural order have been deeply threatening. Such controversy emerged in the wake of the announcement in 1998 that human stem cells had been derived from human embryos (Thomson *et al.* 1998). Human embryonic stem cell research forces debate about the meaning of life. It has deep symbolic significance. Scrutiny of public debates and policy choices regarding this controversial science offers insights into contemporary politics, policy-making and the design of effective governance systems (Mintrom 2009; Mintrom and Bollard 2009).

The work of policy entrepreneurs is given a central place in this contribution. Policy entrepreneurs are political actors who seek policy changes that shift the *status quo* in given areas of public policy. Through case studies of policy entrepreneurship and human embryonic stem cell research in the United Kingdom (UK) and Italy, this contribution shows how policy entrepreneurs have sought to promote more funding and less restrictive regulation for stem cell science, with mixed results. In each case, those efforts have met with significant opposition owing to the morality issues at stake. This study enhances our knowledge, first, of the nature and limits of policy entrepreneurship and, second, of morality policies and the politics surrounding them.

THE WORK OF POLICY ENTREPRENEURS

Among contemporary theories of policy-making, three offer valuable insights into the dynamics of policy change, how the conditions arise that generate change, and the structures of interest groups and other alliances that provide the social capacity for change initiatives. Frank Baumgartner and Bryan Jones's (1993) theory of agendas and instability in government combines knowledge of factors that propel major change with Charles Lindblom's (1959) concept of boundedly rational actors engaging in incremental change. Baumgartner and Jones argued that patterns of change in most policy domains exhibit 'punctuated equilibrium' – that is, periods of deep and rapid change that are both preceded and followed by much longer periods of quiet, business-as-usual. John Kingdon's (1984) theory of independent streams suggests that policy change occurs in windows of opportunity where specific political events, the current state of the policy conversation among policy élites and particular pressing problems align in ways that allow for disruptive agenda-setting. Paul Sabatier's (1988, 1993) theory of advocacy coalitions – the advocacy coalition framework – attends to interactions among diverse stakeholders. Here, the norm-shaping nature of discourse within coalitions over a sustained period of time serves both to generate ideas for policy change and focus the political forces needed to achieve that change. Within all three theories, the role of change agents – or *policy entrepreneurs* – has been recognized, but it has not been given careful attention.

The focus on policy entrepreneurs is a recent phenomenon. Michael Mintrom and collaborators have identified the actions taken by policy entrepreneurs (Mintrom and Vergari 1996, 1998), the ways that contextual factors serve to support or inhibit their actions (Mintrom 1997, 2000), and the compatibility between these more detailed understandings of the work of policy entrepreneurs and broader theories of policy-making (Mintrom and Norman 2009). Those conceptual and empirical investigations suggest policy entrepreneurs are identifiable not so much by their success in securing policy change but by the actions they take in pursuit of that goal. Policy entrepreneurs tend to work hard at (1) defining and framing problems, (2) building powerful teams that tap relevant knowledge networks, (3) amassing evidence to show the workability of their proposals; and (4) creating strong coalitions of diverse supporters.

Original theorizing about policy entrepreneurs drew on evidence from the United States. However, scholars have adapted and applied the concept of policy entrepreneurship in the European context. Falk Daviter (2007) and Daniel Béland (2009) indicated the importance of policy framing as a tool for promoting policy change, and highlighted examples policy entrepreneurs using policy framing to good effect. Marcel Braun (2009) and Dimitrios C. Christopoulos (2006) each explored the actions of policy entrepreneurs within European policy networks and how they leveraged their network resources to promote policy change. Use of evidence by policy entrepreneurs in the European context has been explored by Giandomenico Majone (1989) and Arco Timmermans and Peter Scholten (2006). Finally, Geoffrey Dudley and Jeremy Richardson (1999) and David Natali (2004) used case studies to illustrate how policy entrepreneurs use broad-based advocacy coalitions to help achieve their policy goals.

By definition, policy entrepreneurs seek to change *status quo* policy arrangements. This distinguishes them from many interest group leaders, for whom maintenance of current power relations and institutional settings are accorded highest priority. The attention policy entrepreneurs give to specific issues and their willingness to work with others increase the likelihood of them securing the policy outcomes they desire. But two points should be remembered. First, competency matters. Some policy entrepreneurs will be more adept than others at negotiating their operating context. Second, the operating context matters. Just as athletic performance is influenced by conditions on the day, so too policy outcomes are influenced by the broader authorizing context.

For policy entrepreneurs wishing to change regimes governing controversial science, the authorizing environment is shaped by several factors. In the case of human embryonic stem cell research, these factors can include the relative power and ascendancy of specific interest groups, like the Catholic Church or the local scientific community. Their context can also be shaped by the composition of elected officials in the legislature and relations between those officials and other powerful decision-makers (i.e., presidents or the judiciary). These contextual influences on the effectiveness of policy entrepreneurs have been discussed in detail by Michael Mintrom (2000). The impact of contextual factors on governance of human embryonic stem cell research at the state level in the United States has been tested quantitatively by Andrew Karch (2012) and Michael Mintrom (2009). Differences in contextual factors can significantly influence the time needed for policy entrepreneurs to achieve desired policy outcomes. In turn, they can affect the nature of the work they do in the development and co-ordination of advocacy coalitions. Jocelyn Crowley (2003, 2008) has documented examples of policy entrepreneurship spanning several decades.

HUMAN EMBRYONIC STEM CELL RESEARCH

Stem cell research in itself need not necessarily be controversial. Although all cells within an organism contain the same genetic information, as they develop they become specialized, which allows them to carry out very different and specific functions throughout the body. In contrast to specialized cells, stem cells are uncommitted cells serving no specific purpose. They remain uncommitted until they receive signals to develop into specialized cells. Scientists have speculated about stem cells and their qualities for over a century (Ramalho-Santos and Willenbring 2007). The existence of stem cells was discovered mainly through investigations into animals, particularly mice. Stem cells are known to exist in both adults and embryos, and stem cell researchers have studied the behaviour of both adult stem cells and embryonic stem cells. However, questions remain concerning the plasticity of non-embryonic stem cells – that is, their ability to transform into a variety of specialized cells (National Institutes of Health 2006).

In 1981, researchers from Cambridge University in the United Kingdom reported methods for growing mouse embryonic stem cells (Evans and Kaufman 1981). In 1998, James Thomson and his team of researchers from the University of Wisconsin – Madison reported the isolation of human embryonic stem cells (Thomson et al. 1998). Embryonic stem cells are derived from cells called the inner cell mass, which is part of several-days-old embryos, or blastocysts. If left in the right environment, these cells would develop into an embryo. Once removed from the blastocyst, the cells of the inner cell mass can be cultured into embryonic stem cells. These embryonic stem cells are not themselves embryos and evidence has shown that these cells do not behave in the laboratory as they would in the developing embryo. After researchers have isolated stem cells from a human embryo, the cells can often replicate indefinitely if kept in the correct environment. This creates what is termed a 'cell line'.

The ability of the Wisconsin team to isolate human embryonic stem cells and cultivate stem cell lines was a significant scientific breakthrough. Evidence subsequently emerged that these cells are capable of becoming almost all of the specialized cells of the body and may have the potential to generate replacement cells for a large number of tissues and organs, such as the heart, the pancreas and the nervous system. Because of this, stem cells are seen as having several important scientific and medical applications. These include being used for repair or replacement of cells or tissues that are damaged or destroyed by a variety of diseases and disabilities, testing new drugs in a controlled and safe setting, and studying genetic function and development processes (National Institutes of Health 2001).

Morality politics associated with human embryonic stem cell research

What is the moral status of the human embryo? The question of what constitutes independent human life is central to the debate regarding the use of human embryonic stem cells in research and research-based therapies. The question can be further broken down. First, does life begin at conception – at the moment when the human egg is fertilized – or at some later stage of development? Second, at what point in the development of the embryo or foetus should human rights and other legal protections be assigned to this life form? Human embryonic stem cell research is controversial science precisely because it forces explicit consideration of what counts as human life and who gets to decide that.

Some religious groups – including representatives of the Roman Catholic Church and other Christian traditions – contend that human life indeed begins at conception and from that point forward the embryo or foetus should be accorded full respect and full rights as a human being. That position immediately renders destruction of the embryo as immoral and de-legitimates any justification for the destructions of embryos. Questions concerning trade-offs between the protection of the life of the human embryo, on the one hand, and the quality of life of people who could benefit from advances in human embryonic stem cell research, on the other, inherently involve relativist judgements. But relativism has no place in what is an inherently absolutist world view. Given this, in jurisdictions where politicians depend upon the support of organized religious groups to obtain and maintain decision-making roles – and those religious groups view human life in absolute terms – promoters of human embryonic stem cell research are likely to be stymied in their efforts. In contrast, in jurisdictions where relativism and more pragmatic arguments are able to hold sway, opportunities emerge for advocates to promote government funding and permissive regulation of human embryonic stem cell research. Simon Fink (2008) has shown that across 21 countries that have adopted laws on human embryonic stem cell research, the most restrictive laws have been adopted in countries where Roman Catholicism is a dominant religion and/or Christian democratic parties have been in ascendance.

Proponents of human embryonic stem cell research have pointed out that in the natural reproductive process, human eggs are often fertilized but fail to implant in the uterus. A fertilized egg, they argue, while it may have the potential for human life, cannot be considered equivalent to a human being until it has at least been successfully implanted in a woman's uterus (American Association for the Advancement of Science 2007).

While some have considered embryonic stem cell research to be justifiable for the advancement of scientific knowledge, they have worried greatly about the future (Fukuyama 2005). Looking ahead, the possibility arises of extensive growth in markets for the trading of human eggs. This would create incentives for women to produce and sell eggs that would then be fertilized to create embryos solely for the purpose of destroying them at the blastocyst stage to harvest the stem cells. As is, trading of human eggs has become common in response to the demands of infertile couples to gain access to donor eggs for making babies (Withrow 2007). Scientists seeking to work with human embryos for stem cell research obtain human eggs from in vitro fertilization clinics. In the process of treating infertility, more eggs are produced than are used for the purposes of creating viable embryos. Surplus eggs can be stored, discarded or donated to research (Trivedi 2007). Proponents of embryonic stem cell research have held that it is morally permissible to use surplus embryos for potentially life-saving biomedical research. Opponents have objected to this argument, however, saying that such research would still condone the destruction of embryos.

Some stem cell research is non-controversial. This includes stem cell research using animals and research using cells derived from human placentas discarded at birth or tissue from adult human skin cells. Indeed, work by James Thomson and his Wisconsin team announced in 2007 could eventually take much of the heat away from the controversy over embryonic stem cell research. That is because Thomson's team discovered how to use genetic modification to reprogram non-embryonic human cells so that they exhibit the essential characteristics of embryonic stem cells (Yu *et al.* 2007). This work holds promise because it allows for the possibility of using a patient's own skin cells to create genetically matched stem cells that could be used to make replacement cells and tissues for that patient, without the risk of rejection by the immune system. However, questions remain about the distinction between embryonic stem cells and stem cells derived through genetic modification, making ongoing work with human embryonic stem cells crucial to the advancement of this scientific work (Kolata 2007).

Issues surrounding human cloning also arise in the management of human embryos and the harvesting of embryonic stem cells. That is because the only technique known so far for growing stem cells genetically matched to a subject has involved injecting cells from that subject into a human egg to clone that person and then extract the embryonic stem cells from the blastocyst. Such a procedure and the moral issues associated with it could also be rendered redundant through the research into reprogramming of non-embryonic human cells into stem cells. However, the issue of cloning has created another point of deep controversy surrounding this research (Fukuyama 2005).

A number of previous studies have explored the politics associated with the governance of human embryonic stem cell research (Banchoff 2005; Fink 2008; Karch 2012; Mintrom 2009). This study is the first to focus on the activities of policy entrepreneurs in this issue area.

THE GEOGRAPHY OF HUMAN EMBRYONIC STEM CELL RESEARCH

Publication of original research articles exploring aspects of stem cell science have routinely appeared in two of the world's leading scientific publications: *Science* and *Nature*. Since 2007, another top scientific journal, *Cell*, has published articles on stem cell research in *Cell Stem Cell*. Following Mintrom and Bollard (2009), a place-of-origin analysis was performed on articles published in those journals in the period from January 1998 through to December 2011. This analysis counted original research publications where the term 'stem cell' appeared in either the title or the abstract. Across the three journals during this period, authorship of articles was attributed to scientists located in 24 countries. Of those countries, 20 were members of the Organization for Economic Co-operation and Development (OECD) and 16 were home of at least one university ranked as being among the world's top 100 in the Academic Ranking of World Universities, 2011 (Shanghai Ranking Consultancy 2011).

Additionally, almost perfect correlations existed between the proportions of publications by place-of-origin across the three journals.

In all three journals, well over half of the publications were based on science conducted in the United States. The second-most common place of origin was Japan. Among European nations, scientists from the United Kingdom led the publication count, followed by Germany. Publications from other European countries were sporadic. This pattern indicates that the primary predictor of a country hosting stem cell research is not the religious mix of the population but the wealth of the country and the commitments that successive governments have made to the funding of their research universities. Among countries hosting universities ranked in the world's top 100 in 2011, the United States hosted 54, the United Kingdom hosted 11, and Germany and Japan hosted 5 each. France, Sweden and Switzerland each hosted 3 top-ranked universities, while other European countries hosted two, one or none. This analysis suggests that in some countries the public debates over stem cell research represent little more than political and moral posturing because general, long-term government commitment to funding of premier scientific facilities (for any kind of science) has been lacking.

POLICY ENTREPRENEURS AND THE PROMOTION OF HUMAN EMBRYONIC STEM CELL RESEARCH

Studies of policy entrepreneurship have flourished in the past three decades (Mintrom and Norman 2009). Following John Kingdon's (1984) path-breaking discussion of what policy entrepreneurs do, research on the activities of policy entrepreneurs has tended to employ case study techniques. There have been exceptions. For example, Mintrom (1997, 2000) used event history analysis to quantitatively test the impact of policy entrepreneurs and various contextual conditions on legislative agenda setting and policy change. However, to achieve adequate control of other explanations of policy change, quantitative investigations of policy entrepreneurship require high levels of institutional isomorphism across the jurisdictions included in the study. Such isomorphism is present in many federalism systems but is rarely found across independent countries. A major challenge for policy researchers lies in establishing tractable ways to conduct cross-national studies of policy entrepreneurship.

For the present study, the research question was: how have policy entrepreneurs shaped the governance of human embryonic stem cell research in European countries? The geography of stem cell research served to limit the set of countries relevant to the study. To date, scientists based in just 11 European countries have published the results of stem cell research in *Science, Nature or Cell Stem Cell*. Those countries are: Austria; Belgium; Denmark; France; Germany; Italy; the Netherlands; Spain; Sweden; Switzerland; and the United Kingdom. Since the research work was to be exploratory in nature, I chose to follow the 'diverse case' selection approach (Gerring 2007). Two countries were selected as cases, each offering distinctive contexts with respect to the generation of human embryonic stem cell research and the broader political environment. The two countries were the United Kingdom and Italy. In each case, enough documented evidence was available to assist in the interpretation of the role policy entrepreneurs have played in each country. Analysis of aggregate statistics confirms the appropriateness of this choice of cases. Among European countries, the United Kingdom has one of the lowest populations of adults professing the Roman Catholic faith (at around 9 per cent). In contrast, Italy has the highest population of adults professing Roman Catholicism (at around 90 per cent). Further, comparing across European countries with respect to the mean levels of professionals working in the broad field of research and development (R&D), Italy tends to have a much less developed R&D sector than does the United Kingdom. In addition, proportionate to population size, among European countries Italian universities generate comparatively low levels of science graduates per year, while the United Kingdom generates comparatively high levels.[1]

Substantively, the governance of human embryonic stem cell research is not dichotomous. Rather, it represents a continuum made up of several variables, including the permissiveness of regulations relating to what researchers can do and the willingness of governments to fund that research. European countries differ considerably in their governance of human embryonic stem cell research. On a continuum, Italy lies at the highly restrictive end, while the United Kingdom lies at the permissive end. In their analysis of policy approaches to embryonic stem cell research in 50 countries, Rosario Isasi and Bartha Knoppers (2006) noted that the United Kingdom had a liberal policy regime and Italy a regime that essentially banned this form of research. In both instances, supporters of human embryonic stem cell research have faced significant political opposition based on moral principles. In reviewing each case, attention is paid to how advocates of stem cell research have sought to (1) define and frame problems, (2) build teams tapping relevant knowledge networks, (3) amass evidence to show the workability of their proposals, and (4) create strong coalitions of diverse supporters.

The United Kingdom

A permissive approach has been taken in the United Kingdom to the regulation of human embryonic stem cell research. While human reproductive cloning is banned, the current regime permits the creation of embryos for research purposes as well as for the derivation of stem cell lines and for cloning for research purposes. This permissiveness, and the existence of a long-established, well-supported scientific community has allowed the United Kingdom to stand as a leading jurisdiction for the advancement of human embryonic stem cell research. To the extent that policy entrepreneurship has occurred in this context, it has been undertaken quietly and within an institutional context that has facilitated huge expansion in human embryonic stem cell research. Moral issues have been widely canvassed, and heated debates have occurred, but they have not inhibited scientific research.

Relevant history relating to research on embryos in the United Kingdom dates back to the early 1980s, and what Michael Mulkay (1993) has termed the 'great embryo debate'. In vitro fertilization was producing surplus embryos that were readily accessible material for research. This led to concern over the status of embryos. The medical community, which claimed more research would support better treatment, was opposed by critical voices in public and in parliament. In 1982 the British government established the Committee of Inquiry into Human Fertilization and Embryology, chaired by Mary Warnock, a philosopher. In what now appears as a significant act of policy entrepreneurship, Warnock (1985) and her colleagues recommended that a government agency be established to regulate artificial fertility methods as well as embryonic research. At the outset, Warnock's report upset both scientists – who resisted strict regulation of their work – and religious groups – who wished to protect human embryos. However, following much debate, Warnock's basic proposal was adopted into law. In 1990, the Human Fertilization and Embryology Authority (HFEA) was established, responsible for all issues concerning human fertility and for research with human embryos. The new law resolved prior debate by acknowledging that the moral status of the human embryo is different from any other research object. However, a governing principle was established that the moral value accorded to human embryos may be outweighed by other serious moral considerations (Hauskeller 2004).

When stem cell research became a reality by the end of 1998, embryo research was already a regulated but normal practice in the United Kingdom. The established procedures of the Human Fertilization and Embryology Authority created space for careful discussion of newly arising issues in the field. According to Christine Hauskeller:

> the procedures and practical questions of directing such research to be successful and effective as possible in favour of new therapies was prefigured both in the prevailing structure of ethical reasoning and the resulting institutions. (Hauskeller 2004: 515)

From the beginning, the Human Fertilization and Embryology Authority promoted human embryonic stem cell research. During the period from 1994–2002, the Authority was chaired by Ruth Deech, now Baroness Deech, who subsequently co-authored a book on the Authority's work (see Deech and Smajdor 2007). Deech led the Authority in a manner that created more opportunities for human embryonic stem cell research to be conducted in the United Kingdom. HFEA members are appointed by UK health ministers. The members determine the HFEA's policies. In order that a perspective can be maintained which is independent of the medical-scientific view, the enabling legislation (HFE Act 1990) requires that the chairman, deputy chairman and at least half of the HFEA's membership are neither doctors nor scientists involved in human embryo research. Members are not appointed as representatives of different groups, but bring to the HFEA a broad range of expertise.

As chair of the Human Fertilization and Embryology Authority, Ruth Deech performed many functions consistent with being a policy entrepreneur:

(1) In her role, she had the resources and the stature to work with others to define and frame policy discussions.
(2) Through the Authority's links to the scientific and policy communities, Deech was able to assemble *ad hoc* teams to explore emerging policy issues.
(3) Deech and her colleagues at the Authority continually amassed evidence to show the workability its proposals. Indeed, they took care to be transparent about the scientific work they authorized.
(4) As such, Deech established for herself a powerful position for leading policy debate and gained the support of strong, diverse coalitions.[2]

The quiet, agenda-setting actions of Ruth Deech and the Human Fertilization and Embryology Authority in the United Kingdom are illustrated by the process that led to adoption of the Human Fertilization and Embryology (Research Purposes) Regulations 2001. In 1998, the Authority, in collaboration with the Human Genetics Advisory Commission, established a Working Group chaired by the Reverend Doctor John Polkinghorne, a former professor of mathematical physics at Cambridge University who had subsequently become an Anglican priest. That choice of chair illustrates how Deech and her colleagues sought to appear even-handed in its consideration of issues. In January 1998, the Working Group produced a paper, 'Cloning Issues in Reproduction, Science and Medicine'. It argued that research using cell nuclear replacement (in which the nucleus of an adult cell is fused with an egg which has had its nucleus removed) could lead to new treatments for serious disorders by providing a source of new tissue. In response, in June 1999, the Government announced the establishment of an expert group chaired by the chief medical officer, Professor Liam Donaldson, to advise on whether new areas of research using embryos should be permitted that could lead to broader understanding of, and eventually to new treatments for, a range of disorders where there is disease or damage to tissues or organs. Notably, Donaldson's expert group was not asked to review from first principles the ethical issues of research involving embryos. Rather, it was asked to consider only new ethical issues that might arise from the creation and use of embryos for the extraction of stem cells.

The Donaldson Report was released in August 2000. It proposed the legalization of research with stem cells derived from embryos within 14 days of fertilization. Such research, it contended, should be subject to rigorous scientific and ethical review and it should be conducted primarily with stem cells derived from embryos left over from in vitro fertilization treatments. Following the advice initially promulgated by the Human Fertilization and Embryology Authority's Working Group, Donaldson and his colleagues proposed that the creation and cloning of embryos for biomedical research be allowed. New legislation consistent with this was adopted in December 2000.

The period from August to December of 2000 witnessed considerable debate. While it was initiated by actions of the Human Fertilization and Embryology

Authority, the agency itself remained silent through this period. Statements in support of cloning for research purposes were provided from many quarters, including the Medical Research Council, the Wellcome Trust, the Nuffield Council on Bioethics, the British Medical Association and the Royal Society. Patient's groups, such as the UK Parkinson's Disease Society, also backed the law change. Former American actor Christopher Reeve joined the campaign, and Colin Blakemore of the Medical Research Council described his role as 'very significant' (Gottweis and Prainsack 2006). While scientists, Professor Donaldson, and Members of Parliament (MPs) aligned with the governing Labour Party were most prominent in supporting the law change, Conservative MPs, religious figures and pro-life groups were among its most vocal opponents (Williams *et al.* 2003). This successful action to promote stem cell research in the United Kingdom illustrates how effective policy entrepreneurship can set the terms for subsequent debate. It also illustrates how long-established institutions and the power of entrenched interest groups can assist those promoting policy changes fraught with moral issues.

Italy

In Italy, a virtual ban has existed on human embryonic stem cell research since 2004. This ban is a by-product of an effort to protect and afford citizenship to the embryo from the moment of conception. The Italian Medical Assisted Procreation Law No.40 (2004) stipulates that clinical and experimental research on a human embryo can be conducted only for therapeutic or diagnostic purposes which are exclusively directed to the protection of the embryo's health and development. In vitro fertilization is allowed, but no surplus embryos are to be produced. Since this law is solely focused on the human status of the embryo, Italian scientists are free to work on stem cells lines derived from human embryos, so long as they are imported. (Human stem cell lines, once created, exist outside of the embryo.) However, this kind of research is difficult to sustain in Italy, because national funding for stem cell research is restricted to work using stem cells derived from adult tissues, from cord blood, and from aborted foetuses. The Roman Catholic Church has been active in efforts to restrict research on human embryonic stem cells (Metzler 2007) and in 2006 Cardinal Alfonso Lopez Trujillo expressed his view that excommunication from the Church was merited for researchers who destroyed human embryos (Rosenthal 2006).

The Italian case highlights two conditions that restrict efforts to advance human embryonic stem cell research. First, the Roman Catholic Church – an historically powerful institution in Italian society – has maintained a strong moral stance that accords the human embryo full status as a human being. So morality politics have played against policy entrepreneurs seeking support for human embryonic stem cell research. Second, the limited nature of the funding available to Italian scientists in this field has inhibited the development of institutional support for human embryonic stem cell research. Only when communities of scientists achieve a critical mass do we tend to see their work receive support from entities such as universities, scientific associations and businesses that perceive commercialization potential in the research.

In the face of difficult circumstances, policy entrepreneurs have sought to advance the place of human embryonic stem cell research in Italy. Those policy entrepreneurs comprise a team of scientists lead by Professor Elena Cattaneo, Director of the Center for Stem Cell Research (UniStem) at Università di Milano. Cattaneo has published in *Science* and *Nature* on matters relating to neural stem cells and Huntington's Disease.

To date, the actions of the Italian policy entrepreneurs have not provoked policy change. However, their actions are consistent with efforts of policy entrepreneurs elsewhere to:

(1) define and frame problems;
(2) built teams tapping relevant knowledge networks;
(3) amass evidence to show the workability of their proposals; and
(4) create strong coalitions of diverse supporters.

With respect to (1), defining and framing problems, in 2007 Cattaneo's group known as the Italian Researchers on Embryonic Stem Cells (IES Group) produced its *Manifesto for Scientific Research on Embryonic Stem Cells*. In response to powerful opposition from those who wish to protect the life of human embryos, the signatories to the Manifesto stated:

> we hold there is a moral duty to pursue ... research on embryonic stem cells [because it] is an essential step towards understanding how human tissues are generated and become diseased. In our view, the gaining of this knowledge per se is already ethically sound and sufficient to justify protecting the freedom of scientific research, which is also consistent with [Italy's] Constitution. (IES Group 2007:1)

They also wrote:

> We maintain that embryonic stem cell research is ethically sound and necessary, in particular when performed with cells that are already available, and otherwise destined to be destroyed or wasted. (IES Group 2007:1)

The Italian researchers have also built teams tapping relevant knowledge networks. It is clear from documents associated with their advocacy work that they have gained insights from lobbying practices in other countries (e.g., Cattaneo and Corbellini 2010).

With respect to (3), amassing evidence of the workability of their proposals, Cattaneo and her colleagues have run a series of annual conferences in Italy to bring stem cell researchers together and to showcase for the public the potential benefits of their work with human embryonic stem cells. The creativity of the group has also been evident in their efforts to create strong coalitions of diverse supporters (4). They have targeted young people to educate them in the nature of stem cell research and its potential social benefits. Along with holding public lectures, and days dedicated to high school students, they have been experimenting with social media and collaborating with theatre groups and film makers to get their message across in innovative ways. In March 2012 more than 9,000 students from 160 high schools in 20 cities throughout Italy got together with stem cell researchers to participate in UniStem Day 2012. This was the largest dissemination initiative about stem cells ever held in Italy. Activities on offer included lessons and meetings with researchers, visits to laboratories, games, videos, dance and music. Here we see dedicated scientists battling against powerful opposing forces through creative political activities intended to bring new groups into the discussion and, hence, shift the locus of power in the public debate.

CONCLUSION: POLICY ENTREPRENEURS AND POLICY CHANGE

Policy entrepreneurs are political actors who seek policy changes that shift the *status quo* in given areas of public policy (Mintrom 1997, 2000). The functions and activities of policy entrepreneurs take place within broader contexts that have been effectively theorized through notions of punctuated equilibrium (Baumgartner and Jones 1993), windows of opportunity (Kingdon 1984), and advocacy coalitions (Sabatier 1988). By deepening our knowledge of the political work of these policy actors, we also deepen our knowledge of the applicability of specific policy frameworks to the interpretation of diverse instances of agenda setting and policy change. We come to appreciate the systematic nature of the political practices that connect the dots and make broader changes happen. This contribution has examined instances of policy entrepreneurship in the pursuit of government funding and favourable regulation to advance human embryonic stem cell research. The concept of the policy entrepreneur offers illumination into the governance of human embryonic stem cell research and cross-jurisdictional differences in governance arrangements. However, all forms of policy entrepreneurship take place in contexts that can have significant implications for the effectiveness of advocacy efforts.

The policy entrepreneurship highlighted here has been more effective in the United Kingdom, where there has been a general, long-term government commitment to funding of premier scientific facilities. It should not be a surprise that the most productive scientists working on human embryonic stem cells are located in jurisdictions like the United Kingdom, with significant concentrations of universities ranked among the world's top 100. The well-established and well-supported scientific communities in such jurisdictions appear to have served as strong countervailing forces for religious groups who, on moral grounds, have opposed research on human embryonic stem cells. Nonetheless, the morality politics surrounding this science have been significant everywhere, and they have influenced governance arrangements.

With respect to governing this controversial science, it is clear that a period of intense policy change occurred in the United Kingdom in the 1990s and early

2000s. This period punctuated the longer period of policy equilibrium preceding it, and set the direction for future incremental policy changes. The work of policy entrepreneurs – especially their efforts to shape and direct broader moral debates – was crucial to achieving the major shift in the governance of human embryonic stem cell research in that country. In contrast, the Italian case illustrates the enormity of the agenda-setting task confronting those who wish to challenge an entrenched *status quo* enjoying support from well-established and powerful interest groups. In such instances, efforts to create new advocacy coalitions appear the most effective course of action. However, such work takes concerted effort over an extended period of time. The focus of Italian policy entrepreneurs on educating young people about human stem cell research indicates their acute awareness of the need to engage in efforts targeted at long-term social and ideational change. In that instance, the focus of the policy entrepreneurship has been on coalition building, rather than tactical efforts to secure immediate change.

While the focus of this contribution has been on policy entrepreneurship and a specific scientific agenda, the findings hold implications for those studying the dynamics of change across many substantive areas of public policy. Here, we have gained more clarity around the ways that policy entrepreneurs can pursue their goals in the face of intense moral debates. We have also gained greater awareness of how the work of policy entrepreneurs can be both supported and inhibited by ideas, institutions, and interest-group politics.

Biographical note: Michael Mintrom is a Professor of Public Sector Management at Monash University in Melbourne, Australia. He is jointly appointed as the Monash Chair at the Australia and New Zealand School of Government.

NOTES

1 Author's calculations using population data from the CIA's *World Factbook* (2012) and the OECD's (2010) databases on science and technology indicators.
2 I am grateful to Baroness Deech for verifying this interpretation of her activities at the HFEA.

REFERENCES

American Association for the Advancement of Science (2007) *AAAS Policy Brief: Stem Cell Research*, Washington DC: American Association for the Advancement of Science.
Banchoff, T. (2005) 'Path dependencies and value-driven issues: the comparative politics of stem cell research', *World Politics* 57: 200–30.
Baumgartner, F.R. and Jones, B.D. (1993) *Agendas and Instability in American Politics*, Chicago, IL: University of Chicago Press.

Béland, D. (2009) 'Ideas, institutions, and policy change', *Journal of European Public Policy* 16: 701–18.
Braun, M. (2009) 'The evolution of emissions trading in the European Union – the role of policy networks, knowledge and policy entrepreneurs', *Accounting, Organizations and Society* 34: 469–87.
Cattaneo, E. and Corbellini, G. (2010) 'Science under politics: an Italian nightmare', *European Molecular Biology Organization Reports* 1–4.
Central Intelligence Agency (CIA) (2012) *The World Factbook*, available at https://www.cia.gov/library/publications/the-world-factbook/index.html, accessed 29 January 2013.
Christopoulos, D.C. (2006) 'Relational attributes of political entrepreneurs: a network perspective', *Journal of European Public Policy* 13: 757–78.
Crowley, J.E. (2003) *The Politics of Child Support in America*, New York: Cambridge University Press.
Crowley, J.E. (2008) *Defiant Dads: Fathers' Rights Activists in America*, Ithaca, NY: Cornell University Press.
Daviter, F. (2007) 'Policy framing in the European Union', *Journal of European Public Policy* 14: 654–66.
Deech, R. and Smajdor, A. (2007) *From IVF to Immortality: Controversy in the Era of Reproductive Technology*, Oxford: Oxford University Press.
Dudley, G. and Richardson, J. (1999) 'Competing advocacy coalitions and the process of "frame reflection": a longitudinal analysis of EU steel policy', *Journal of European Public Policy* 6: 225–48.
Evans, M.J. and Kaufman, M.H. (1981) 'Establishment in culture of pluripotential cells from mouse embryos', *Nature* 292: 154–56.
Fink, S. (2008) 'Politics as usual or bringing religion back in? The influence of parties, institutions, economic interests, and religion on embryo research laws', *Comparative Political Studies* 41: 1631–56.
Fukuyama, F. (2005) 'Human biomedicine and the problem of governance', *Perspectives in Biology and Medicine* 48(2): 195–200.
Gerring, J. (2007) *Case Study Research: Principles and Practices*, New York: Cambridge University Press.
Gottweis, H. and Prainsack, B. (2006) 'Emotion in political discourse: contrasting approaches to stem cell governance in the USA, UK, Israel and Germany', *Regenerative Medicine* 1: 823–29.
Hauskeller, C. (2004) 'How traditions of ethical reasoning and institutional processes shape stem cell research in Britain', *Journal of Medicine and Philosophy: A Forum for Bioethics and Philosophy of Medicine* 29: 509–32.
IES Group (2007) *Manifesto for the Scientific Research on Embryonic Stem Cells: On the Ethics of a 'New Frontier'*, Rome: IES Group, available at http://archive.eurostemcell.org/Documents/News/2007_ROMA_Manifesto_12J, accessed 29 January 2013.
Isasi, R.M. and Knoppers, B.M. (2006) 'Mind the gap: approaches to embryonic stem cell and cloning research in 50 countries', *European Journal of Health Law* 13: 9–26.
Karch, A. (2012) 'Vertical diffusion and the policy-making process: the politics of embryonic stem cell research', *Political Research Quarterly* 65: 48–61.
Kingdon, J.W. (1984) *Agendas, Alternatives, and Public Policies*, 2nd edn, Boston, MA: Little Brown.
Kolata, G. (2007) 'Researcher who helped start stem cell war may now end it', *The New York Times*, 22 November, A1.
Lindblom, C.E. (1959) 'The science of "muddling through"', *Public Administration Review* 19: 79–88.
Majone, G. (1989) 'Evidence, argument, and persuasion in the policy process', New Haven, CT: Yale University Press.

Metzler, I. (2007) '"Nationalizing embryos": the politics of human embryonic stem cell research in Italy', *BioSocieties* 2: 413–27.
Mintrom, M. (1997) 'Policy entrepreneurs and the diffusion of innovation', *American Journal of Political Science* 41: 738–70.
Mintrom, M. (2000) *Policy Entrepreneurs and School Choice*, Washington, DC: Georgetown University Press.
Mintrom, M. (2009) 'Competitive federalism and the governance of controversial science', *Publius: The Journal of Federalism* 39: 606–31.
Mintrom, M. and Bollard, R. (2009) 'Governing controversial science: lessons from stem cell research', *Policy and Society* 28: 301–14.
Mintrom, M. and Norman, P. (2009) 'Policy entrepreneurship and policy change', *Policy Studies Journal* 37: 649–67.
Mintrom, M. and Vergari, S. (1996) 'Advocacy coalitions, policy entrepreneurs, and policy change', *Policy Studies Journal* 24: 420–34.
Mintrom, M. and Vergari, S. (1998) 'Policy networks and innovation diffusion: the case of state education reforms', *Journal of Politics* 60: 126–48.
Mulkay, M. (1993) 'Rhetorics of hope and fear in the great embryo debate', *Social Studies of Science* 23: 721–42.
Natali, D. (2004) 'Europeanization, policy arenas, and creative opportunism: the politics of welfare state reforms in Italy', *Journal of European Public Policy* 11: 1077–95.
National Institutes of Health (2001) *Stem Cells: Scientific Progress and Future Research Directions*, Bethesda, MD: National Institutes of Health.
National Institutes of Health (2006) *Regenerative Medicine*, Bethesda, MD: National Institutes of Health.
OECD (2010) *OECD Science, Technology and Industry Scoreboard*, Paris: OECD.
Ramalho-Santos, M. and Willenbring, H. (2007) 'On the origin of the term "stem cell"', *Cell Stem Cell* 1(1): 35–8.
Rosenthal, E. (2006) 'Excommunication is sought for stem cell researchers', *The New York Times*, 1 July, A3.
Sabatier, P.A. (1988) 'An advocacy coalition framework of policy change and the role of policy oriented learning therein', *Policy Sciences* 21: 129–68.
Sabatier, P.A. (1993) 'Policy change over a decade or more', in P.A. Sabatier and H.C. Jenkins-Smith (eds), *Policy Change and Learning: An Advocacy Coalition*, Boulder, CO: Westview Press, pp. 13–39.
Shanghai Ranking Consultancy (2011) *Academic Ranking of World Universities, 2011*, available at http://www.shanghairanking.com/ARWU2011.html, accessed 29 January 2013.
Thomson, J.A. et al. (1998) 'Embryonic stem cell lines derived from human blastocysts', *Science* 282: 1145–7.
Timmermans, A. and Scholten, P. (2006) 'The political flow of wisdom: science institutions as policy venues in the Netherlands', *Journal of European Public Policy* 13: 1104–18.
Trivedi, B. (2007) 'Researchers detour around stem-cell rules', *Chronicle of Higher Education*, 5 October.
Warnock, M. (1985) *A Question of Life: The Warnock Report on Human Fertilisation and Embryology*, Oxford: Basil Blackwell.
Williams, C., Kitzinger, J. and Henderson, L. (2003) 'Envisaging the embryo in stem cell research: rhetorical strategies and media reporting of the ethical debates', *Sociology of Health and Illness* 25: 793–814.
Withrow, E. (2007) 'Global trade in human eggs thriving', *The Washington Post*, 27 January.
Yu, J. et al. (2007) 'Induced pluripotent stem cell lines derived from human somatic cells', *Science*, 20 November: 115–26.

Index

abortion 18, 27, 28, 29, 31–2, 46, 52, 55 and attitudes to ESCR 106–7; policy patterns 35; policy timeline 33–4; political partisanship 19, 102; religious world 36, 37; secular world 38, 39, 40; venues by country 54
addictive behaviour 4, 12, 70 Germany and Netherland 64–80; religious influences 17, *see also* drug and gambling
advocacy coalitions 135, 136, 146, 147
agenda-setting 20, 30 by judicial system 21; subsystem and macro level 30
Albæk, E. 38, 45, 51
Albright, E.A. 86
Albritton, R.B. 18
Andeweg, R.B. 32
ART (assisted reproductive technologies) 27, 28, 29, 46, 52 and ESCR 101, 107, 108–9, 110, 111, 112, 113; policy timelines 33–4, 35; religious world 36, 37; secular world 38, 39, 40; venues by country 54
Austria 41, 51, 53, 105, 140

Banchoff, T. 1, 27, 29, 99, 100, 101, 112, 139
Baumgartner, F.R. 30, 58, 67, 84, 135, 146
Beckstein, Günther 93
behavioural change: policy effects 12–13
Béland, D. 135
Belgium 41, 48, 51, 53; ESCR 99, 104, 105, 109, 110, 140
Belz, A. 75, 76
Berlusconi governments 123–4, 125
Bernauer, T. 103
Berrington, E. 89
Berry, W.D. 103
biotechnology 99, 102, 103–4
Birkland, T.A. 16, 82, 84, 85, 86, 87, 95
Blair, Tony 86, 88, 91, 92
Blakemore, Colin 144
Bleiklie, I. 27, 46, 51, 100
blended issues 66
Blofield, M. 20, 29
Bloomberg, Michael 6–7
Boin, A. 83, 84, 85, 95, 96

Bollard, R. 134, 139
Böllinger, L. 73
Braun, M. 136
Breeman, G. 36, 65
Brooks, S. 100
Brossard, D. 104
Brown, C. 88
Burstein, P. 103
Butler, D. 47, 48

Cagossi, A. 45–63
Caiffa, P. 126
Calfano, B.R. 18
Calvo, K. 119
Capano, G. 113
capital punishment 46, 47, 52, 55; venues by country 54
Cashore, B. 10, 14
Castles, F.G. 17, 58
Catholic Church 17, 18, 29, 32, 103, 117 and ESCR 136, 138, 144; Italy 124–6, 141; Spain 128–9; in UK 141; as veto player 131
Cattaneo, E. 145
Cell Stem Cell 139, 140
change *see* policy change
change and blocking coalitions 120, 121–2, 126; Spain 126–9
Chapman, S. 87
Chaqués, L. 32, 36, 37, 128
Chiesa Cattolica Italiana (CCI) 125
Christian Democratic parties 28, 29, 49
conflict and debate 30–1; Erfurt shooting 93; and ESCR 102, 106, 110–11; on gambling 75; Italy 124, 125; Netherlands 32, 36, 37
Christoph, J.B. 48
Christopoulos, D.C. 136
church attendance, cross-national 36, 37
Church-State cleavage 17–18, 30
Classification frames 3; policy-based approach 3–4, 11; politics-based approach 2–3, 11; sub-fields 4, 12
cloning 34, 139, 143, 144
Cobb, R.W. 84

INDEX

Cohan, A.S. 48
Cohen, S. 7, 83
compliance 7–8, 13
confessional parties 28, 30–2, 35–6, 38, 41
conflict 27, 40
Congregation for the Doctrine of the Faith (CDF) 124
conscience, issues of 11–12; parliamentary voting 48
Consejo de Estado 119
Constantelos, J. 122
Corbellini, G. 145
Council of Europe 47; death penalty abolition 48, 51
Cowley, P. 11, 20, 38, 48, 50, 51
criminalization of behaviour 15, 22, 68
cross-country analyses 27–42, 45–60
Crowley, J.E. 136
Cullen, Lord (Report) 86, 92
cultural opportunity structure 5, 6, 78

Dahl, R. 103
Danna, D. 119
Davies, P.L. 101
Daviter, F. 135
Daynes, B. 2, 29, 45, 47, 48, 49
De Vries, M.S. 86
Debus, M. 14
decentralization 53, 54–5, 56, 57, 58–9
Deech, Ruth 142–3
definitions of morality policies 11–12
Denmark 40, 51, 53, 57; ESCR 104, 105, 106, 109, 111, 140; policy pattern 33–4; policy timelines 38–40; referendums 51; same-sex marriage 33, 35; secular world 28, 32
discourse network analysis 83, 87–8, 91–6
Donaldson, Liam (Report) 143, 144
Donovan, T. 49
Döring, H. 47
drug and gambling policies, framing 64–80; analysis 76–8; case selection 65–6; economic and fiscal frame 69, 70, 74, 75; Germany 72–3, 75–6; health and social frame 69, 70, 71, 72, 74, 75–6; hypotheses 66–8, 76; method and data 68–71; morality frame 69, 70, 72, 74, 75, 76; Netherlands 71–2, 73–5; and policy choices 67–8; and politics 66; redefining issues 67–8; security and public order frame 69, 70, 71, 72, 74, 75; shifts in 72, 73, 75–7; theoretical framework 66–8; value shifting 66–7
Dudley, G. 136
Dunblane shooting 83, 86; discourse network 91–2, 95; media coverage 89–90; policy consequences 86, 92
Dunphy, R. 21
Durham, M. 45

Duval, R.D. 45–63

economic costs/benefits 5
economic and fiscal frame 69, 70, 74, 75
Eeckhout, B. 47, 48
effects, policy 12–13
Elvins, M. 21
embryonic stem cell research (ESCR) 27, 28, 29, 46, 52 and ART 101, 107, 108–9, 110, 111, 112, 113; controversial aspects 138, 139; data and methods 104–12; development of 136–7; diverging regulatory paths 99–100, 104–7; explaining 107–12 geography of 139–40; hypotheses 101–5; Italy 140, 141, 144–6, 147; morality issues 137–9; party politics 100, 101–3, 106, 108–9, 110–12; path dependency 99, 100, 101, 109–12; policy entrepreneurs 134–47; policy timelines 33–4, 35; public opinion 100, 103–4, 106–7, 112–13; regulatory paths 99–114; and religious cleavages 106, 108–9, 110, 112, 113; in secular world 38, 39, 40; truth table 108–9; UK 140, 141–4; and university funding 140, 146
Engeli, I. 3, 6, 7, 8, 11, 18, 20, 22, 27–44, 45, 46, 49, 50, 51, 58, 64, 66, 67, 99–116, 119–20
Epp, C.R. 21
Erfurt shooting 83, 86–7; actors 89, 90; discourse network 92–3, 95; policy consequences 87, 93
Ernst & Young *Biotechnology Report* 99
Ertman, T. 30
ESCR *see* embryonic stem cell research
Euchner, E.-M. 8, 11, 64–81, 83, 117–33
European Union institutions 22, 47
euthanasia 27, 28, 46, 52; active 34; policy timelines 33–4, 35; religious world 36, 37; secular world 39–40; venues by country 54
Evans, M.J. 137
Evans, R.J. 51
executive-legislative relations 47, 48
external shocks 16, 82–3, 86, 96; framing 84, 85; from human failure 96

feminist movement: Italy 126
Fink, S. 1, 17, 27, 29, 49, 100, 102–3, 112, 119, 120, 121, 138, 139
Finland 51, 53; ESCR 104, 105, 106, 109
firearms *see* gun policy; shooting
Flanagan, S.C. 67
Flowe, M. 15
focusing events 83, 84–5, 95
framing 11, 69, 70, 72, 74, 75, 84, 85; by policy entrepreneurs 135–6; frame shifts 65, 66, 68, 76–8; morality/non-morality 3; religious influence 66
France 41, 51, 53; ESCR 99, 104, 105, 106, 109, 111, 140

INDEX

Frank, D.J. 22
freedoms, individual 4, 12, 20–1, 83
Freeman, G.P. 48
Frum, D. 7
Fukuyama, F. 138, 139
fundamental problems 16

Gallagher, M. 48, 51
gambling policy; frame shifts 73–4, 75–8; Germany 75–6; Netherlands 73–5, *see also* drug and gambling policies
Germany 41, 51, 52, 53; drug policy 72–3; ESCR 99, 101, 104, 105, 106, 109, 111–12, 140; gambling policy 75–6; same-sex unions 14, *see also* Erfurt
Gerring, J. 140
Gindulis, E. 15, 21
Gottweis, H. 100, 103, 144
Gould, A. 15
Greasley, K. 16
Greece 51, 52, 53; ESCR 104, 105, 109, 110
Green-Pedersen, C. 13, 18, 20, 27–44, 49, 50, 102, 106, 112
Grießler, E. 50
gun policy 7, 16; coalition cohesion 85–6; discursive complexity 85–6; Dunblane consequences 86; Erfurt consequences 87; as latent morality policy 83, *see also* shooting rampages
Gunther, R. 126

Hadolt, B. 50
Haider-Markel, D.P. 19, 66, 82, 84
Hall, P. 13, 14, 120
Hamann, K. 127
Hauskeller, C. 142
health and social frame 69, 70, 71, 75
Heichel, S. 3, 7, 8, 10–26, 64–81, 83, 96, 118, 119, 131
Hewitt, K. 82
Highton, B. 19
Ho, S.S. 104
homosexuality 38; Italy 119, *see also* same-sex unions
Hood, C. 86
Hood, R. 47, 48
Hooghe, L. 51
Howlett, M. 10, 14, 113
Human Fertilization and Embryology Authority (UK) 142–4
human rights issues 47, 57
Hurka, S. 7, 8, 16, 67, 82–98

Iceland 51, 52, 53; ESCR 104, 105, 109
implementation of policies 7–8; deficits 13; judicial system 21
independent streams, theory of 135

individual freedoms 4, 12
Inglehart, R. 19, 36, 58, 66
institutional theories *see* policy type; two worlds
interest groups 38, 39, 40, 135; institutionalized religion 17, 20; and policy entrepreneurship 144, 147; as veto players 120–1, 125
international influences 21–2
Ireland 41, 51, 53, 55–7, 105
Irwin, G. 32
ISAD 71
Isasi, R.M. 141
Italy 51, 53, 55–8, 117; ESCR 99, 104, 105, 109, 111, 134, 140, 141, 144–6, 147; policy-making 122–6; prostitution 118–19, 123, 124, 125–6; referendums 51; same-sex unions 118, 119, 123–5
IVF (in-vitro fertilization) 33, 112

Jaenicke, D.W. 19
Jasanoff, S. 100, 101, 103
Jemphrey, A. 89
Johnson, P. 16
Jones, B.D. 30, 58, 67, 84, 135, 146
Joslyn, M.R. 82, 84
judicial intervention 48, 52, 53–4, 55, 56 and change 15, 20–1; and legislature 21; sexual behaviour issues 21

Kaider-Markel, D.P. 13
Kalke, J. 73
Kalyvas, S. 31
Karch, A. 136, 139
Karp, A. 92, 95
Kaufman, M.H. 137
Kaufman, M.S. 19
Keck, M. 59
Keck, T.M. 21
Kilburn, H.W. 19
Kilvington, J. 119
Kingdon, J.W. 83, 84, 95, 96, 135, 140, 146
Kingma, S.F. 64, 77
Knill, C. 1–9, 10–26, 65, 66, 78, 83, 96, 100, 112
Knoppers, B.M. 141
Kolata, G. 139
Kollman, K. 22, 27
Krabbendam, H. 45
Krippendorff, K. 68
Kurzer, P. 47

Larsen, L.T. 27–44, 68, 102, 112
latent morality policies 5, 6, 83
Latin America: same-sex marriage 21
Laver, M. 47
Lawrence, R.G. 82, 85, 87
Lee, A.-R. 67
Lee, M.-H. 19

153

INDEX

leftist parties 29 and biomedical issues 102–3
legislature and judicial system 21
Leifeld, P. 83, 87, 89, 91
life and death issues 4, 12, 16, 17, 46, 65; judicial intervention 21
Lijphart, A. 51, 58
Lindaman, K. 19
Lindblom, C.E 135
Linton, A. 103
Littler, A. 15, 21, 74
Littleton (US) shooting 87
Lodge, M. 86
Longo, V. 126
López, S. 128, 129
lotteries 75, 76, 77
Lovenduski, J. 39
Lowi, T.J. 3, 48
Luxembourg 51, 53

McBride Stetson, D. 102
Majone, G. 48, 136
Major, John 86, 91, 92, 95
Mancuso, A. 125
manifest morality policies 4–5; time/place dynamics 6–7
Manow, P. 30
March, D. 51
Mazur, A. 29
measurement of policy change 10, 12–15; alternative approach 14–15
medical interest groups 39, 40, 41
Meier, K.J. 1, 13, 66, 68
Mellor, David 91, 92, 95
Metzler, I. 144
Millns, S. 39
Minkenberg, M. 17, 27, 29, 49
Mintrom, M. 8, 59, 134–49
Montero, J. 126, 131
Montpetit, E. 27, 29, 46, 48, 51, 59, 100
Mooney, C.Z. 1, 2, 4, 13, 19, 29, 45, 49, 64, 103, 120, 121
moral panics 7, 83
morality charge 6, 78
morality frame *see* framing
morality policies characteristics 1; concepts of 2–4, 11–12; content-based approach 3–4; contents and effects 7–8; cross-country analysis 27–42, 45–60; data and methods 51–2; findings 52–8; definitions 11–12; future research 8, 22; latent and manifest 4–7, 83; list of 46; as policy types 2–3; and politics 2–3, 11; types of 4–7, *see also* non-morality
Mucciaroni, G. 3, 11, 65, 66, 69
Mudu, P. 123, 124
Mulkay, M. 142

Nadelmann, E.A. 59

Natali, D. 136
Nature 139, 140, 145
Nebel, K. 7, 8, 16, 64–81, 82–98
Netherlands 40, 51, 53; abortion 36, 37; ART 110; assisted suicide 21; Christian Democrats 31, 32, 36, 37; drug policy 71–2; normalization principle 71; ESCR 104, 105, 106, 109, 110–11, 140; euthanasia 34, 36; gambling policy 73–5; policy dynamics 35–8; policy pattern 33–4; policy timelines 35; political parties 32; religious world 28; same-sex marriage 34, 35; secularization 37
New York, sugary drinks issue 6–7
Nielsen, H.T. 103
Nisbet, C. 104
Nisbet, M.C. 104
Nohrstedt, D. 86
non-compliant behaviour 7–8
non-morality policies 3–4, 5–6, 11
Norman, P. 135, 140
Norrander, B. 19
Norris, P. 36, 58
Norway 51, 53; ESCR 104, 105, 106, 109, 111

O'Connell, C. 47
Oldmixon, E.A. 18
outputs, policy 12, 13; as change indicators 13; and Church-State relations 17; instrument settings 14; paradigm changes 13
Outshoorn, J. 36, 48, 50, 51, 119, 129
Overby, L.M. 19

Page, B.I. 103
Palau, A.M. 128
paradigm shifts 13, 14
party government model 46–8
party politics and ESCR 100, 101–3; left-right cleavage 102; religious cleavages 102, *see also* political parties
Paternotte, D. 47, 48, 119
path dependency, ESCR 99, 100, 101, 109–12
Patton, D. 13
Pennings, P. 50
permissiveness, cross-national variation 27–42; case selection 32–5; existing explanations 29–30; religious world 35–8; secular world 35, 38–40
Pickel, G. 67
Pierceson, J. 21
Pierson, P. 101
Platero, R. 37, 119
policy change 7–8, 10–11; analytical peculiarities 15–22, 23; judicial intervention 20–1; measuring 10, 12–15; problem pressure 16; theories of 135; and veto players 118, 120–2
policy entrepreneurs 134–47; characteristics of 135–6; competency of 136; Italian ESCR 144–

INDEX

5; operating context 136; and policy framing 135–6; Ruth Deech 143
policy monopolies 78
policy process 30–2, 45–6; international influences 21–2; religious influences 20, 30–1
policy type theory 2–3, 45, 48–9, 59; findings 52–5
policy-based approach 3–4
political parties 19–20, 49; confessional 27, 28, 30–2, 35–6, 38, 40, 41; conflict between 28–9, 30–1, 32; left-wing 29, 102–3; Netherlands 32; secular 27, 28, 32; Spain 32
politics dimension 4, 66
politics-based approach 2–3, 11
Polkinghorne, John 143
Pollack, D. 67
pornography regulations: UK 16
Portugal 41, 51, 53, 55; ESCR 104, 105, 106, 109, 110; referendums 51
Prainsack, B. 144
Preidel, C. 117–33
problem definition/perception 77–8, 95
problem pressure 16, 77, 78; critical mass 16
Prodi governments 123, 124–5
prostitution and same-sex marriage 117–32; actor coalitions and regulation 130; change and blocking coalitions 120, 121–2, 126, 131; Italy 130; research question 117; Spain 126–9, 130; Sweden 15; theoretical approach 120–2; veto players 118, 120–2
public opinion 100, 103–4, 106–7, 112–13; ESCR 100, 103–4, 106–7; and societal values 18–19
public order frame 69, 70, 71, 72
punctuated equilibrium 67, 135, 146

Raaflaub, C. 95
Radaelli, C. 100
Ragin, Ch. 100, 106, 107
Ramalho-Santos, M. 137
Ramjoué, C. 102
Ranney, A. 47, 48
Rasch, B.E. 47
Raschzok, A. 64–81
Read, M. 51
Reeve, Christopher 144
referendums 48, 50, 53, 54, 55, 56
reframing issues 65 *see also* framing
regulation 7–8; convergence hypothesis 99–100
religion 4, 17–18 and ESCR 106–7, 108–9, 110, 112, 113; impact on policies 29–31; institutionalized 20
religious world 28, 49; conflict and debate 31–2; policy dynamics 35–8; policy timelines 35; secularization in 36–8, 40
Reuband, K.H. 64, 77
Richards, P.G. 48, 51

Richardson, J. 136
Rihoux, B. 106
Rochefort, D.A. 84
Roqué, A.M.P. 32, 36, 37
Rose, R. 101
Rosenthal, E. 144
Rossi Barilli, G. 125
Rothmayr Allison, C. 8, 29, 59, 99–116

Sabatier, P.A. 84, 135, 146
same-sex unions 27, 28, 29, 46, 52; Germany 14; judicial activism 21; policy timelines 33–5; religious world 36, 37; secular world 38, 39, 40; Spain 127–8; venues by country 54, *see also* prostitution and same-sex
sanctions 8, 13, 15, 71
Sanders, D. 21
Schattschneider mobilization 30
Schiffino, N. 1
Schily, Otto 93
Schmitt, S. 7, 8, 10–26, 85, 117–33
Scholten, P. 110, 136
Schröder, Chancellor 111
Schwartz, M.A. 17, 119
Science 139, 140, 145
secular parties 27, 28, 32
secular world 28–9, 32, 49; issue variation 38–40; policy timelines 35
secularization 6, 27, 28, 31, 67; Germany and Netherlands 65–6, 76–7; Italy and Spain 131; in religious world 36–8, 40
security and public order frame 69, 70, 71, 72, 74, 75
Serdült, U. 102
sexual behaviour issues 4, 12, 46; judicial intervention 21; religious influences 17, *see also* prostitution
Shapiro, R.Y. 103
Sheldon, S. 39
Shepsle, K.A. 47
shooting rampages: actors and frames 89–90; comparative analysis 82–97; discourse network analysis 87–8, 91–5; Dunblane 86; Erfurt 86–7; Littleton (US) 87; media categories 89; method and data 87–9; Port Arthur (Australia) 87; role of framing 83; statements per frame 90; Zug 87
Sieberer, U. 47
Sikkink, K. 59
slot machine gambling 74–5, 76
Smajdor, A. 142
Smith, J.D. 15
Smith, K. 46
Smith, M. 21
Smith, T.A. 1, 29, 45, 47, 48, 49, 58, 64, 67
Snowdrop Campaign 92, 95
social class 47

social mobilization 6, 16
social order 69, 70
social values *see* values
Soroka, S.N. 103
Soule, S.A. 104
Spain 40, 51, 53; abortion 35, 36, 37; change coalition 128, 129; ESCR 104, 105, 106, 109, 140; morality policy-making 126–9, 130; parliamentary initiatives 127–8, 129; policy dynamics 35–8; policy pattern 33–4; political parties 32; prostitution 117, 118, 119, 127, 128–9, 130; religious world 28; same-sex unions 117, 118, 119; marriage 34, 35, 127–8; secularization 37–8; veto players 126, 127, 128–9, 130, 131
Steel, David 39
stem cell research *see* embryonic stem cell
Stetson, D.M. 27, 29
Steunenberg, B. 21
Stimson, J.A. 103
Stone, D. 84
Strøm, K. 121
Studlar, D.T. 7, 8, 45–63, 66, 68
sub-fields 4, 12, 16
suicide, assisted 16, 21, 34 *see also* euthanasia
Sweden 51, 53; ESCR 104, 105, 109, 111, 140; prostitution 15
Switzerland 41, 51, 52, 53, 55; ESCR 104, 105, 106, 109, 111, 140; referendums 51, *see also* Zug

Tatalovich, R. 1, 2, 17, 29, 45, 47, 48, 49, 58, 64, 67, 119
Tate, C.N. 48
Taylor, R. 120
Ten Napel, H.-M. 45
Thomson, J.A. 134, 137, 139
threshold policies 16
Tiberghien, Y. 99
time/place dynamics 6–7
Timmermans, A. 36, 48, 50, 58, 65, 110, 136
Toggenburg, G.N. 47
Tosun, J. 3, 12
transnational influences 21–2
Tremblay, M. 60n
Trivedi, B. 138
True, J. 59
Trujillo, Cardinal Alfonso Lopez 144
Tsebelis, G. 47, 58, 118, 120, 121
two worlds model 30, 49–51, 55–8, 59; hypotheses 50, 56–7, *see also* religious; secular
typologies 2–3

United Kingdom 40, 51, 53; ESCR 99, 101, 104, 105, 109, 110, 134, 140, 141–4; policy entrepreneurship 143; interest groups 38, 39, 40; policy pattern 33–4; policy timelines 38–40; pornography regulations 16; same-sex marriage 35; secular world 28, 32, *see also* Dunblane
United States policy processes 49
universities, ranking 139
research funding 140, 146
Utøya shooting 82

Valiente Fernández, C. 119
Vallinder, T. 48
value conflicts 1, 2, 4, 48–9; defining morality policies 12; gun policy 83; manifest policies 4–5; and paradigm change 14; and politics 4, 10
values 18–19; changes 78; cultural dispositions 6; individual 4; latent and manifest policies 4–5; shifts 66–7, 76–7; societal 18–19, 70
Van Hees, M. 21
van Kersbergen, K. 30, 31, 49
Varone, F. 29, 100, 101, 104, 107
Vatican 122–3, 124, 131
venues 50, 51, 52, 55–7; number by country 53–4; religious worlds 55–7; secular 55–6, 57
Vergari, S. 135
veto players 118, 120–2; Catholic Church 131; institutional 123; societal 123, 124; Spain 126, 127, 128–9, 130, 131
Vianello, F. 126

Warner, C.M. 17
Warnock, Mary (Report) 142
Weisberg, H.F. 103
Welzel, C. 19
West, J. 119
Wetstein, M.E. 18
Wilcox, C. 19
Willenbring, H. 137
Williams, C. 144
windows of opportunity 84, 96, 135, 146
Withrow, E. 138
Wlezien, Ch. 103
World Value Surveys (WVS) 36, 37, 131; secularization 65–6

Yamane, D. 18
Yu, J. 139

Zapatero, J.L. Rodriguez 37, 127
Zug shooting 83, 87; actors 89–90; consequences 94–5; discourse network 94–5

www.routledge.com/9780415624749

Related titles from Routledge

Economic Patriotism in Open Economies

Edited by Ben Clift and Cornelia Woll

The recent financial crisis has demonstrated that governments continuously seek to steer their economies rather than leaving them to free markets. Some politicians even proudly evoke "economic patriotism" to justify their choices.

This volume links such populism to a specific set of tensions – the paradox of neo-liberal democracy – and argues that the phenomenon is ubiquitous. The mandate of politicians is to defend the economic interests of their constituents under conditions where large parts of economic governance are no longer exclusively within their control. Economic patriotism is one possible reaction to this tension. As old-style industrial policy and interventionism gained a bad reputation, governments had to become creative to assure traditional economic policy objectives with new means.

Ben Clift is Senior Lecturer in Political Economy at the University of Warwick.

Cornelia Woll is Associate Research Professor at Sciences Po Paris and Research Fellow at the Max Planck Institute for the Study of Societies in Cologne.

Dec 2012: 246 x 174: 160pp
Hb: 978-0-415-62474-9
£85 / $145

For more information and to order a copy visit
www.routledge.com/9780415624749

Available from all good bookshops

www.routledge.com/9780415627337

Related titles from Routledge

Political Marketing in Retrospective and Prospective

Edited by Christine B. Williams and Bruce I. Newman

Political marketing coalesced as a subfield in the mid-1990s, and in 2002 the *Journal of Political Marketing* began publication. This anniversary collection reviews the existing theory, empirical evidence and practice of political marketing and explores emerging topics and lines of inquiry within the field. While political candidates and their campaigns are a major focus, it also considers the broader range of issue advocacy and lobbying. The selections expand beyond the U.S. context to offer a much needed comparative perspective. The volume includes material on the effects of new media and technology, posing questions about their direction and consequences for political actors and institutions, citizens and governmental systems. Collectively, the chapters illustrate the breadth and depth of a maturing field of inquiry, taking the reader through a retrospective and prospective examination of the intellectual grounding and scholarship that comprise political marketing.

This book was published as a special issue of the *Journal of Political Marketing*.

Christine B. Williams is a Professor of Political Science at Bentley University, USA.

Bruce I. Newman, Professor of Marketing, DePaul University, USA.

Dec 2012: 246 x 174: 152pp
Hb: 978-0-415-62733-7
£90 / $145

For more information and to order a copy visit
www.routledge.com/9780415627337

Available from all good bookshops

www.routledge.com/9780415696180

Related titles from Routledge

The Nature of Belief Systems Reconsidered

Edited by Jeffrey Friedman

In the foundational document of modern public-opinion research, Philip E. Converse's "The Nature of Belief Systems in Mass Publics" (1964) established the U.S. public's startling political ignorance. This volume makes Converse's long out-of-print article available again and brings together a variety of scholars, including Converse himself, to reflect on Converse's findings after nearly half a century of further research.

This book was originally published as a special issue of *Critical Review: A Journal of Politics and Society*.

Jeffrey Friedman, a visiting scholar in the Department of Government, University of Texas at Austin, received a Ph.D. in Political Science from Yale University.

Shterna Friedman received an MFA from the Iowa Writers' Workshop, University of Iowa.

April 2012: 216 x 138: 416pp
Hb: 978-0-415-69618-0
£100 / $160

For more information and to order a copy visit
www.routledge.com/9780415696180

Available from all good bookshops